# TEXTUAL SILENCE

# TEXTUAL SILENCE

## Unreadability and the Holocaust

JESSICA LANG

RUTGERS UNIVERSITY PRESS
New Brunswick, Camden, and Newark, New Jersey, and London

Library of Congress Cataloging-in-Publication Data

Names: Lang, Jessica, 1973- author.
Title: Textual silence : unreadability and the Holocaust / Jessica Lang.
Other titles: Unreadability and the Holocaust
Description: New Brunswick, New Jersey : Rutgers University Press, 2017. | Includes bibliographical references and index.
Identifiers: LCCN 2016044027| ISBN 9780813589909 (hardback) | ISBN 9780813589916 (pbk.) | ISBN 9780813589923 (e-book (epub)) | ISBN 9780813589930 (e-book (Web PDF)) | ISBN 9780813589947 (e-book (Mobi))
Subjects: LCSH: Holocaust, Jewish (1939-1945), in literature. | Silence in literature. | Memory in literature. | Mimesis in literature. | Realism in literature. | Literature, Modern—20th century—History and criticism. | Literature, Modern—21st century—History and criticism. | BISAC: LITERARY CRITICISM / Jewish.
Classification: LCC PN56.H55 L36 2017 | DDC 809/.93358405318—dc23
LC record available at https://lccn.loc.gov/2016044027



♾ The paper used in this publication meets the requirements of the American National Standard for Information Sciences—Permanence of Paper for Printed Library Materials, ANSI Z39.48–1992.

www.rutgersuniversitypress.org

Manufactured in the United States of America

To my family

# CONTENTS

# TEXTUAL SILENCE

# INTRODUCTION

> At certain levels, we are not meant to understand at all, and our interpretation, indeed our reading itself, is an intrusion.
>
> —George Steiner, *On Difficulty and Other Essays*

Reading Holocaust texts is difficult, nearly impossible in fact.[1] Such a statement seems a contradiction in terms for, once the skills behind reading are mastered, reading becomes almost instinctual or automatic. It is difficult *not* to read when faced with a text—an aspect of reading (and audience) that has long been recognized and assumed, as evidenced by the multitude of public texts all around us. Moreover, given the sheer number of texts that invoke the Holocaust, texts that position the Holocaust as either primary or secondary, the claim that we *cannot* read these works when precisely that task—reading—appears fundamental to so many of these works' origins and aims seems itself misguided, a failure to understand. Yet, as I make clear throughout the chapters of this book, reading texts that hold at their core traumatic memory and experience depends on our *in*ability to read them and, more broadly, on their inability or refusal to be read. The Holocaust is, for reasons I enumerate, perhaps the best example of this. That is, these texts bear within them an element of inaccessibility that is an important—indeed, fundamental—aspect of the text.

At the heart of this project lies an exploration of the tension between the will and desire to read and our ultimate inability to do so as it applies to Holocaust literature. It may well be the case that unreadability as I understand it is a concept that applies to a wider range of trauma literature than I discuss here. I have chosen to focus on Holocaust literature for a number of reasons. First, perhaps more than in any other literary genre or category, questions about Holocaust representation—how we write, draw, narrate, exhibit, present, speak about that event—beginning with the very fact that so much representation exists, have been thoughtfully and determinedly examined by survivors, authors, scholars, artists, and others. However, questions of how that representation is processed, or for this book, how representations are read, have received relatively little attention. Because I understand scholarship to be closely tied to the act of reading and the assertion of a readerly identity, for me understanding reading is not subordinate to or detached from questions of representation; rather, reading and representation are necessary counterparts to each other—one cannot function without the other.

Second, and perhaps more than other readers, I feel comfortable with the idea of the presence of the unreadable. I attribute this in large part to my sense of Jewish tradition. Jewish textuality is often accompanied by a fundamental ethos of the unreadable, one that is understood as reverential. The most primal example of this is the reading of God's name in the recitation of prayers or the Torah. The Hebrew letters "yud," "hay," "vav," "hay," when combined, spell God's name. But this word is itself never literally pronounced or read. Instead the reader substitutes another name for God for that contextualized one. I do not mean to suggest, in introducing a Jewish textual ethos of unreadability, that Holocaust texts are all Jewish. To the contrary: one of my accompanying arguments in this book is that Holocaust literature, especially more recent Holocaust literature (post-1990s), captures a far wider and more diverse designation than has previously been acknowledged. But recognizing that at least one significant precedent acknowledges the possibility of unreadability opens the way for contemporary readers to conceive of and approach the unreadable in their own relationships to texts.

Last, the presence of the unreadable is made all the more pointed and powerful as more time imposes itself between the actual historical moment in history that Holocaust texts refer to and the act of reading. We as contemporary readers must recognize that the body of Holocaust texts is gradually taking the place of the body of the eyewitness. The sentiment expressed by so many survivors, that language is insufficient to describe their experiences, can, should be, and very much *is* part of the reading experience. That is, a relationship exists—this book explores it—between the limitations of representation in terms of expression by an author and the limits of understanding or processing on the part of a reader.

I point to the literary gaps or silences within texts that impose limitations on the act of reading. Here I provide evidence not only for the idea that limits to the act of reading do exist but also that these limits contain within them implications for the moral aspect of reading, which signal to readers what can and cannot be—what should and should not be—available for interpretation, analysis, and imaginative recourse. To put it bluntly, when it comes to reading the Holocaust, we as readers are condemned to fail. And this failure both is morally justified—necessary, even—and bears significant import. We cannot, ultimately, read the unreadable. But, as I go on to illustrate, many contemporary authors attempt to do just this. The devices these authors employ, instead of drawing readers closer, in terms of their comprehension or otherwise, to the historical trauma of the Holocaust inadvertently challenge precisely what they attempt to accomplish, namely, a more intimate understanding of a Holocaustal event through enhanced readability.

"Unreadability" is an elusive term because of its range of implied meanings. For my purposes here, it does *not* mean that the physical act of reading (that is, of reading aloud or to oneself a sentence, paragraph, page, or work) cannot be accomplished—although I do think, and my students and others have confirmed, that this physical reading experience, when applied to trauma narratives, often differs from other kinds of reading experiences, with readers unable to read with the same facility that they otherwise employ. Indeed, it seems clear to me that the physical act of reading is impacted by the deeper, often more intuitive exercise of reading that I explore here. Reading (or attempting to read) about trauma causes us to respond physically as well as intellectually, analytically, and of course, emotionally. In the years I have been working on this project, many people have talked to me about their reading experiences and how their responses reflect a kind of un-reading. So, for example, readers may speed through passages, skim pages, stop at a single word, or find themselves unable to continue. Other readers note that they cannot accurately or thoroughly recall the details of what they have read. Others read with a kind of careless urgency that recognizes both a necessity and a reluctance to face a text that is painful to process, even in the most basic and mechanical way. Reading trauma is at times perceived as a form of memorialization, a painful experience, one that in some way the reader wants to escape or end quickly—this in contrast to the escape that reading more typically offers. While all of these reactions point to a strong sense of distress regarding the subject they are confronting, they are not the sorts of unreadability I explore here. Nevertheless, they are significant markers of the act of reading traumatic text and signal the deeper quality of inaccessibility that I describe here and which informs Holocaust texts.

Thus, "unreadability" does not refer to the physical or emotional inability or unwillingness to continue reading. The term pertains rather to a textual quality or condition of inaccessibility—blankness, illegibility. Perhaps the best synonym for "unreadability" is "textual silence," by which I mean a kind of silence that is itself read, similar to a substantial blank space covering an entire page or pages, a silence that challenges the norms of reading. Sometimes this quality of silence emerges through a mode of literary interruption—a series of dashes, ellipses, spaces, or a sentence or thought that is literally cut off in the middle and remains incomplete. At other times this quality emerges quite self-consciously from the author. Ruth Kluger notes in the opening pages of her memoir *Still Alive* (2003) that "the familiar words, black ink on dry white paper, interfere with the mute and essentially wordless suffering—the ooze of pain, if I may so call it—they aim to communicate."[2] In keeping with this idea, "unreadability" refers to a moment or series of moments of "non-illumination" in the reading process—aspects of the text that simply cannot be opened, accessed, interpreted, or decoded, no matter what apparatus or methodology is applied. Indeed, as Kluger notes, to the contrary: language, words, the reading itself all interfere with the system of communication they more typically enable.

Furthermore, rather than implying any absence of textual substance, my understanding of the unreadable claims it to be irrepressible as a force bearing meaning. It is, in my view, an intrinsic element of traumatic text, necessary and fundamental to texts that document trauma. It is transcendent. The unreadable both binds the text to the world of the reader—we hold it in our hands, we turn the pages—and moves it away from all things which that world is made of—from the normal limitations inscribed by reading. Because readers are unable to read the unreadable does not in any way make it less real or less valuable. Indeed, I argue here that the unreadable is a central marker of Holocaust texts and serves as a key aspect in realizing their purpose of recalling the Holocaust. Unreadability, then, is part of a wide array of texts and, as I explore in this book, certainly a quality that marks Holocaust texts; it is integral to those texts and the experience of reading them even when readers are not specifically conscious of this feature.

In contrast to unreadability, I define "readability" as the unforced realization or comprehension in the relationship among authors, readers, and texts. It is a sustained moment where a sense of intentional understanding and interpretation exists that links readers to one another, even if the interpretations vary drastically from intended or authorial meaning to read meaning, and from reader to reader. Generally, my use of the verb "to read" in this study does not refer to the technical psycholinguistic processing of symbols, a sounding out of letters, words, and sentences; rather, it refers to a relationship with and to the text. The nature of that relationship is determined by the extent to which the text allows or enables the reader's own faculties to be engaged.[3]

This process involves a number of related questions, all focused on the event of the Holocaust itself. How do authors of Holocaust texts—from those who wrote eyewitness accounts to those born decades after the Holocaust, composing fiction and memoir—conceive of their readers or viewers? How do they themselves read? Given the enormity of the trauma experienced by so many in the Holocaust and the well-established challenges to representation that these narratives present, how do authors attempt to direct or inform their readers and their reading experience? Do authors, eyewitness or otherwise, anticipate what I define here as "unreadability" or "textual silence" as part of the reader's experience of their text? On the part of the reader, what constitutes our experience of reading a Holocaust text? What happens as we parse the signs and symbols that come together to form a Holocaust narrative? How do we modify, adjust, or change our understanding of a particular Holocaust text, and the Holocaust more generally, as we read?

We read narratives of trauma, and especially Holocaust narratives, differently from other texts. In many ways this is a broadly accepted point. In his essay "Why I Write," Elie Wiesel notes that the "word has deserted the meaning it was intended to convey—one can no longer make them coincide." The language of the concentration camp, he continues, "negated all other language and took its place. Rather than link people, it became a wall between them. Could the wall be scaled? Could the reader be brought to the other side? I knew the answer to be

No, and yet I also knew that No had to become Yes."[4] Wiesel positions himself as not only the survivor-writer but also as the survivor-reader. He is not alone. Almost invariably the act of bearing witness takes into account both some form of representation and also an acknowledgment of audience, of how that representation is perceived, understood, and read. Yet the duality tied to bearing witness has been, knowingly or not, weighted toward the side of representation and explores how the magnitude and implications of the Holocaust are portrayed, referenced, and pictured in literature and art.

Many books and essays investigate the limits of Holocaust representation—the limitations and subordination of language, imagination, and art in depicting an event as catastrophic as the Holocaust. In this book I redress the imbalance through a close examination of the other side of that equation: the role of the reader and the process of reading. The act of "reading the Holocaust" places a different set of demands on readers, one that is distinct from writing about the Holocaust and one that is distinct from the process of reading that we engage in for other, nontraumatic texts. In his work *Transgressions of Reading* (1993), in which he explains how readers engage personally with specific and nontraumatic narratives, Robert Newman claims that the adjustments made by a reader in decoding text imitate the authorial process of writing.[5] I am interested here in investigating how, for traumatic material, these same adjustments either cannot be made or are made in response to different pressures and with different results.

Virtually no sustained exploration about reading Holocaust representation exists. In this work, I aim not merely to understand why that is but also to offer a methodology for reading that takes into account its correlative: the unrepresentable and the unimaginable. In large part because I deal with silence and the implications of reading and reading differently, defining a theoretical framework for it proves challenging. The questions I examine tend to fall outside the traditional lines of academic inquiry and can be—need to be—considered through a multi- and interdisciplinary approach rather than focused through a narrower lens. My own formalist training as a reader and literary scholar certainly plays a role in my understanding of text, and in each section of the book I linger over the act of reading itself as a means of illustrating its function, its interpretive possibilities, and also the limits of the reader. I adopt a number of methodological approaches and analytic tools developed by a diverse range of scholars working on the Holocaust or—separately—on conceptions of reading. These scholars reside intellectually in area studies such as Holocaust studies, gender studies, trauma studies, literary studies, and cultural studies, as well as in the better defined disciplines such as psychology, literature, history, and philosophy. This wide range of disciplinary influences strikes me as fitting since our roles as readers cross disciplines, cultures, and often histories. Central to my study of reading Holocaust literature is the recognition of the fluidity of definitions and boundaries that attempt to separate those who supposedly belong from those who do not.

I consider a diverse set of Holocaust texts that include within them memoir, autobiographical fiction, poetry, fiction, and archival matter. These include texts widely known and read such as Primo Levi's *Survival in Auschwitz* (1996), for example, and other texts such as diaries, which have a far more limited audience. In a similar vein, in addition to considering texts indisputably catalogued as "Holocaust texts," often because they are written by Holocaust survivors and their immediate descendants, I examine—and broaden—this designation of belonging, understanding the genre as relevant to functions of reading in addition to personal history and the relationship of the author to the Holocaust. As the connection between authors and the Holocaust grows more tenuous over time, I refer also to writers who might be categorized as third- or even fourth-generation, proposing that for them the act of writing and reading draws closer together in terms of imaginative authority. That is, author and reader, as figures on both sides of the page, must navigate their understanding of the Holocaust primarily through text and through the imagination rather than through personal experience in acquainting themselves with a Holocaust narrative. The risk, as I illustrate is the case with certain texts, is that the essential quality of unreadability is violated, thus subverting the aim of greater comprehension.

The guiding organizational principal at work in this book is chronological and, within that framework, generational divisions. Thus, after an opening chapter on theoretical concepts of reading, I turn to three chapters on memoirs as divided by generation: eyewitness memoir, followed by second-generation memoir, followed by "third" or post-Holocaust memoir, a designation that refers to contemporary nonfiction literature written about the Holocaust. The concept of belonging to or identifying with these conventionally accepted categories is a topic I address throughout. The second section of this book addresses the enormous field of American Holocaust fiction that has emerged since 1945 and, as with memoir, is roughly broken down by generation.

In addition to bringing together a wide array of sources in order to consider them together and to shine attention on texts that have long lived in the shadows of other texts, my aim is to trace the qualities, conditions, and meanings behind the act of reading about the Holocaust through time and genre. My purpose here is to lead readers to examine a behavior that feels like second nature in an effort to better comprehend and value Holocaust texts. I identify here three modes of unreadability that—while roughly compatible with the three-generational structure of post-Holocaust authorship commonly referenced by scholars and readers—adjust, challenge, and expand notions of belonging in connection to these groups. That is, the quality of textual silence or unreadability distinguishes one generation from the next not only chronologically but in substance and form *and* in unreadability. Eyewitness authors deal with reading in a highly self-conscious way, recognizing reading as an experimentation with silence. Author-eyewitnesses write not only with an audience in mind but often, with painful awareness, record their experiences and memories while recognizing that their writing inadequately represents their experience and that their readers will fail to grasp fully even what they do write.

The presence and role of unreadability or textual silence is further problematized with second-generation Holocaust writers who document their quest to discover a narrative that can be written—that is, a narrative rendered readable—of their parents' wartime experiences. In the absence of their parents' own texts, second-generation writers bear a more complex relation to what they write than do eyewitnesses. Beyond testimony, their search for a possible narrative structure involves and reveals them not only as writers, that is, telling the narrative of the earlier generation, but also in the position of readers and of readers who are themselves thwarted. That is, second-generation writers recognize the boundaries of unreadability in Holocaust experiences that are not theirs and of which they are not direct witnesses.

Third-generation or post-Holocaust authors often strive, because of the historical distance that separates them from the event itself, to recover the unreadable narrative. Because of historical distance, they typically have no direct relation to the events, and so recovery occurs through the experience of textuality, that is, through the act of reading the unreadable. Texts authored by third-generation writers of necessity obscure the fact and nature of unreadability, precisely because the grounds of a "pre-relationship" between writer and reader, which rests on a remembering or a memorializing of precisely that moment, is no longer possible. In this sense, third-generation Holocaust literature as a whole is a marker of loss. Such loss of a direct relationship to the events that are unreadable presents this literature as eminently readable—precisely because readability is an essential condition for representation in the absence of the events themselves.

The final two chapters of this text focus on contemporary Jewish Holocaust fiction. Here I investigate how the use of the Holocaust as background setting serves both to enable discussions about it but also, and significantly, to marginalize its role. Chapter 5 is devoted to the fiction of Chaim Potok, Cynthia Ozick, and Philip Roth, and earlier conceptions of the Holocaust in American literature. Chapter 6 explores the more contemporary work of Aryeh Lev Stollman and Nicole Krauss. Indeed, the representation of the Holocaust in these novels may be read as an early witness to a future of Holocaust literature where imagination and history—both Holocaust and non-Holocaust history—are interpolated and read exclusively as a hybrid genre.

In part because I came of age in the 1980s, my reading of survivor and children-of-survivor memoirs a generation or more removed from me reflected that distance. The closest members of my family who perished in the Holocaust were largely unknown to me (my grandmother's first cousins and their children), separated by generations and geography. My long-standing engagement with the Holocaust historically and culturally was built primarily on books, museums, and artifacts. In other words, my identity as a reader, listener, and viewer is the primary means through which I came to know whatever I do about the Holocaust. I realize that the majority of my peers are in the same position, since the majority of American and indeed world Jewry has little direct connection to the Holocaust. In spite of this—perhaps because of it—Holocaust literature, film, and art remain a major component of Jewish culture and consciousness.

This history leads me to first define the roots of unreadability in eyewitness texts and then trace this quality with its transformations through second-generation literature and into contemporary works of memoir, fiction, and art. My aim here is to show how recent publications fit into—and complicate—the trajectory of Holocaust productions that has, until recently, been described primarily in linear and chronological terms. I attempt this without in any way minimizing the impact of eyewitness testimony and second-generation literature; their contribution to postmodernism and even, retroactively, to earlier literary and artistic eras, is inestimable. Rather, I wish here not only to consider the influence and effect of earlier Holocaust texts on those written in the past decade or two but also to reflect further on memory and memorialization through the reading of contemporary texts. I wish to show how, in moving retroactively as well as progressively, we as readers more fully understand the essential quality of unreadability that continues to affect the reading and writing of Holocaust texts even until today.

# 1 • READABILITY AND UNREADABILITY

## A Fractured Dialogue

> The Holocaust belongs to the type of enormous experience which reduces one to silence. Any utterance, any statement, any "answer" is tiny, meaningless, and occasionally ridiculous.
>
> —Aharon Appelfeld, *Beyond Despair*

The two opening images of Primo Levi's *La Tregua—The Truce* (published in the United States as *The Reawakening*), which describes his liberation from Auschwitz and his long journey home, shift between his own act of reading and ours.[1] I use these images here as a means to introduce the concept of readability and unreadability—in contrast to postwar and ongoing discussions around the process of reading itself, including theories that investigate how meaning and interpretation emerge from reading. After Auschwitz was liberated by the Russians, Levi is ill and weak and is hoisted into a cart along with other sick and dying men and taken to the infirmary in the main part of Auschwitz: "While the slow steps of Yankel's horses drew me towards remote liberty, for the last time there filed before my eyes the huts where I had suffered and matured, the roll-call square where the gallows and the gigantic Christmas tree still towered side by side, and the gate to slavery, on which one could still read the three, now hollow, words of derision: 'Arbeit Macht Frei,' 'Work Gives Freedom.' "[2] These are the words that Levi first encounters upon entering the camp. He records this moment in *Survival in Auschwitz*: the gate is "brightly illuminated (its memory still strikes me in my dreams)."[3] The shift Levi notes in his own reading of the words that demarcate the boundary of Auschwitz are telling: from "brightly illuminated" as he enters the camp, to hollow and derisive on his departure, to continuing to "strike" him in his dreams decades after the war, all these effects reflect the "proverbial work" the sign purportedly advances.[4] The sign itself identifies Auschwitz as a place of work "where the nonproper, the nonworking—and, it is thus insinuated, the already dead—are once more put to death, in order that the proper, the society of work, can emerge as the product of its own labor. It defines murder as the work of life on itself."[5] The bitter hollowness with which Levi reads the sign on his departure underscores the mockery found in each word—"work"; "making"; "freedom"—each of which is rendered void of its original meaning in Auschwitz, the place that ultimately concentrates on the unmaking of its *Häftlinge* (Levi's preferred word for prisoners like himself).

Levi's second initiation of reading anticipates his reader. As he recovers in the infirmary in the days following liberation, he finds in a neighboring bed a child about three years old who is paralyzed, cannot speak, and has no name but who others around him have taken to calling Hurbinek. A Hungarian teenager in another bunk devotes himself to Hurbinek's care and declares after a week of tending to the child "that Hurbinek 'could say a word.' What word? He did not know, a difficult word, not Hungarian: something like 'mass-klo,' 'mastiklo.' . . . In the following days everybody listened to him in silence, anxious to understand, and among us there were speakers of all the languages of Europe; but Hurbinek's word remained secret." Levi's tone shifts in the next sentence, addressing his readers as much as those who are with him, puzzling out Hurbinek's syllables: "No, it was certainly not a message, it was not a revelation; perhaps it was his name, if it had ever fallen to his lot to be given a name; perhaps (according to one of our hypotheses) it meant 'to eat,' 'bread'; or perhaps 'meat' in Bohemian, as one of us who knew that language maintained." And then Levi concludes magisterially: "Hurbinek, who was three years old and perhaps had been born in Auschwitz and had never seen a tree; Hurbinek, who had fought like a man, to the last breath, to gain his entry into the world of men, from which a bestial power had excluded him; Hurbinek, the nameless, whose tiny forearm—even his bore the tattoo of Auschwitz; Hurbinek died in the first days of March 1945, free but not redeemed. Nothing remains of him: he bears witness through these words of mine."[6]

By concentrating on language and more specifically on reading, or (as I believe it is better described) on unreading, as marking his way into and out of Auschwitz, Levi invites those who are reading about his reading—namely, us—to reflect on our own actions, positions, and interpretations. In the first instance, Levi bears witness through the act of reading; in the second, he narrates and records, navigating between the non-witness reader (again, us) and the voiceless non-survivor. What is most significant here is the sense that Levi recognizes not only our limits of comprehension but also, and quite willingly, his own. The "secret" word that Hurbinek repeats bears import through the act of repetition—originating with the child, reproduced by Levi, read by us. Repetition and not (necessarily) comprehension is, Levi both illustrates and advises, a legitimate form of bearing witness. In recording Hurbinek's testimony, in declaring its incomprehensibility and also its value as testimony Levi not only makes room for the unreadable but becomes a protector or preserver of it, recognizing how easy it would be to modify—and so reduce—its unknown meaning to something more manageable and more accessible, more identifiable, such as a name or a plea for food. In many ways the foreignness of Hurbinek's language and testimony resonates with the discomfort with which readers encounter the unreadable. Levi recognizes this tension and not so much resolves it as makes room for it, using the legibility of his language to imbed the illegibility of the murdered witness.

Taking together these two moments in Levi's *The Reawakening* illustrates the need and function behind reconsidering our relationship to the act of reading, both the language that is readable and accessible and the language that subverts our understanding, language that falls into textual silence. In some way, my understanding of the unreadable can be aligned with Giorgio Agamben's understanding of bearing witness. "What is borne witness to cannot already be language or writing. It can only be something to which no one has borne witness. And this is the sound that arises from the lacuna, the non-language that one speaks when one is alone, the non-language to which language answers, in which language is born. It is necessary to reflect on the nature of that to which no one has borne witness, on this non-language."[7] Hurbinek's initial silence is transposed into a language that is inaccessible to all those around him. But, Levi reminds us, meaning derived from the absence of meaning is an essential component of witnessing.

Indeed, I would go so far as to say that Levi not only articulates an important difference between reading as a survivor and reading otherwise but in doing so gestures toward a tension between memory and experience that is transfigured for post-Holocaust readers. Our memory is a memory of that fragmented textual experience made available to us by the survivor-writer. The memory is for the most part intact—we have the book right in front of us! The experience it captures and the experience it *is* itself as a text that has been read are both well within our reach to describe, discuss, process, read, and re-read. In effect, our ability to read distracts us from what is arguably the most delicate, essential, and hard to access element of the text, namely, the silence that accompanies the language, imagery, and style of the original text—an overture, in other words, to read the unreadable. Here language and narrative both do and do not allow for the presence of the unreadable with the intention of illuminating its importance and value. An alternate formulation of this turn appears in Kalí Tal's *Worlds of Hurt* (1996) with the suggestion that one strategy of coping culturally with traumatic narrative is to mythologize it, "turning it from a frightening and uncontrollable event into a contained and predictable narrative. . . . Traumatic events are written and rewritten until they become codified and narrative form gradually replaces content as the focus of attention."[8] One might add here that mythologizing is a product of reading as well as writing. The reductive nature of a text or texts that have gone through the process of mythologizing gestures toward the necessity of defining and preserving the quality of the unreadable that was part of the text's original creation.

The process of reading is typically understood as a moment or series of moments of illumination, from which readers derive certain meanings through a complex processing of words or images and placing them in a continuum of individual and textual memory of contexts and usages. Mikhail Bakhtin understands reading as a dialogic enterprise, one intrinsically open to outside influences in which no word is limited to a single meaning. The main thrust behind Bakhtin's understanding of reading is that readers cannot and do not converge around a single meaning with a given text. Rather, language and thus also reading are fundamentally relational. Readers and texts, and the cultural influences that form them, come together to produce the multiple meanings that inform reading. Bakhtin claims that

> no living word relates to its object in a *singular* way: between the word and its object, between the word and the speaking subject, there exists an elastic environment of other, alien words about the same object, the same theme, and this is an environment that it is often difficult to penetrate.... The way in which the word conceives its object is complicated by a dialogic interaction within the object between various aspects of its socio-verbal intelligibility. And an artistic representation, an "image" of the object, may be penetrated by this dialogic play of verbal intentions that meet and are interwoven in it.[9]

Bakhtin's thesis here is clear: meaning and thus reading always exceed the singular definition found within a text's individual words.

Bakhtin's definition is significant both in its understanding of the process of reading and in its gesture toward what cannot be read: if language opens on a multiplicity of meaning, not only will the value attached to any one reading vary among readers but the possibility of meaning existing outside of or eluding any one reading is a constant presence. This does not mean that all acts of reading are equal. Nor does it mean that the limits of reading and what lies beyond them—namely, the unreadable or the silent—play a prominent role in every text. Rather, this points to an underlying anxiety that often accompanies the act of reading and acknowledging or identifying our limitations as readers. Claiming that we cannot or do not read (even as we all seem to) appears to fly in the face of our understanding of ourselves even as individuals. Yet, in keeping with Bakhtin's notion of the elasticity of language, the meaning that emerges from reading is so various and divergent that also unattainable meaning becomes a possibility. Holocaust texts, and in particular survivor testimonies, challenge the normative practices behind reading. What this means in connection to Bakhtin's understanding of dialogism is that, while many meanings behind reading Holocaust literature certainly exist, one of them is and must be the presence of textual silence or unreadability.

One central cause behind the "unreadability" of Holocaust texts lies in the tension between memory and experience. Survivor-novelist Aharon Appelfeld best situates these two distinct but overlapping concepts when he notes that anyone "who underwent the Holocaust will be as wary of memory as of fire. . . . It was impossible to live after the Holocaust except by silencing memory. Memory became your enemy." Appelfeld documents the moment for him when "memory burst forth from the prison where it had been sent." As an author, the challenge then was corralling memory in such a way that it would give "a new order to facts" and touch upon the "heart of the experience."[10] Memory can never be conveyed in its wholeness; rather, the tools of the writer—Appelfeld lists them as "the sense of alternatives, of proportion, the choice of words"—lend themselves to a more fragmented description of experience. The unreadable, then, is a recognition of the gap between the memory and the experience that Appelfeld and so many other Holocaust eyewitnesses who write about their memories regularly note; the sense that their documentation is necessarily limited and incomplete and yet, at the same time, necessary. "The question facing me was no longer what happened, but what had to have happened," Appelfeld notes as he reflects on the shift between not writing and writing about the Holocaust. Memory serves to represent the past even as it stands for what cannot be represented.

To return to Bakhtin's conception of reading, in many ways he and postwar writing about reading by the philosopher Jean-Paul Sartre and literary theorists Roland Barthes and Wolfgang Iser all combine to express renewed interest in defining the relationship between writing and reading, essentially investigating a cross-section of phenomenology and epistemology. These thinkers largely recognized that the process of writing involves a special sort of partnership, with a "dialectic correlative" (in Sartre's words), which links the process of writing to the process of reading: "these two interdependent acts require two differently active people [whose] combined efforts . . . bring into being the concrete and imaginary object which is the work of the mind."[11] Iser moves one step further, describing the reading process as a "dynamic *interaction* between text and reader."[12] Iser, in part, is responding to Barthes's claims in his 1968 essay "The Death of the Author" that the existence of a text "lies not in its origin but in its destination." Yet this destination cannot any longer be personal. The reader "is without history, biography, psychology; he is simply that *someone* who holds together in a single field all the traces by which the written text is constituted."[13] This move requires the author to be "removed."[14]

## THE ROLE OF THE READER

Barthes's provocatively titled essay and extreme position required theorists to consider more seriously the role of the reader in relation to the author. What these several views share is the principle that the act of reading is comprised of a series of constructive moments *for the reader*, a process of production where symbols become characters, characters become sentences, sentences become stories, stories become worlds. Whereas previously the notion of creation and creativity was attributed solely to the act of authorship, with a reader dutifully reading for a proscribed meaning, increasingly in the twentieth century the reader is considered part of the creative process that, when successful, results in a more extended or even open meaning.

Among the many theorists who build on Bakhtin's understanding of language, reading, and writing, the general consensus emerges in which the author is in fact quite removed from the relationship and interaction between the reader and the text. The reader and the text essentially meet in an arena that is open to cultural influences, mediation, and experience.[15] In effect, these are causal constructions of reading: readers are able to read and understand narrative because they devise a system of comprehension that contextualizes current reading in a continuum of past reading and personal experience.[16] In his book *Understanding Reading* (1971), the psycholinguist Frank Smith makes the point that reading works on a predictive model. That is, the uncertainty with which any reader faces a text "is limited to a few probable alternatives" that are predicted before the actual reading of a given sentence. The act of reading a sentence "indicate[s] which predicted alternative is appropriate" and thus "comprehension occurs."[17] Smith's understanding of reading, in keeping with other postwar theorists, positions readers as participants in bringing meaning to text, which they do through a limited set of predictions and expectations about the text before and as they read.

In a similar vein, Paul Ricoeur extends the "dialectical structure of reading" by thinking of it in unequal terms: "With writing, the verbal meaning of the text no longer coincides with the mental meaning or intention of the text. This intention is both fulfilled and abolished by the text, which is no longer the voice of someone present. The text is mute. An asymmetric relation obtains between text and reader, in which only one of the partners speaks for the two. . . . Consequently, to understand is not merely to repeat the speech event in a similar event, it is to generate a new event beginning from the text in which the initial event has been objectified."[18] Ricoeur understands meaningful reading as taking place through "emplotment," that is, reading is situated not only in relation to prior texts but also in anticipation of future texts. Another way of thinking about emplotment is as a sequence of events " 'configured' ('grasped together') in such a way as to represent 'symbolically' what would otherwise be unutterable in language."[19] For Ricoeur, reading narrative is the opposite of passively imbibing the ideas—historical, fictional, or otherwise—of the author. Rather, the reader "works up the material given in perception and reflection, fashions it, and creates something new."[20]

In his study *Becoming a Reader* (1994), J. A. Appleyard largely concurs with Frank Smith's view that readers extract meaning from the text as they read: "The text is a system of response-inviting structures that the author has organized by reference to a repertory of social and literary codes shared by author and reader. But it does not simply cause or limit the reader's response, nor does the reader passively digest the text. Rather, reader and text interact in a feedback loop. The reader brings expectations derived from a literary and life experience to bear on the text, and the text feeds back these expectations or it does not."[21] In considering the relationships between author, text, and reader, increasingly it is the interaction between the text and the reader that is explored, with the author's role diminished. The figure of control, then, the figure who is instrumental in lending a text meaning and presence, is the reader.

Understanding the role of the reader in the twentieth and twenty-first centuries is part and parcel of the larger movement established by postmodern theorists to reject methodologies that invest heavily or exclusively in the power of the author as a single powerful figure. And in many ways Holocaust literature deeply identifies with the sweeping rejections espoused by postmodern theorists. Postmodernists, anxious to revise the traditional conception of authorial authority, diminish the role of the author as the dominant component of textual meaning. The philosopher Thelma Lavine notes that from postmodern theorists came "a passionate anti-Cartesian, anti-Enlightenment anti-rationalism; anti-foundationalism; anti-realism; and anti-humanism. They rejected claims to axiomatic truths that mirror reality; they rejected an autonomous, rational, constituting self and all totalizing theories of history, society, and politics. . . . This outcome is expressed by some postmodernists in the dire and apocalyptically exciting pronouncements of the end of philosophy, the end of history, the end of capitalism, the end of society, the end of art, and the death of man."[22]

Yet here we arrive at an important intersection between functional theories of reading and those evident in Holocaust survivor literature: the presence of the survivor-author both asserts a powerful presence over the text and, as Levi makes clear, stands for those who cannot write or speak. Central to the telling and the retelling, the reading and the re-reading of Levi's recounting of Hurbinek's story is the absence of one author, Hurbinek, and the presence of another—namely, Levi, the eyewitness author. In acknowledging both Hurbinek's role in testifying and the need for the reader to read and to *not* understand, Levi establishes a possibility that some texts cannot and, more crucially, *should not* be decoded—that, indeed, the idea of participation and predictive modeling or emplotment lose their relevance when applied to reading experiences that encompass as profound a transformation in language, meaning, and representation as the Holocaust does. In short, ideas that work convincingly in more normative reading experiences lose their sense of purpose and applicability in representations centered on extreme trauma. I do not claim that the textual silence or unreadability that is present in eyewitness literature is a rejection of more conventional standards of reading; rather, what Levi and other survivor-writers note in their work through demarcating the limits of representation is an accompanying counterpart: the limits of reading. We read even what we cannot access.

Paul Celan's poem "Todesfuge," or "Deathfugue," is another extraordinary example of the presence and absence of the authorial figure in its interaction with readers. Composed in 1944, "Todesfuge" opens with an invocation of the first person plural, "we":

> Black milk of daybreak we drink it at evening
> we drink it at midday and morning we drink it at night
> we drink and we drink[23]

The repetition of "we drink" recalls, as John Felstiner notes, the boisterous music and beat of "much-loved German songs—from the Munich beer-hall, let us say, where Nazism arose . . . until you remember who it is in Celan's poem that is saying *wir* ('we')."[24] While not immediately evident, as the poem progresses, it becomes increasingly clear that the "we" refers to the Jews, the infamous "other" established by the Nazi government. In "Todesfuge," Celan takes a common German trope, one that pairs music, rhythm, and death (think, for example, of Franz Schubert's "Erlkönig"), and inverts it. Instead of the first person referring to a German hegemonic "we," an appropriate reference given Germany's predominance in the arts and culture since the eighteenth century, it assumes the voice of the powerless, the voiceless, the dead. The relocation of power does not end here, however. Celan's "wir" wraps around those who were cast out of society, but "wir" involves the reader, too. As we, the reader, read the "we" of the text we, too, become the ghost-like associations of those whose absence haunts the poem. Like countless other Holocaust texts, Celan's "Todesfuge" resonates with Barthes's idea of the death of the author. Where Celan's poem presses forward is not so much in inviting as forcing readers to identify with the wrenching violence of this absence.

Authorship during the Third Reich, then, became either a totalizing experience of authority and autonomy or something punishable in extreme ways. By looking toward the reader in the decades following World War II and recognizing the role of the reader in determining the meaning behind textuality, postmodernists worked to diffuse the kind of totalitarian system that in their view marked the institutionalism of modernism. Indeed, Theodor Adorno's often quoted sentiment to "write poetry after Auschwitz is barbaric," seen in its original context, explicitly confirms the suspicions of postmodern theorists against the institutions that flourished before the Holocaust:

> The traditional transcendent critique of ideology is obsolete. . . . In the open-air prison which the world is becoming, it is no longer so important to know what depends on what, such is the extent to which everything is one. . . . There are no

> more ideologies in the authentic sense of false consciousness, only advertisements for the world through its duplication and the provocative lie which does not seek belief but commands silence. . . . Neutralized and ready-made, traditional culture has become worthless today. . . . The more total society becomes, the greater the reification of the mind and the more paradoxical its effort to escape reification on its own. Even the most extreme consciousness of doom threatens to degenerate into idle chatter. Cultural criticism finds itself faced with the final stage of the dialectic of culture and barbarism. To write poetry after Auschwitz is barbaric. And this corrodes even the knowledge of why it has become impossible to write poetry today.[25]

Adorno here talks more generally about the production of culture that, in his mind, has contributed to the mass destruction of the Holocaust and World War II; he argues for a "silence" to quell the "idle chatter," for inner reflection to replace public and "false consciousness." Would Adorno also claim that to *read* poetry after Auschwitz is barbaric? The production of "neutralized" culture depends on its consumption and dissemination in order for it to have life. Insofar as reading enables this kind of public presence, yes, Adorno's statement can be understood to include it. That is, to the extent the reader is regarded as a consumer of culture, that consumption, too, contributes to the barbarity of poetry. Yet at least some reading after Auschwitz—specifically that about Auschwitz—leaves untouched the aspect of the text that I call here the "unreadable."[26] Recognizing the unreadable aspect of a text serves to reestablish the initial wholeness of poetry and culture more broadly. Textual silence, the places in Holocaust literature where meaning is found in what we cannot access precisely because of its tacit presence as what remains unspoken and uninterpreted secures it from "false consciousness" and "idle chatter"—falls outside Adorno's claim about the ethics of literacy after the Holocaust.

So, yes, the focus on the reader in the postwar era is complicated by the voice of the survivor and, with it, the devastating power of witnessing that, after the war, came to the reader/listener/viewer's attention by way of survivor testimony—either oral, visual, or in the written word. Shoshana Felman and Dori Laub note the special authority with which the eyewitness remembers and relates what he or she saw and experienced: "Since the testimony cannot be simply relayed, repeated or reported by another without losing its function as a testimony, the burden of the witness—in spite of his or her alignment with other witnesses—is a radically unique, noninterchangeable and solitary burden."[27] The necessity for testimony to be read, heard, and viewed and the impossibility, through these very acts, of having it remain "only" testimonial, make for an intrinsically unreadable aspect to Holocaust testimony. This tension can and ought to be extended to literature that relies on testimony, even (perhaps especially) testimony written decades after the Holocaust took place. The necessity found in wanting to access testimony and not being able to do so fuels readers to return repeatedly to the act of reading or experiencing testimony, in spite of the trauma or pain this reading may incur.

The few literary theorists who have taken up the role of the reader in relation to reading Holocaust texts have differed in their understanding of the relations among author, text, and reader. In his powerful essay "Interpreting Literary Testimony," James Young considers both the role of the witness and that of his or her readers. First, the witness:

> It is almost as if violent events—perceived as aberrations or ruptures in the cultural continuum—demand their retelling, their *narration*, back into traditions and structures they would otherwise defy. At the same time, however, there seems also to be a parallel and contradictory impulse on the part of writers to preserve in narrative the very *dis*continuity that lends events their violent character, the same discontinuity that is so effectively neutralized by its narrative rendering.[28]

Second, the reader:

> For inasmuch as the diarists and memoirists see themselves as traces of experiences, and their words as extensions of themselves, the link between words and events seems quite literally *self*-evident: that which has touched the writer's hand would now touch the reader. . . . But for the reader with only words on a page, the authority for this link is absent. The words in a reproduced Holocaust diary are no longer "traces" of the crime, as they were for the writer who inscribed them; what was evidence for the writer at the moment he wrote is now, after it leaves his hand, only a detached and free-floating sign, at the mercy of all who would read and misread it. Once he withdraws from his words, the writer has in effect also withdrawn the word's evidentiary authority, the only link it ever had to its object in the world. The writer's absence thus becomes the absence of authority for the word itself, making it nothing more than a signifier that gestures back toward the writer and his experiences, but which is now only a gesture, a fugitive report.[29]

The reproduction of testimony is a process of mechanization and, consequently, erasure. The physical reproduction of testimony divorces it not only from its creator, the survivor-witness, but also from its reader. Indeed, once testimony becomes a text that is read, re-read, and misread—that is, once it exists beyond the author's self—it becomes significantly something less than what it originally was. Cynthia Ozick, in her impassioned essay "Who Owns Anne Frank?," declares that just such a thing has occurred with the popularity of Anne Frank's *Diary of a Young Girl*: "In celebrating Anne Frank's years in the secret annex, the nature and meaning of her death has been, in effect, forestalled. The diary's keen lens is helplessly opaque to the diarist's explicit doom—and this opacity, *replicated in young readers in particular*, has led to . . . the shamelessness of appropriation" (my italics).[30] Both Young and Ozick agree, then, that one function of reading is a process of replication, one that serves—even if inadvertently—to erase or mute, to the point of extinction, the subject of the text read.

Young and Ozick claim on the one hand the disappearance of testimony through the act of reading or listening and, on the other hand, the necessity of creating a new kind of listener or reader capable of absorbing eyewitness testimony. Indeed, Ozick goes so far in the conclusion of "Who Owns Anne Frank?" as to suggest a shocking yet "more salvational outcome" to the misappropriation of Anne Frank's legacy: "Anne Frank's diary burned, vanished, lost—saved from a world that made of it all things, some of them true, while floating lightly over the heavier truth of named and inhabited evil."[31] The possibility is posed here of redemption in the idea of rendering texts physically unavailable. This element of inaccessibility, however, already exists in eyewitness literature.

Instead of literalizing its silence through physical destruction, however, I propose a new method of reading and theorizing reading. A counterpart to this new methodology is explored by Michael Levine who, in *The Belated Witness* (2006), references witnessing as limited to a "performative speech act . . . open to the possibility of failure, to the possibility of *not* reaching its destination." Levine concentrates his inquiry on "the fluid space of transmission opened between the precariously fluctuating positions of the witness and the witness to the witness."[32] While he examines both spoken and written testimony, Levine's main goal is to "invent" a new method of listening that takes into account the repetition of oral testimony, its gaps and silences, and creates a dialogic relationship between speaker and listener. The necessity of oral testimony, Levine argues, lies in having a listener who can adequately serve as "a witness to the witness" and, in so doing, enable the witness to exist. I propose creating a mode of reading that leaves room for the inaccessible, the illegible, the silent, and the unreadable. The participation of the reader in these acts of perceived "failure" in fact leads to a more complete version of what we conceive of as reading.

What *happens* when we read Holocaust texts? While my argument here is not a proposal for a middle ground between the creation of a new kind of receptivity and the elimination of any need for it, I do want to underscore the "moment" of criticism on which these critical "readers" focus in common: an *unreadable* aspect of Holocaust texts which is in my view foundational to Holocaust texts. Standard theories of reading do not apply to Holocaust texts because they presuppose a "text" or event that is readable, a story or history emplotted or predicted into narrative structures that are personally familiar to the reader. Theoretical explorations of the act of reading argue that readability is in general dependent on a dialectical contract between reader and text, but the trauma of the Holocaust effectively fractures this relationship, creating a space and position where reading is interrupted and finally impossible. Unreadability in these terms is a characteristic aspect of texts about the Holocaust that, although more difficult to identify in texts further removed from it, is as essential to second- and third-generation accounts as to eyewitness accounts. Indeed, unreadability is one of few textual qualities that link all Holocaust texts, from all periods and all authors. Thus my claim that "readability" itself is called into question in Holocaust literature. Indeed, the shifts in this literature between first- and second-generation literature and again between second-generation and more contemporary Holocaust works suggest the inadequacy of standard and even postmodernist reading theory because in these works the very concept of readability is itself evolving. Understanding the problematics of these generational shifts, which literature of the Holocaust clearly marks, allows us at once to critique theories of reading and to revise them.

While the concept of representation, through language or imagery, is an aspect of Holocaust literature and art that has been fruitfully studied and analyzed, reading has generated much less scholarly attention insofar as it applies to the Holocaust. And this in spite of the fact that every act of representation assumes some form of receptivity. The question at the heart of this book asks the following: How do we read acts of trauma that are unrecognizable, not replicable, and have no historical resonance? Theories of reading that are most commonly accepted essentially place comprehension on a spectrum of available possible experience. Indeed, as understood by theorists as varied as Mikhail Bakhtin and Louise Rosenblatt, or Susan Suleiman and Martin Nystrand, reading is now commonly understood to rely on the experience of the reader at least as much as the experience of the writer. Readers make sense of what they read by connecting words, ideas, and even narrative to their own experiences—both lived and read—of precisely those words, ideas, and narrative. For example, readers have a special affiliation to first-person narrative because the "I" stands as a familiar and known point of reference for all individuals. Reading comprehension can be built and furthered by text—we can think of this as developing a reading history and a reading future—but all textual meaning must be based in the possibility or reality of experience. Read meaning is cumulative and anticipatory; it relies as much on universal history as it does on personal history; it is located in between the experienced past and the projected future.

Read meaning, then, is fluid and relies on narrations of possibility, that is, for a reader to read, a text has to fall within the range of not only possible but also replicable or recognizable human experience, history, and expression. Yet, as George Steiner notes, the "sphere of language," while once encompassing "nearly the whole of experience and reality," has today "narrowed tremendously." "The world of words has shrunk."[33] Jean Améry (born Hanns Chaim Mayer), the Jewish Austrian essayist and Holocaust survivor, reflects on the time it took for him to "learn the ordinary language of freedom" once he had been liberated. Even after reeducating himself, he speaks "with discomfort and without real trust in its validity."[34] For Améry, language "ultimately proves inadequate as a cure for the precarious condition of a man losing faith in the world again daily when, on getting up, he sees his Auschwitz number tattooed on his forearm."[35] Elie Wiesel—in many of his works, including *The Gates of the Forest*—notes the failure of language to adequately represent trauma. Cynthia Ozick and Berel Lang both advocate selective silence or the absence of art or literature representing the Holocaust as preferable—preferable because they are more truthful, more accurate—to representations of the Holocaust that are historical, narrative, or ethical distortions.[36] In her essay "The Rights of History and the Rights of Imagination," Ozick honors the "scrupulous" voices of Elie Wiesel and Primo Levi as well as "the stumbling voices of witnesses who have no fame and have no voice, yet whose eloquence rises up through the scars and stammerings of remembered suffering."[37] But as language increasingly "break[s] through the gates of memory into the freer fields of parable, myth, analogy, symbol, story," Ozick writes, the result "is to dilute and to obscure, and ultimately to expunge, the real nature of the Holocaust."[38]

These various declarations regarding the limitations of language bear out on the understanding of language that takes place through reading in general and through reading trauma—which, because it lies at the extreme end of experience is especially subject to a linguistic narrowing. In many texts written about the Holocaust a tense relationship emerges that, on the one hand, asserts the unavailability of adequate vocabulary and signs and, on the other, resorts to implementing available vocabulary and signs in the absence of other possibilities. In spite of the by now well-established idea that language and art intended to represent aspects of the Holocaust are inadequate, much has nonetheless been written about that event. Regardless of whether the many words and images devoted to the Holocaust are indeed representational, all of these texts involve some kind of relationship with audience.

Just as the Holocaust has been explored as lying at the outer limits of representation and imagination, and so tied to the terms "un-representable" and "unimaginable," here I position Holocaust textuality as at the limits of the readable, bearing an essential aspect of unreadability that both imposes distance between memory and experience and also draws them as close together as possible. Understanding and valuing the unreadable in Holocaust texts lends the reader reading them some imperfect fragment of meaning; and this in spite of the fact that the very notion of unreadability means that the relation of the reader to the text—the making and processing of meaning that comes through the collaboration between reader, author, and text—is disrupted or thwarted. Likewise, by *not* allowing for the unreadable, readers risk distancing themselves even more profoundly from the text than is already entailed by a position marked by historical distance and inherited memory. Failing to make room for the unreadable is possible, as I trace in the following chapters, but doing so comes at the expense of precisely the role post-Holocaust texts are meant to preserve, namely, a means to remember an atrocity that redefined local and global landscapes. This failure has key literary, historical, and ethical consequences: at its most severe, it discredits survivor testimony and memory. Recognizing the unreadable—allowing for it, preserving it—entails revising our understanding of the reading process by enlarging it and redefining its limits.

## THE ETHICS OF UNREADING

I turn now to an additional but essential aspect of textual silence in Holocaust narratives, namely, the moral imperative underlying their unreadability. The phrase "the ethics of reading" comes from J. Hillis Miller's work by that name in which he investigates reading in relation to six authors: Immanuel Kant, Paul de Man, T. S. Eliot, Anthony Trollope, Henry James, and Walter Benjamin. "The ethical moment in the act of reading," argues Miller, "faces in two directions. On the one hand it is a response to something, responsible to it, responsive to it, respectful of it. . . . On the other hand, the ethical moment in reading leads to an act. It enters into the social, institutional, political realms, for example in what the teacher says to the class or in what the critic writes."[39] Miller arrives at his definition of the ethics of reading only after establishing that "ethics and narration cannot be kept separate."[40] While largely in agreement with Miller's understanding of the entwined relationship between reading and ethics, I understand the ethical nature of reading as moving in a distinct third direction: beyond serving as "a response to something," and in addition to playing out in the public arena, reading has a self-reflexive quality. This self-reflexivity occupies an inner negative space, that is, a space characterized by absence rather than presence, by silence rather than sound, by unknowing or not knowing rather than comprehension. Because of its personal nature, reading—and reading ethically—necessarily involves qualities attached to inner-ness, to knowledge of the self, together with the limits to this knowledge. Accordingly, reading is not only responsive, not only proactive, but self-defining. Reading creates memories and informs existing memory—of the act of reading, but also of the self interacting with the text moment by moment. In short, reading moves us inward on a path that, at its most modest, may mirror and parallel the two directions Miller describes but, at its most emphatic, overtakes them completely. As I will elaborate later, the quality of unreadability becomes increasingly marginalized and indirect as the Holocaust recedes into history. The ethical implications behind losing the ability to recognize unreading or to experience unreadability are immense, affecting notions of collective memory and public history and memorializations but also personal and private remembering.

Even in its most public iteration, reading is an intensely private and intimate experience. This is perhaps most dramatically depicted in fifteenth-century Renaissance art where images of the eye—detached from the body, enlarged and bulging, often bearing a pair of wings—illuminate the power of observation and sight in absorbing knowledge and bringing what lies external to the body into the mind. Daniel Schwarz advocates for a method of reading that he calls "humanistic formalism," in which he imagines reading "as a series of hypotheses rather than as a final product," one that "is inclusive rather than exclusive. Even as we answer each question and pursue each line of inquiry, we become aware that each explanation is partial."[41] Schwarz thus urges a return to "the more modest Socratic question and answer structure in order that we leave rhetorical space for other explanations."[42]

In his thoughtful work *Narrative Ethics* (1995), Adam Newton, even more emphatically than Miller or Schwarz, ties ethics and narration together, making the case for "narrative *as* ethics: the ethical consequences of narrating story and fictionalizing person, and the reciprocal claims binding teller, listener, witness, and reader in that process."[43] Newton further distinguishes his work on ethics and narrative by acknowledging that "reading sometimes demands the contrary sign of looking away, of stopping short, of realizing that texts, like persons, cannot entirely be known, that they must keep some of their secrets. It is, finally, the sign of interruption which identifies the reader's share in the act of telling the self to others, the dialectic of revelation and concealment, of leaving home and looking away, of knowing and acknowledging, that is narrative ethics."[44] Newton's point coincides, at least in part, with the unknowability of the Holocaust experience. In this way Newton recognizes that the negative or interior "rhetorical space" of what I call textual silence bears insistently on the reading process; it is a moment in the text that precludes the experience of a fully realized relationship to the text, an experience that is itself integral to the act of reading.

The image of "rhetorical space" resonates with understanding reading as an act that, in addition to its other impulses, also moves inward. Because it is self-directed and self-informed, the notion of "rhetorical space" is valuable, literally opening up a possibility of absence. "Rhetorical space" can refer to a product of reading, a specific interpretation, but it can also refer to a gap, one that the reader recognizes but is unable or unwilling to fill. If readers can read responsively and with an awareness of the world around them, as Miller proposes, and if they can read, as Schwarz recommends, with an even greater capacity for divergent interpretations, then they must also be able to read the space as itself, which is what I mean by "unreading." That is, in moments of unreading, readers recognize the limits of their authority over text: whether the printed word is referenced by the author or even printed on the page, readers acknowledge, first, that text exists and, second, that text is impervious to the act of reading. While readers can interpret the unreading of the moment or passage, the exact text itself is not available to interpretation or explanation. The identification of qualities of textuality—for example, the sense (whether explicit or implicit) that "words are beyond us"—endures even when the text itself cannot be accessed or sought through reading; this is what I mean by the "ethics of unreading."[45]

While recognizing that the presence of "rhetorical space" and the act of "looking away" are integral to the reading process, Schwarz and Newton—as with the scholars whose work they build on, including Wayne Booth, Paul Ricoeur, Louise Rosenblatt, and Martha Nussbaum—conceive of these places and actions as embedded within the reading process, a transitory moment that exists side by side with "revelation" or alternative and multiple "explanations."[46] At most they appear as equal, correspondent, and comparable to one another. At the very least, the moment of interruption or concealment is so fractured as to occupy only a small place in the expanse of reading and read narrative.

It is here that I want to introduce the alternate model of unreading and *its* ethical imperative. For, while every reading act is accompanied to some degree by moments of unreading, when it comes to the presence of unreading, not all texts are equal. Some texts are more available to reading and interpretation than others, and the aspect of unreadability in these texts asserts itself less forcefully in them. Wayne Booth, in *The Company We Keep* (1988), establishes as his subject "the ethical value of the stories we tell each other as 'imitations of life,' whether or not they in fact claim to depict actual events."[47] Booth establishes an "ethics *of* readers," the notion that readers have responsibilities toward stories, understanding a given narrative as "ethical" or "unethical."[48] While in principle Booth claims that his subject "must be all narrative," and he theoretically applies his argument of ethics to all literary representation, in fact he recognizes that "we simply read differently when we believe that a story claims to be true than we do when we take it as 'made-up.' . . . As Samuel Johnson insisted, biographies present some kind of ethical power and risk that either are not met in fictions or are met there only in different form."[49]

I would further emphasize the distinction Booth makes by acknowledging that, while many texts have the interpretive quality Booth notes, for others their power comes in a different form. At their most extreme, these texts position unreadability as central to their meaning. To attempt to read the unreadable as if it *were* readable not only reduces the meaning and value of the text but also diminishes the integrity of the reader. Authors of third-generation memoir (see chapter 4) often cannot resist reimagining or reinventing the most violent moments of persecution their loved ones may have experienced. In a move dramatically different from the ambivalent distance established in second-generation memoir (ambivalent because there is a longing to close it and at the same time an understanding that it cannot be done), third-generation memoirists often attempt to record the moments from which earlier generations of writers have backed away. These authors recognize the moral risk at hand; this comes through in their tentativeness to claim their vision as truth. Phrases like "it is possible" and verbs such as "would" qualify the claims the texts otherwise make, pushing them close to certain boundaries of representation and misrepresentation and thus to the near transformation of the unreadable into the readable.

In her article on interpretation and psychoanalysis, Shoshana Felman makes the point that the "readable and the unreadable are by no means simply comparable but neither are they simply opposed, since above all they are not symmetrical, they are not mirror-images of each other."[50] It is not enough—far from it—to count the unreadable as equal in part and measure to the moments of readability that accompany most narrative investigations. Felman suggests that an appropriate corrective would be "not so much to read the unreadable as a variant of the readable, but, to the very contrary, to rethink the readable itself, and hence, to attempt to read it as a variant of the unreadable."[51]

Contrary systems, however, are by their very nature defined by that which they oppose. While Felman acknowledges that reading and unreading, and with them the readable and the unreadable, are not equal and opposite, even when they are linguistically situated in that form, I suggest an approach that further elevates unreadability: the identification of texts that tend more than others to address the necessity of recognizing textuality and, with it, an essential quality of unreadability—essential to understanding the text as it relates to the reader and to the larger world. Imre Kertész's memoir *Dossier K.* (2006) opens with a vivid and telling exchange about precisely this set of interactions. Written in response to the various profiles, reports, and inquiries published about his work after he was named a Nobel Laureate in 2002, *Dossier K.* is a "so-called 'in-depth' interview." Like much of Kertész's work, the memoir is more a conversation or interrogation with and by himself—conducted between the author and his friend and editor Zoltán Hafner between 2003 and 2004.[52] The questioner returns multiple times to the intertwined relationship between fiction and reality that plays such a prominent role in Kertész's work, only to be rebuffed. When inquiring about the label of "autobiographical novel" to *Fatelessness*, Kertész concludes:

> [Kertész:] No such genre [as autobiographical fiction] exists. A book is either autobiography or a novel. If it's autobiography you evoke the past, you try as scrupulously as possible to stick to your recollections; it's a matter of extraordinary importance that you write everything down exactly the way it happened . . . that you don't varnish the facts one little bit. . . . In a novel, by contrast, it's not the facts that matter, but precisely what you add to the facts.
>
> [Questioner:] *But as far as I'm aware—and it's something that you have repeatedly confirmed in statements you have made—your novel is absolutely authentic; every facet of the story is based on documented facts.*
>
> [Kertész:] That's not inconsistent with its being fictional. . . . The world of fiction is a sovereign world that comes to life in the author's head and follows the rules of art, of literature. And that is the major difference that is reflected in the

> form of the work, in its language and its plot. An author invents every aspect of a fiction, every detail.
>
> [Questioner:] *But you can't mean to say that you invented Auschwitz?*
>
> [Kertész:] But in a certain sense that is exactly so. In the novel I did have to invent Auschwitz and bring it to life; I could not fall back on externalities, on so-called historical facts outside the novel; everything had to come into being hermetically, through the magic of the language and composition. . . . From the very first lines you can already get a feeling that you have entered a strange sovereign realm in which everything or, to be more accurate, anything can happen. As the story progresses, the sense of being abandoned increasingly takes hold of the reader; there is a growing sense of losing one's footing.[53]

Perhaps more than any other author considered in this study, Kertész is not only a self-conscious writer but also a self-conscious reader. Aware that Auschwitz both cannot be invented and cannot not be invented (the underlying premise of his line "There is no explanation for Auschwitz," which the narrator/author spends a great deal of time investigating in *Kaddish for an Unborn Child* [1990]), Kertész deliberately positions the reader in a place of increased isolation, remoteness, and strangeness until, ultimately, the growing sense of "losing one's footing" becomes an actuality: the reader is lost. In short, Kertész creates a fiction that bears all the familiar landmarks only to gradually move the reader farther away from them, creating a sense of inaccessibility and unreadability with a text that is characterized on its surface by precisely its qualities of legibility, access, and readability.

By my reckoning, certain kinds of narrative—Kertész's is one powerful example—encompass a subject so extreme in nature that they fall outside the more common normative practices of reading and analysis. Because of historical and cultural repercussions, the production of narrative in the face of genocide, including literary representations of the Holocaust, demand a different kind of reading, one that not only allows for but elevates the significance of the act of unreading and the existence of the unreadable. This does not mean that the ethics tied to reading Holocaust text is any the less relevant. To the contrary: the ethical aspect of reading becomes heightened; it acquires a greater sense of urgency and a more visible presence precisely because the reading of such texts lies on the margins of reading experiences. Ozick presents an example of just this in her short story "A Mercenary." The protagonist, Stanislaw Lushinski, urges his girlfriend to put down the "stories" and "tales" about the Holocaust: "Imagination is romance. Romance blurs. Instead count the number of freight trains."[54] Narrative—and reading narrative, also—invites interpretation, and interpretation of Holocaust history, in whatever form it takes, "blurs" and thus diminishes, by rendering less truthful, the history of the Holocaust. Instead of reading, Lushinski counsels, "count." Ozick's impulse here is one that we as readers share, namely, a desire to "do right" by these texts and the history and memory they encompass, even if our understanding of precisely that quality of moral sensitivity, when it comes to reading and interpretation, may vary.

Indeed, this is where acknowledging the presence of the unreadable, and acknowledging the ethics of unreading, becomes crucial: participating in the act of unreading creates a shared and common experience and memory, particularly among readers removed from eyewitness narrative, those belonging to subsequent generations and varying geographies. In thinking about the act, let alone the ethics, of reading, we no longer make claims about shared or common experiences. As Booth notes, for "any individual reader, the only story that will have ethical power is the one that is heard or read *as* it is heard or read."[55] But this is one of several fundamental differences between the ethics of reading and the ethics of *un*reading. That is, the ethical power of unreading comes in part from the collective understanding and recognition of it. Unreading is a shared experience, one based around—as opposed to within—text. In the earlier example of unreadability found in *Dossier K.*, Kertész identifies the abandonment, the undermining of confidence, of "the reader." That is, Kertész acknowledges that one central feature of reading his work is the way in which readers locate themselves in relation to it. Where the reader becomes isolated and lost—what I call unreading—is a communal experience in the sense that it is shared with other readers.

What, then, are the ethical implications of the role of memory in the "unreading" of Holocaust fiction and memoir? The literary devices used and manipulated in imaginative literature of the Holocaust subject the reader and the reader's relationship with both text and author to a different set of pressures and exchanges from those found in reading eyewitness testimony. In his volume of essays addressing Holocaust literature, Berel Lang notes "that there is a significant relation between the moral implications of the Holocaust and the means of its literary expression. . . . What constraints, whether in the use of fact or in the reach of the imagination, are imposed on authors or readers by the subject of the Holocaust? How does that subject shape the perspectives from which it is viewed?"[56] In his later work, *Act and Idea in the Nazi Genocide* (1990), Lang states even more strongly that "the process of literary representation is viewed as itself constituting a moral act" and "subject to moral judgment."[57]

Building on these questions about the ethics between readers and writers of the Holocaust and the texts they share is the volume of collected essays by Jakob Lothe, Susan Suleiman, and James Phelan, *After Testimony* (2012). As they note in their introduction, "authors writing about the Holocaust often subject conventional forms of narrative to unusual and even extreme transformations. . . . Even as these techniques emphasize their authors' difficulty in coming to terms with the Holocaust, they simultaneously challenge—and often place a considerable interpretive burden on—their audiences. In this way, the authors' efforts to find the appropriate aesthetic forms of representation raise questions about the ethics of their relationship to their audiences. The authors inevitably address an ethics of the told (in their attention to the specific experiences of perpetrators, victims, bystanders, and others), while their techniques also direct attention to the ethics of their telling."[58] I would respond to the ideas posited here and in Lang's work by making two points. First, readers, as active participants in decoding, remembering, and interpreting texts, are, in addition to authors, subject to the moral component found in literary representation. While this point is well argued and documented in work on the ethics of reading more generally (as explored above in relation to Newman, Booth, and Miller), it virtually goes unidentified when thinking about the audience in relation to Holocaust literature. Second, the role—obligation—of the reader is to recognize not only the "ethics of the told" but also the ethics of that which resists being told, narrated, or represented and, consequently, that which resists being read. Here I wish, again, to connect the ethics of reading—and unreading—Holocaust literature to analyses of the ethics of reading more broadly. The negative or interior space that defines "unreading" is present in all acts of reading; the ethical obligation of recognizing this interior space grows with its centrality and urgency in relation to the text.

The moral responsibilities of reading eyewitness literature are more clear-cut than those demanded by reading Holocaust fiction. Whereas the problem with reading testimony can roughly be understood as the challenge of preserving the element of unreadability by resisting what is in fact a common and even cultivated impulse toward identification or assimilation with the narrative's subject, the problem with reading Holocaust fiction is less clear-cut. The many analytical works that analyze eyewitness memoir often acknowledge a sign of their unreadability, for example Sarah Horowitz's work on muteness, James Young's exploration of presence in the face of absence, Alvin Rosenfeld's metaphor of doubling. Each of these, and many more, work both to analyze eyewitness testimony and to acknowledge its unreadable, and central, features. In contrast, because the premise of fiction more generally is to invite readers, as Louise Rosenblatt notes, to focus their attention on the actual experience they are living through during the reading event, the notion of unreadability can be understood as an undoing of the narrative effort. Reading fiction "permits the whole range of responses generated by the text to enter into the center of awareness, and out of these materials [the reader] selects and weaves what he sees as the literary work of art."[59]

In commenting on Martin Amis's Holocaust novel *Time's Arrow*, James Phelan identifies "readerly dynamics" and "readerly judgments."[60] The former are experiential (i.e., the reader's experience of text), the latter determinative (i.e., the judgments that readers "are guided to make" about the text) and work together to decode what has been encoded.[61] Neither Rosenblatt nor Phelan distinguishes between readerly demands for different kinds of aesthetic texts; where they differ is in their recognition of the role of memory for the reader and in the act of reading. Rosenblatt declares that the "reader of any text must actively draw upon past experience" but also understands aesthetic reading as being "*centered directly on what [the reader] is living through during his relationship with that particular text*."[62] Phelan's even-handed conception of textual dynamics carefully accounts for Amis's artistic technique, claiming that it is "part and parcel of an artistic response to the Holocaust that is at once aesthetically innovative and ethically valuable," but he gives no account of memory or history in his various definitions of readerliness, rhetoric, or narrative.[63]

## READERLY MEMORY

In fact, it is a heightened sense of what I call "readerly memory" that both distinguishes traumatic reading from other kinds of reading and accounts in large part for the ethical component enacted through reading Holocaust texts. Readerly memory is an awareness of the past that distinguishes between personal and vicarious experience, for example, as read. In reading eyewitness literature of the Holocaust, the presence and role of readerly memory tempers the reader's "center of awareness," informing his or her relationship with a particular text. Readerly memory also serves a specific role in Holocaust literature: in recognizing the inevitability of the role that the Holocaust has and will continue to take in the textual world, readerly memory serves as a means to factualize the imagination. By this I mean that the act of reading shifts from centering on a process of experience that solely engages the reader to centering on a process of experience that includes an awareness of a past that lies outside of the reader's experience and, indeed, outside the reader's memory. Unreading and the ethics of unreading are closely tied to readerly memory: the former addresses the experience of reading text through its inaccessibility, and the latter upholds the memory of reading this absence, this negative inner space. Readerly memory encompasses a shared experience of unreading that is unique to texts like those about the Holocaust, in which the unreadable is central to meaning. In contrast, more typical reading is highly individualized, relying on a specific reader's experiences.

Fiction that places the Holocaust in its background is well positioned to connect unreading to readerly memory. On the one hand, the Holocaust's more marginal role reflects its receding historical place and its corresponding position in human memory—this is part of the experience of reading (ethically, of course) these texts; on the other hand, the deliberate move to both include and exclude the Holocaust in these works illustrates the acts of unreading that take place interiorly, in a "negative space," that lies beyond the reach of the reader. To be sure, there are different means by which fiction limits the Holocaust to the background. Ozick's language, Stollman's understanding of queerness, Potok's vision of historical violence, Roth's employment of the body, Krauss's use of the page all work from different directions to achieve a quality of unreadability. I suggest that it is this quality, the space given for unreading and unreadability, that defines both the aesthetic and the ethical richness of a text. For the two—art and ethics—are not only tied through the act of reading but are yoked together, at times even more tightly than otherwise, through the quality of unreading that they present.

Readerly memory and its role in ethical reading is a feature of all acts of reading but becomes illuminated in reading experiences that stand outside of normative experiences and, at the same time, attempt to gain access to them. Holocaust eyewitness narrative and literature stemming from the second generation (see chapters 2 and 3) not only identify the unreadable in texts that engage them as readers but also recognize, for eyewitnesses, the impossibility of reading about the Holocaust otherwise. This unreadability emerges out of an ethical understanding of readerly memory—for survivor testimony there is no other kind—and its accompanying insistence of unreading. Second-generation readers and authors as a whole observe the integrity of unreadability, even as they seek to uncover its edges: to know, and through this knowing to grow closer to their parents through the act of reading, a gesture that is as necessary as it is futile. This is the push and pull of unreading, and second-generation authors regularly document the pain it causes: a recognition that textuality exists and yet lies at a measure beyond reading.

Authors (and readers) of contemporary Holocaust memoir and fiction are in the most tenuous position when it comes to the ethics of unreading. Given their position in history, they bear both the greatest risk of violating the ethics of unreading (and reading) and, at the same time, stand to gain the most through their recognition and honoring of it. The third-generation Holocaust memoir, in an attempt to bridge the distance of time and memory, tends to document the author's wish for an affiliative experience, one in which, through reading, the author can better understand and remember the history of the Holocaust. In fact, however, the conflation of history with the personal motivations of the author pressures and flattens the quality of readerly memory that works to enliven the text. The effect ultimately is the opposite of that which the author strives to achieve: instead of bridging space, time, and memory the compression of readerly memory serves to further detach the reader from history and from its remembering; the experience of unreading, with all of its unifying implications, is largely forgone. The ethical implications are deeply unsettling. In the name of a moral imperative to remember, we in fact come closer to forgetting—and this through taking action, through reading and writing about the Holocaust.

Yet, as I illustrate in each chapter that addresses contemporary Holocaust textuality, failure to recognize the unreadable is not inevitable, far from that. In many ways contemporary readers are uniquely positioned to understand what, precisely, is at stake—the future of Holocaust memory. The distance from the eyewitness associated with third-generation readers is often understood as a first step in an inevitable progression of the deterioration of Holocaust memory. However, this does not have to be the case and, indeed, often is not. By forcing us to confront the relationship between reading and unreading, third-generation readers demand that we examine the ethics behind remembering and reading, behind the history of the Holocaust and the present. These authors enable us as readers to design a new method of memorialization, one that looks forward, backward, and inward, and one that has taken root, appropriately, in a new generation.

# PART I GENERATIONAL DIFFERENCES IN HOLOCAUST LITERATURE

# 2 • BEFORE, DURING, AND AFTER

## Reading and the Eyewitness

Do you know why I write so much?
Because as long as you read, we are together.

—Ann Kirschner, *Sala's Gift*

Writing in his unpublished diary, Polish Jew Kalman Rotgeber recorded many of his observations from his hiding place on the Aryan side of Warsaw not long after he and his wife escaped from the ghetto, where they had witnessed the deportation of their son. In the earliest pages of his diary, Rotgeber addresses his anticipated reader:

> The person into whose hands this diary should happen to fall is strongly urged not to discard it, or to destroy it. . . . In case it is not possible to deliver it to the intended address—one is kindly asked to give it over to competent hands so that a future historian might ladle out the true evidence, illuminating at least partially those terrible days of ours full of murder, conflagration, blood, and tears unprecedented in the history of the world, the suffering of a defenseless nation.[1]

In analyzing this diary Alexandra Garbarini interprets Rotgeber's defensive posture as stemming from his fear that he will not be believed in spite of being an eyewitness to genocide. But more central to this entry is Rotgeber's identification of a question—a problem—about readership. Not only does he confront the question of "Who will read this?" but he also asks "How will the reader read this?" Garbarini points to Rotgeber's emphasis on the historical factuality of his experience, conveyed through his use of the words "true" and "unprecedented." More significant, though, is the word "ladle," which recognizes the power of the historian to dole out bowlfuls of truth, atrocity, and trauma. Through this word Rotgeber suggests that a reader without a specific kind of training will be unable to read more than some fragmentary portion of what his diary contains or may be unable to understand or make meaning of its contents in their entirety. In short, Rotgeber not only asks "How will the reader read this?," a question of audience often posed by writers, he also suggests a possible rationale: that if it is understood in small doses even as a joint or communal exercise, his history will be only "partially illuminated."

How does Rotgeber's sense of readership shape his writing and how is our understanding of his text informed by that? Survivor-authors, as Rotgeber demonstrates, clue in readers on *how* to read, in addition to providing them with *what* to read. As Rotgeber's entry illustrates, eyewitness testimony anticipates limitations that his future readers face in reading their narratives. But while this anticipation of the limitations of future readers and of reading specific to this type of writing allows the reading to proceed in one sense, it cannot replace the consensual or contractual relationship between reader and text as defined in standard theories of reading. Full readability—that moment of unforced realization or comprehension between author, reader, and text—is not possible here because the act of collaboration between those three entities and the creation of meaning that reading is founded on cannot exist on the basis of the destruction and trauma that has preceded it.

The idea that the reading that has *not* taken place also offers the most promise of access to both memory and experience is suggested in Paul de Man's *Allegories of Reading* (1979), where he invokes both the terms "the unreadable" and the "impossibility of reading." Writing about Jean-Jacques Rousseau, de Man states that certain texts (Rousseau's *Profession de foi* among them) "can literally be called 'unreadable' in that they lead to a set of assertions that radically exclude each other. . . . They compel us to choose while destroying the foundation of any choice. They tell the allegory of a judicial decision that is neither judicious nor just. As in the plays of Kleist, the verdict repeats the crime it condemns. . . . One sees from this that the impossibility of reading should not be taken too lightly."[2]

Clearly, de Man considers and allows for the concept of unreadability. Furthermore, while it may seem that there is no connection between his understanding of the unreadable and my attempt here to connect the quality of unreadablility to Holocaust literature, in fact he recognizes that textual unreadability bears traces of the traumatic within its very conception, within its very existence.[3] The inscribed memory that fails to make a place for itself haunts—obsessively—the memory of what actually took place.[4] For de Man, as with my own definition, the impossibility of reading is not a reflection of textual indeterminacy. Rather, "the allegory of reading narrates the impossibility of reading"; or, as J. Hillis Miller rightly explains, "only someone who can *read,* that is, who can interpret the allegory, which seems to say one thing but in fact says something else, will be able to see that what is really being narrated is the failure to read. But that act of reading will no doubt commit another version of the same error of the failure to read, and then again, in a perpetual fugacity of final clarity."[5]

"Unreadability" as I apply it here differs from de Man's definition. The nature of the event that is depicted in the text renders impossible any relation between the reader and the text; it requires a conception of reading that is both novel and fluid, one that allows for un-interpreted moments of reading, for a non-understanding of text to exist.[6] That is, the words may be physically parsed, and so in some sense they can be literally and mechanically "read," but their meaning eludes the reader. They cannot be grasped because no relationship, no anticipatory or predictive model, no continuum in which a typical reader's history, present life, and future can be built on or around texts of the Holocaust. I want, too, not only to consider here the secondary experience of the reading of eyewitness testimony by non-eyewitnesses but also to examine reading *by* the eyewitness. It is significant that eyewitness authors both reflect on the limitations of their audience and also often document their own experiences with text as part of their experience under fascism. The act of reading invariably recalls the memory of a former life, one that then figures into the trauma of the one documented. The cyclical nature of reading, remembering, and writing is compressed in eyewitness narrative, and the results are a series of crucial shifts in meaning and presentation.

Survivor literature, because its testimonial quality openly acknowledges the limitations of language and power of reading, presents us with a crucial test: the formation of a relation between reader and text is foundational to theories of reading. If no relation can be formed (as I argue for Holocaust texts), then these theories cannot account for reading as an act, because the fundamental assumption of readers and authors coming together through a common experience of text—on which the entire theory of reading is built—is absent. The question regarding the availability of what is readable becomes: How does the reader engage in an act that requires a relationship when that relationship exceeds or even denies its necessary conditions?

In response to this question, and in relation to eyewitness literature, I examine here three instances of reading: the interaction between reader and eyewitness author; the eyewitness as reader; the conception of the reader and the eyewitness postwar. Through all three relationships what remains clear is the self-aware depiction by eyewitness authors that reading is an experience transformed by trauma, so much so that what can be read is useful because it demarcates the space containing that which cannot be read. The examples I examine here both anticipate and explore the problematized relation of the reader to the text. They represent a range of settings from which the act of reading by an eyewitness can be considered: an entry in a diary recorded by the author while he is in hiding in which he anticipates the response and inability of future readers to read his narrative; autobiographies written after the end of the war that carefully record a number of different scenarios involving textuality and the act of reading, both as they were conceived of before the war and then, in pitched contrast, as they are understood in the war's aftermath; an autobiographical novel that describes a determinedly self-reflective protagonist author considering the profound impact the Holocaust has held on even his most regular communications.

While Rotgeber addresses his future reader more directly than many other eyewitness-authors, two other examples (among many) of writers who acknowledge the limitations of language and text that their readers will inevitably experience in reading their work include Charlotte Delbo and Primo Levi. Charlotte Delbo, who was arrested and sent to Auschwitz with a group of 230 other Frenchwomen involved in the Resistance, notes at the beginning of her autobiographical work, *Days and Memory* (1990), that memory can be understood either as "external" ("memory connected with thinking processes") or as "deep" (memory that "preserves sensations, physical imprints . . . the memory of the senses"). Words are not "swollen with emotional charge," Delbo writes. "Otherwise, someone who has been tortured by thirst for weeks on end could never again say, 'I'm thirsty. How about a cup of tea.' This word has also split in two. *Thirst* has turned back into a word for commonplace use. But if I dream of the thirst I suffered in Birkenau, I once again see the person I was, haggard, halfway crazed, near to collapse; I physically feel that real thirst and it is an atrocious nightmare."[7] On one hand, a word such as "thirst" bears the more pedestrian meaning that all readers can identify; on the other, however, it carries a meaning specific to torture, a meaning that few readers will recall. As we read Delbo's twofold understanding of this word—and this one word is surely representative of an entire language of duality—we as readers are able to glean a sense of the torment behind the deep memory of "thirst" that Delbo records. This fraction of understanding, however, is achieved only through our external memory of "thirst." That is, we know (through the description that Delbo and others provide) that the thirst Delbo refers to is *not* the thirst of our understanding and experience but the thirst of some other kind entirely; what it *is*, precisely, we cannot know. The fracturing of this single word's meaning carries with it a sense of telling violence as the meaning of language is wrenched away from the reader.

In *Auschwitz and After* (1995), Delbo expands upon the meaning of thirst in Auschwitz in a chapter with that title. She introduces the word in all its familiarity: "Thirst is an explorer's tale, you know, in the books we read as children. It takes place in the desert." After presenting to her readers the kind of thirst with which they are familiar, Delbo promptly shifts direction: "But the thirst of the marsh is more searing than that of the desert. . . . There is the thirst of the morning and the thirst of the evening, the thirst of the day and the thirst of the night. . . . Anguish fills your whole being, an anguish as gripping as that of dreams. Is this what it means to be dead?"[8] Again, as with her earlier discussion of the word "thirst," Delbo acknowledges the limitations of her reader's ability to read about thirst in the context of Auschwitz. Our understanding of thirst, Delbo suggests, is a world apart from hers and can only be minimally accessed through the language and the words we hold in common.

Using the readable to identify the presence of the unreadable is also a strategy employed repeatedly by Primo Levi in his memoir *Survival in Auschwitz* (1996). Many words are recorded in single quotation marks, suggesting the presence of more than one meaning associated with even the most basic terms: 'down'; 'they'; 'bed'; as well as more complex words: 'good'; 'evil'; 'just'; 'unjust.'[9] Levi takes pains to define these and other words, addressing his reader's limitations quite openly. When describing the various articles of clothing allotted to *Häftlinge*, or prisoners (and we should recognize that Levi's insistence on leaving certain words in their "native" tongue is yet another acknowledgment that reading places unusual demands and pressure on readers), Levi lingers on shoes: "And do not think that shoes form a factor of secondary importance in the life of the Lager. Death begins with the shoes; for most of us, they show themselves to be instruments of torture, which after a few hours of marching cause painful sores which become fatally infected."[10] Levi exhorts his readers to not read the word "shoes" in its deeply familiar and conventional meaning, but rather to think of "shoes" as like a foreign object. Where typically shoes are merely an accessory that provide comfort and protection, in the Lager shoes have the capacity to become instruments of torture and death that prisoners have no recourse but to wear, every step an agonizing combination of suffering that is both self-inflicted and imposed. As with Delbo's discussion of the word "thirst," Levi accesses what readers do not know—indeed, what we *cannot* know—from what we do. Together Rotgeber, Delbo, and Levi recognize the limitations of readers' abilities—paired with the limitations of language—to read about the Holocaust in the same way that readers approach most other texts, namely, as a dialogic, interactive, and predictive experience.

What Rotgeber illustrates explicitly and Levi and Delbo more implicitly is an awareness of reading that falls short of the meaning they wish to convey. To be clear: neither Delbo nor Levi nor Rotgeber changes—or even attempts to change—the meanings of words that readers read as we peruse their writing. They are aware of how readers read words like "shoe" or "thirst" or even "murder," and they recognize, in writing that addresses their readers, how these normative meanings fall short of the meaning that would more accurately depict their memory, even as they acknowledge the limitations attached to the best of their representation. The tension between these two reading structures—the former, which is quite literally a word on the page of the book, and the latter, which is an element engraved on the mind of the author—ultimately creates a mode of unreading that is as important to recognize (if not more important) than the actual reading accomplished.

I pause here to think more concretely about the relationship between the word that is recorded and read by outsiders and the knowledge that escapes in this very process, a relationship acknowledged by the author. Consider, then, reading

Levi's "shoe," a word with a great deal of personal valence and yet, also, a word that has ultimately achieved an extraordinarily public postwar invigoration through Holocaust memorials built on multiplying the symbolic value of that humble necessity. Levi first writes about shoes in *Survival in Auschwitz* and then returns to them in *The Reawakening*, which documents his lengthy journey back to Turin after his liberation from Auschwitz. In traveling from Auschwitz to Cracow, Levi meets a Greek Jew, Mordo Nahum, who initially appears to be "nothing exceptional, except for his shoes (of leather, almost new, of elegant design: a real portent, given the time and the place)."[11] Levi's own shoes fall apart after twenty minutes of walking. Nahum interrogates Levi, asking him his age and profession and then calmly declares that a "man who has no shoes is a fool." Levi reflects on this injunction: "Few times in my life, before or after, have I felt such concrete wisdom weigh upon me. There was little to say in reply. The validity of the argument was manifest, plain: the two shapeless pieces of trash on my feet, and the two shining marvels on his. There was no justification. I was no longer a slave; but after my first steps on the path of liberty, here was I seated by the road, with my feet in my hands clumsy and useless like the broken-down locomotive we had just left. Was I really entitled to my liberty?"[12] Levi and the Greek return to the subject of shoes once safely ensconced in barracks in Cracow: "He explained to me that to be without shoes is a very serious fault. When war is waging, one has to think of two things before all others: in the first place of one's shoes, in the second place of food to eat; and not vice versa, as the common herd believes, because he who has shoes can search for food, but the inverse is not true. 'But the war is over,' I objected. . . . 'There is always war,' replied Mordo Nahum memorably."[13]

Traces of humor inform this passage, a humor that is noticeably absent in Levi's introduction of shoes in *Survival in Auschwitz,* but also, and more notably, Levi conveys a sense of wonderment that the transformation of his own status, his liberation from the tyranny of the death camps, does not carry with it an accompanying transformation of language or meaning. "Death begins with shoes," Levi declares in *Survival in Auschwitz,* the initial meaning—one that resonates with our understanding of the word—voided and replaced with a value different and far darker than its initial one. Indeed, Levi himself, in *The Reawakening,* is reminded of this transformed meaning by the Greek. The point here is to understand (i.e., read) not only the original meaning along with the newly acquired one but also the notion behind the loss of meaning. In addressing the reader, Levi recognizes the "unreading" that will inevitably occur if the reader is not made aware of the life-and-death power of shoes—that is, a definition Levi can provide. The definition he cannot provide is the awareness that the moment of lost comprehension accompanies that of lost meaning.

While Levi can adjust our understanding of the transformative role of shoes in and after Auschwitz, what we as readers do not and cannot read is the violent and wrenching gesture accompanying meaning that is lost, taken away, stolen, or even—murdered. And we likewise cannot read the act of substituting or refilling original meaning with a different and starker one. We cannot read the tension or delicate balance necessitated by the moment of loss and then that word's fitful and scarred reemergence. We cannot read the darkness conveyed by a newer meaning that is both dependent on the existence of original meaning and also dependent on its absence. All of that, and certainly more, escapes our understanding, even as we read Levi define and redefine the word "shoe" on behalf of his readers.

David Krell notes that writers write "always . . . on the verge of both remembrance and oblivion alike."[14] Levi openly acknowledges the truthfulness of precisely these conditions as he writes, both by acknowledging the meaning that language once had but no longer has and also by despairing over the sense that, once modified, language will never return to its former "self." Reading, however, because it is a secondary experience that is built both on textuality and on the experience of the reader, operates under a different set of conditions, one where in the place of "oblivion," or what Maurice Blanchot calls "what one cannot remember," there is a void, a moment of textual silence.[15]

Meaning does not stand still, and that was never more true than with the word "shoe" and its post-Holocaust life. In the 1961 trial of Adolf Eichmann, Dr. Adolf Avraham Berman testifies that when he visited Treblinka in January 1945 he saw "scattered skulls, bones, tens of thousands. And heaps of shoes. Piles of shoes."[16] He then carefully unwraps a tiny pair of shoes that he had picked up and saved, calling them "precious," a memory of the deaths of a million other children. One observer noted that "no one who attended the sessions that day will ever forget the sight of these two tiny tot's shoes, held aloft in the Jerusalem courtroom. For seemingly endless seconds, we were gripped by the spell cast by this symbol of all that was left of a million children. Time stood still, while each in his own way tried to fit flesh to the shoes, multiply by a million, and spin the reel back from death."[17]

Since that courtroom exhibit of a single pair, shoes, often in vast numbers and jumbled together, have become one of the most familiar artifacts to be displayed as part of Holocaust memorial sites and museums. Jeffrey Feldman notes that the shoes within these displays "are filled with such tension because they are familiar, but assembled in ways that lead to painful and embodied impressions of the past."[18] On the one hand, shoes and other ordinary objects such as brushes, bowls, suitcases, glasses, and prostheses that were collected by Nazis and are now on display convey a sense of intimacy through their implied use and contact with the body, one with which we are all familiar. On the other hand, however, because of the sheer quantity of objects heaped together and the distance that being part of an exhibit imposes between object and viewer, they have acquired a metaphoric and iconic status used to convey the sense of breadth and brutality of Holocaust history.[19] James Young, while recognizing the power of these displays, is troubled by them: "In great loose piles, these remnants remind us not of the lives that once animated them, so much as the brokenness of lives. For when the memory of a people and its past are reduced to the bits and rags of their belongings, memory of life itself is lost. . . . Nowhere among this debris do we find traces of what bound these people together into a civilization, a nation, a culture."[20] Tim Cole, in pointing to the "authentic relics" that are used to make up "a contrived tourist attraction" he provocatively calls " 'Auschwitz-land,' " claims that by experiencing "a mediated past which has been carefully created for our viewing . . . we perhaps unwittingly enter a 'Holocaust theme-park' rather than a 'Holocaust concentration camp.' "[21]

Authentic artifacts, among them shoes, have become part of the packaging that accompanies Holocaust memorialization, one that, according to Cole, can be understood as a form of voyeurism, satisfying an urge for titillation rather than memory.[22] Using shoes as a point of connection to the Holocaust is not limited to exhibits that carry historical relevance, such as those that can be seen in vast piles at the museums now of Majdanek, Auschwitz, and other camps. Many memorial projects on high school and college campuses involve collecting donated shoes, creating a temporary memorial remembering Holocaust victims out of them, and then sending them off to those in need.[23] These projects, with their charitable aim, reinscribe the brokenness found in exhibits of shoes belonging to Holocaust victims with a sense of moral clarity, a desire to make good out of bad—a gesture that, in its simplicity, serves to further obscure the very event being memorialized.

If these contemporary memorials feel so remote as to be disconnected from Levi's depiction of shoes in and after Auschwitz it is because they are. In thinking about the act of remembering, Michael Bernard-Donals notes that while "we attach names to objects, and see objects as mnemonics for that which is irrevocably lost . . . what has been lost and what is absent exerts a terrible pressure upon both monument and name, and insinuates itself between the two."[24] Exhibits and memorial sites that center on shoes create a monument—ostensibly to those whose lives were taken from them. For Levi, what is lost cannot be monumentalized by physical objects. Instead, the act of remembering needs to accompany that other act that Levi holds dear: the act of reading and the act of reading the silence conveyed by meaning lost.

An awareness of the transformation of the meaning found in reading, because it has been subjected to the immoderate pressure of trauma, is not limited, in eyewitness testimony, to an anticipated postwar reading audience; rather, it is itself experienced and documented by eyewitnesses themselves. Indeed, it is arguably this experience of their own changed relationship to reading and textuality that fuels their recognition of the anticipated experience of other readers reading about the trauma of the Holocaust from a position that is at a further remove, with the intervention of time distancing the reader from the eyewitness's experience. Once again Levi documents this shift in his autobiography, *Survival in Auschwitz,* when he is required to pass a chemistry examination in order to become a "Specialist" with all the privileges and increased chance of survival such a position might entail. Projecting ahead, Levi thinks about the fact that the exam will be in German; that he and the other workers taking the exam will risk runny noses and no handkerchief at hand; that they will hardly be able to stand because of hunger and weakness; that the examiner "will certainly smell our odour." In spite of these thoughts, the examination, which is oral, goes well, with Levi remembering, only through "violent effort" as he stands trembling in front of a "Doktor" in his ill-fitting soiled clothes, wooden clogs, and limited German, the title of his degree thesis: "My poor old 'Measurements of dialectical constants' are of particular interest to this blond Aryan who lives so safely: he asks me if I know English, he shows me Gatterman's book, and even this is absurd and impossible, that down here, on the other side of the barbed wire, a Gatterman should exist, exactly similar to the one I studied in Italy in my fourth year, at home."[25] The book in question is *The Practical Methods of Organic Chemistry,* which quickly became, after its initial publication in 1896, the standard textbook on the subject in most German and many other European universities. It was often identified, as Levi does here, simply by the last name of the author, Professor Ludwig Gattermann (1860–1920), who had a distinguished academic career at the universities of Heidelberg and Freiburg.[26] If the "barbed wire" is the now familiar image of a physical boundary that separates Auschwitz from the rest of the world, for Levi the Gatterman is its intellectual counterpart, its cover creating a boundary between what was once read and familiar in contrast to the setting Levi currently finds himself in, one that is neither readable nor knowable. That a book, and one that investigates the structure and properties of organic matter no less, should exist on the inside of Auschwitz, a place of utter decay, in the same form—with the same cover, divided into the same chapters, containing the same diagrams, conveying the same information—as it did on the outside is, for Levi, "absurd and impossible." Why? Because part of the transformational effect of the concentrationary universe (to use a term first coined by Levi), along with its impact on systems of ethics, religion, wealth, power, and more, is its impact on reading. Levi notes this in *The Drowned and the Saved* (1989), describing how he paid for German lessons with bread in order to understand what "the roars of the Kapos and SS meant, the foolish or ironic mottoes written in Gothic letters on the hut's roof trusses, the meaning of the colors of the triangles we wore on our chests above the registration number. So I realized," notes Levi, "that the German of the Lager—skeletal, howled, studded with obscenities and imprecations—was only vaguely related to the precise, austere language of my chemistry books, or to the melodious, refined German of Heine's poetry that Clara, a classmate of mine, used to recite to me."[27] Seeing the Gatterman creates for Levi a moment of contrast between "here" (i.e., Auschwitz) and "home"; between the examination he currently is undergoing and the one he passed in university, "that spontaneous mobilization of all my logical faculties and all my knowledge, which my friends at university so envied me"; between the sense of fate, in its most ultimate sense, that awaits the results of this exam and the one that was both on offer and was then awarded—*summa cum laude*—a mere three years prior.

I do not suggest that the Gatterman as a text has moved from being readable to unreadable; this is not the case. Rather, through the act of remembering reading, as opposed to reading itself, this scene exposes some of the limits of reading, as revealed by Levi's use of the words "absurd and impossible" upon seeing the Gatterman. In his work *Time and Free Will* (1921), Henri Bergson recognizes the dynamic nature of time and, as a consequence, the impossibility of repeating exactly the same experience (reading or otherwise) more than once. Instead, memory of the past feeds an anticipation of the future.[28] This is true in terms of the larger meaning of a single text in connection with other texts, but it also works on a micro-level, where even reading a single sentence is marked by a prediction of the next, which, once read, moves to the background where it feeds the next expectation. Wolfgang Iser notes that clearly "throughout the reading process there is a continual interplay between modified expectations and transformed memories."[29]

Indeed, this anticipation of the future becomes a part of the memory, even influencing its conception of the past. While Levi never reveals his precise memories associated with reading Gatterman in his fourth year at university, we can safely conclude that his memory of that past reading, colored by whatever future opportunities he may have imagined or associated with the book, never could have anticipated the moment when the book would reappear and when his familiarity with it—that is, his memory of his earlier reading—would mean the difference between life and death. Putting together these two memories in *Survival in Auschwitz*, the original one that included reading the Gatterman while a student and the second one that repositioned the book as transgressing the barbed wire of Auschwitz to find a place profoundly incongruent to its prior one, is "absurd" in the connection it derives between these two worlds and "impossible" because of the distance it implies between the memory of reading and the reality of Auschwitz. Ultimately, Levi's memory of reading allows for a broadening of the continuum on which a theory of reading can and should be understood. That is, while the study of reading investigates the reasons behind the range of meaning a single text can have, that range should also include, at its furthest outreaches, a possibility for impossibility and absurdity—a chance that the conditions for meaning derived from reading cannot be, or can no longer be, met or anticipated.[30]

Like Levi, Charlotte Delbo also documents Auschwitz's effect on the memory of reading, both in the physical form that books take and in the meaning they provide. As she is prying bricks from a pile "covered with ice" and moving them to another pile, two at a time, her friend and fellow inmate Yvonne says to her: "'Why can't I imagine I'm on the Boulevard Saint-Michel, walking to class with an armful of books?' and she propped the two bricks inside her forearm, holding them as students do books. 'It's impossible. One can't imagine either being somebody else or being somewhere else.'" Delbo then shifts in her narrative from thinking about the impossibility of imaginatively replacing the cold weight of bricks with the familiar heft of books to contemplating the role that their contents offered her in Auschwitz:

> In Auschwitz reality was so overwhelming, the suffering, the fatigue, the cold so extreme, that we had no energy left for this type of pretending. When I would recite a poem, when I would tell the comrades beside me what a novel or a play was about while we went on digging in the muck of the swamp, it was to keep myself alive, to preserve my memory, to remain me, to make sure of it. Never did that succeed in nullifying the moment I was living through, not for an instant. To think, to remember was a great victory over the horror, but it never lessened it. Reality was right there, killing. There was no possible getting away from it.[31]

As Levi draws together two contrasting memories of reading—and in so doing delineates the parameters or limits of read meaning—so too does Delbo, for whom remembering reading is remembering a past that provides sharp contrast to the present "horror." Whereas once reading poetry, fiction, or drama presented an opportunity for "getting away from [reality]," it cannot offer the same refuge against the overwhelming presence of Auschwitz. The memory of reading for Delbo is in no way an escape or even a tempering of reality; it does not—cannot—present the reprieve of even an instant of pleasure. Instead, to remember reading is to remember herself engaged in an activity that relied specifically on her person and her mind, and this, too, in contrast to the physical labor, anonymity, and brutalization of the concentration camp. The use of the body for reading—her eyes passing over words, her hands turning the pages—is a far cry from the drudgery of excavating and carrying bricks or "digging in the muck of the swamp." Her interpretation of her reading rests on her own individual history and yet takes place, in remembered form, in a place that erases differences. Delbo marks the process of remembering reading by speaking it aloud, turning what was once private and singular into a public and collective act, reciting and narrating to those around her.[32] Through these distinctions between past and present, between the experience of reading and a memory of it, between reading privately and remembering publicly, Delbo allows for the possibility that, where once reading existed in all its familiarity, the experience of "reading" within Auschwitz is not only distinct but utterly foreign.

The act of reading and not only its recollection also plays a specific and overlooked role in the camp. Shortly after arriving at Auschwitz, Primo Levi describes the washroom of Block 30. It is dark, drafty, and smells revolting. "The walls are covered by curious didactic frescoes" that include captions underneath them. On one wall "an enormous white, red and black louse encamps, with the writing: '*Ein Laus, dein Tod*' (a louse is your death), and the inspired distich: *Nach dem Abort, vor dem Essen / Hände waschen, nicht vergessen.* (After the latrine, before eating, wash your hands, do not forget.)"[33] The remainder of the chapter, entitled "Initiation," is spent analyzing the meaning of this couplet and considering the ways in which it can be read. Initially, the incongruity of a childlike rhyme encouraging hygiene in a setting where the one constant (deliberate and unfailing) is filth in every direction leads Levi to consider the poem some sort of joke, an example of "the Teutonic sense of humor" that he had already witnessed and experienced upon entering the camp—the humor that expressed itself in making two men wear each other's trusses and in wanting to see people hobble about in mismatched shoes and dressed in ill-fitting clothes. Levi assumes that the author of these lines is a member of the camp's administration and so he reads the words with a pained sense of their intended and inadvertently (or perhaps not) tragic irony—while the sentiments of the distich are perfectly familiar and would formerly have been read as simple advice, in the Lager these same words, Levi's initial reading of them suggests, serve in fact to remind prisoners of the basic necessities refused them. Furthermore, Levi's interpretation suggests that the futility of attempting to follow the advice recorded on the washroom wall increases the indignities suffered by the prisoners because it makes them, yet again, the butt of a joke that underscores their degraded status.

Levi modifies his initial reading, however, after a conversation with his friend Steinlauf who, in the process of vigorously washing himself, inquires pointedly and "severely" why Levi too is not washing. Levi lists the many reasons that seem to him both logical and self-evident for not washing: it is a waste of energy, pointless, "a dismal repetition of an extinct rite," takes up too many of the few precious idle moments available. Levi's reasons for not washing in fact serve as a form of protest to his daily reading of the sign. Reading such a sign prior to or outside of the camp would elicit little meaningful response. Either the reader would follow the advice advertised (in accordance with the sign or out of habit or personal desire—it hardly matters), or the reader would ignore it and suffer the possible consequences. But reading in the camp becomes far more complex an exercise, one where the system of rational meaning on which the act of reading typically rests cannot be assumed. In response to the Teutonic humor of the washroom wall art, Levi responds gravely, arguing that since "we are all about to die: if they give me ten minutes . . . I want to dedicate them to something [other than washing]." Steinlauf, however, with "plain, outspoken words," forces Levi to reconsider his initial reading. He argues that washing without soap and in dirty water is necessary in order not to "become beasts" in a place intended to "reduce us to beasts." He continues his list of counter-responses, confronting one by one Levi's argument against washing, and concludes with these words: "We are slaves, deprived of every right, exposed to every insult, condemned to certain death, but we still possess one power, and we must defend it with all our strength for it is the last—the power to refuse our consent."[34]

Part of the thrust behind these final thoughts bears meaningful implications for reading: instead of consenting to read according to a methodology prescribed by an authoritarian regime that determines any and all physical deprivations and punishments, refuse! Read with a sense of intellectual and emotional independence, one that belies and even resists these surroundings and conditions. The advice resonates with Levi who writes that after his conversation with Steinlauf, he "understood that [the fresco's] unknown authors, perhaps without realizing it, were not far from some very important truths. In this place it is practically pointless to wash every day in the turbid water of the filthy washbasins for the purposes of cleanliness and health; but it is most important as a symptom of remaining vitality, and necessary as an instrument of moral survival."[35]

The shift in reading here is quite radical. In assuming that the author writes from a position of authority, Levi reads what confronts him in the washroom ironically, which in effect is a means of resisting reading, understanding the couplet and accompanying picture as yet another disturbing attempt at humor in a place defined by the loss of dignity and life. In adopting Steinlauf's reading, however, Levi is uncertain whether to attribute the authorship to those in charge of the camp. This uncertainty destabilizes his initial reading, allowing (enabling, even) him to read the couplet first literally, as conveying "some very important truths," and then metaphorically, as a message for physical and moral survival.

Levi's reading does not stop here. After describing the washroom and both his initial and revised reading of the distich, largely in the past tense (although with a few interjections that make clear he writes retrospectively), Levi concludes the chapter in the present tense, effectively reading the couplet in Block 30 one last time. "No," writes Levi, "the wisdom and virtue of Steinlauf, certainly good for him, is not enough for me. In the face of this complicated world my ideas of damnation are confused; is it really necessary to elaborate a system and put it into practice? Or would it not be better to acknowledge one's lack of a system?"[36] The system Levi questions here is a "moral system" and pulls one back to his revised reading of the couplet painted on the washroom wall, inspired by Steinlauf (who reads the words with an eye toward psychological and perhaps physical well-being), a reading that understood the refrain's simple advice as a directive toward, as Levi himself writes, "moral survival." Upon reflection, however, Levi questions not only the moral system that informed his modified reading within the camp but also the apparatus that "put it into practice." In short, Levi questions the very act of reading that served to implement Steinlauf's system. Levi's final and concluding question—"would it not be better to acknowledge one's lack of a system?"—goes to the core of "Initiation" and, arguably, *Survival in Auschwitz* as a whole, implicating the existence of *any* moral system within the camps and implicating any system of reading within it as well.

Levi's deliberate reading of the washroom walls is unusual not so much in its far-reaching implications or in its description of reading and re-reading. Rather, few examples exist of public reading in the camps, as the walls of the washroom inevitably were. This, in part, enables Levi to think about reading not only empirically, which he also does, but systematically and theoretically. Far more typical, although also significant, are the many examples described and included in eyewitness narratives of the reading of private letters, notes from fellow prisoners, letters from outside that somehow manage to cross the barbed wire, postcards sent from those inside the camp to loved ones elsewhere, and diaries that manage to survive the war. The reading of these texts is challenged as much by what they fail to convey as by what they do—a quality that in itself is regularly noted and recorded. In her memoir about her experience in Birkenau, Giuliana Tedeschi describes her friend Bianca Maria bursting into tears after receiving and reading a letter from her son, who was in hiding. "Why are you crying?" the author inquires. Bianca Maria responds: "You know how it is. . . . Your nerves can hold out just so long, then you reach a point when you can't handle it anymore. And when I saw his writing . . . you know. . . . Oh, I can't stand it, I can't, I'll never go back." One woman who witnesses this exchange remarks, "That letter . . . with everything it didn't say" was more dangerous having been received and read than otherwise.[37]

Reading and re-reading also preoccupies Hélène Berr when she receives the first postcard from her father who has been arrested and taken to Drancy, the internment camp outside of Paris.[38] "When I read the sender details, 'Berr Raymond registration number 11 943, Drancy Camp,' I didn't understand—now and again there are flashes of understanding. I read and reread it as I climbed the stairs trying to convince myself this was all real. . . . Yet as I looked at the postcard I still could not grasp the reality: Papa's handwriting just reminded me of the letters he used to write when he was away from home. . . . I could not manage to reconcile the handwriting with what it said, with the meaning of the words."[39] In anticipation of Berr's journal being published, sixty-four years after its last entry, Berr's onetime fiancé, Jean Morawiecki, considers how reading it has affected him: "The *Journal* of Hélène Berr has always been part of my life in both its forms—as a manuscript, and as one of the typescript copies. It was the latter that I reread from time to time. The original was too charged with emotion. Hélène's writing, her 'hand,' wiped out the years that had passed, and if it made her more present, it only emphasized the cruelty of her irremediable absence: a pale and frozen hand stretched out toward me so I could bring it back to life."[40]

Similar to what Delbo and Levi note when thinking about reading and the memory of reading during their time in Auschwitz, these three accounts of reading all express the overwhelming incompatibility between seeing the familiar handwriting of a loved one and an awareness that this may well be (in Morawiecki's case, it most certainly was) the last trace of them they see. Reading the letter becomes charged with a range of emotions. As Berr notes, she is joyful "at knowing what [her father] was doing out there." Yet she is also aware that "between the Papa of home and the one out there who wrote this postcard, a gap is yawning open."[41] Berr's reaction echoes Morawiecki's emotional response to reading her journal in its original form, with the pages marked by Berr's handwriting. An interesting if tragic triangulation emerges through the reading of primary documents, where Berr and Morawiecki independently and yet ultimately in chorus recognize the element of the unreadable that the text of the original document, recorded under the strain of the Third Reich, yields. For Berr this is articulated as the blank gaps (her word) between "flashes of understanding"; for Morawiecki this comes through a sense of Berr's "irremediable absence."

Bianca Maria's repeated assertion—which she continues to declare through a debilitating illness as she "read[s] that one letter over and over": "I'll never go back"—points to this same gap, one that separates, even severs, the connection that links past and present, memory and experience. That is to say, the feedback loop through which a reader typically relates to text—by bringing with her or him, and reading through, a set of personal expectations and predictions derived from a range of self-experiences—simply breaks down.[42] While there is room in theories of reading for expectations and predictions by the reader not to be validated by the text, and when this occurs readers would then modify or revise their anticipations, in the case of Auschwitz and perhaps in all traumatic experience, it is the process of adjustment that ultimately becomes nullified. However readers respond to the text, their responses rely on a system that the concentration camp has made obsolete. The response "I'll never go back" is as much a declaration of awareness of the fate likely in store for the young mother as it is an awareness of an inability to move backward in time, to reclaim not only a life and a child but a system of understanding and thought, a system that also undergirds acts of reading and analysis.

These examples of unreadability emerge from a sense of textuality under extreme pressure, where survivor-authors document the transformation that the reading process undergoes when conducted under traumatic conditions, a transformation that moves reading from the realm of the familiar and daily to a space of bewilderment, senselessness, and absurdity. In considering applications of unreadability to a range of eyewitness accounts, I consider a final example of unreadability that appears in Imre Kertész's novel *Kaddish for a Child Not Born*.[43] First published in 1990, this is the third novel of an autobiographically informed tetralogy that includes *Fatelessness* (1975), *Fiasco* (1988), and *Liquidation* (2003). In *Kaddish for a Child Not Born*, the novel's narrator—identified only as B., a middle-aged Hungarian Jewish Auschwitz survivor who works as a writer and literary translator—is asked if he has a child. The novel is a study on both the question and his instinctive, immediate response (and the opening word of the novel): "No!"

At one point the narrator reviews a statement he made years before at the social gathering where he first met his now ex-wife. Reading his own words, for in this novel the narrator/writer is also a fixedly self-conscious reader, and speaking of himself in the third person, B., "after proper but, of course, quite futile clearing of the throat, in a voice still hoarse with emotion, declares 'There is no explanation for Auschwitz' " (*Kaddish*, 33). It is an emphatic and definitive statement, received as such by his audience who "accepted, analyzed, and debated this simplistic statement, scrutinizing it this way and that" (*Kaddish*, 33). Years later, as he records the statement and re-reads it, his own understanding of it shifts. For each successive reading of the statement (six of them in a handful of pages following the initial depiction), he prefaces the reviewed statement—"There is no explanation for Auschwitz"—with another statement, "I most probably must have said . . .":

> I most probably must have said that this statement, which is to say the statement "There is no explanation for Auschwitz," is faulty in purely formal terms, since for something that *is* there is always an explanation, even if, of course, merely an arbitrary, erroneous, so-so kind of explanation; nevertheless, it is a fact that a fact has at least two lives, one a factive life and another, so to say, cerebral life, a cerebral mode of existence, and this is none other than an explanation, the explanations or, better still, set of explanations that overexplain the facts to death, which is to say ultimately annihilate or at least obscure the facts, and this hapless statement that "There is no explanation for Auschwitz" itself is an explanation, being used by its hapless author to explain that it would be better for us to remain silent about Auschwitz, that Auschwitz does not (or did not) exist, because, you see, the only thing for which there is no explanation is something that does not or did not exist. (*Kaddish*, 36)

As the narrator moves from speech to text, from living in the immediate shadow cast by the event to reflecting on the event years later as he moves from society and an active social life to a rarely interrupted solitude, as he moves from being a virile young man, meeting his future wife, to middle age with a failed marriage behind him, two major shifts occur in his understanding of his statement: "There is no explanation for Auschwitz."

First, the statement itself is emptied of precisely the meaning that the writer wants—but fails—to convey: Auschwitz does and does not exist; it has always and has never existed; the statement of non-explanation is, in fact, an explanation. De Man's invocation of the "impossibility of reading"—the failure to read that is enacted through the act of reading—is at work here. But Kertész's obsessive reflections yield a second shift, too.

Not only does the statement become impossible to read, but even its existence becomes questionable, shifting from a firm declaration in its first iteration (he "declares") to a puzzled indeterminate state of mind ("I most probably must have said") with every subsequent reading. "I most probably must have said" is an odd locution, one that opens with indeterminacy ("most probably") but is colored by the succeeding implementation of the modal verb "must have," an indicator that the statement is surely true. The narrator's own attempt to read the narrator's locution, then, not only renders unreadable the statement, "There is no explanation for Auschwitz," but also—even!—the narrator's own presence as an Auschwitz survivor, which is precisely the problem with which the narrator (and Kertész) struggle. If the statement "there is no explanation for Auschwitz" is read as meaning that Auschwitz never existed, then the survivor of Auschwitz, too, is rendered either impossible or unexplainable. And, indeed, B. writes: "I am nothing" (*Kaddish*, 15).

If the novel's opening repetition of "I most probably must have said" provides readers with the narrator's denied quest for affirmation, the phrase that emerges toward the novel's end is the more definitive: "I told my wife . . ." Between the two iterations Mr. B recounts the conversation, letter by letter, that inspires his opening "No!"—opening with his wife's request to have a child:

> ". . . no other wholeness could substitute for the one and only, total, unsurpassable, *true* wholeness, said my wife—in other words, she wanted my child, yes, indeed and
>
> 'No!' I said immediately and forthwith, without hesitation and spontaneously, so to say, for it is quite obvious that our instincts actually work against our instincts, so that, so to say, our anti-instincts act instead of or even for our instincts; and either that this
>
> 'No!' was not a decisive enough
>
> 'No!' or an unexpected response, given my unpredictability, and my wife only laughed at me. She does understand me, she said later, she knows from how deep inside this 'No!' sprang, and how much I have to struggle and conquer within me in order to make it a '*Yes*.' And I answered her, I believed I understood her and knew what she was thinking but that the
>
> 'No!' was a
>
> 'No!' Not some sort of Jewish 'no,' which she probably had in mind, no, I was quite certain of this, as certain as I was uncertain as to the nature of the
>
> 'No!' only that it was a
>
> 'No!' I said, even though, as concerns Jewishness, there would be plenty of reasons, for I could imagine a desperate and wretched conversation, I said . . ." (*Kaddish*, 68)

The word "no" comes in every form imaginable. The wife, whose plea opens the passage, starts with the word "no" in anticipation of her husband's negative response. "No other wholeness," she says, attempting to turn negation into real, quantifiable presence, "could substitute . . . for *true* wholeness." Mr. B's response is immediate, unhesitating, spontaneous, and declarative: "No!" Yet, he considers, perhaps it was instinctual enough to be anti-instinctual, so certain as to be uncertain. The word itself is an emphatic gesture toward negation, its implementation interrupts sentences and thoughts—and yet at the same time, "No!" as a statement completes and enables them, becoming not only a response to the prospect of a child, but emblematic of his own sense of being, a being that resists being read and being heard: "I am nothing."

The iterative and reiterative nature of Kertész's autobiographical novel, its commitment to circling back repeatedly to lines spoken, read, and heard, gestures not only to the language that engulfs the translator-narrator, language that comes from the people around him (i.e., his wife) and the books he owns (references to Celan and Nietzsche are displayed most prominently), but also to the text the book is named after and effectively serves as—the "Kaddish," the Jewish prayer of mourning that is read and recited aloud, multiple times within each prayer service, in commemoration of the dead.[44] While the word *kaddish* is Hebrew for "holy," the prayer "Kaddish" is written and recited in Aramaic, the vernacular in the time of the Second Temple, when the practice of saying "Kaddish" was first developed. For all its commitment to textual citation, Kertész's *Kaddish* is most deeply tied to the prayer through the act of repetition. Kertész's "No!"—the simple, declarative word that punctuates his novel most regularly—corresponds to the pronouncement of affirmation with which the reader and congregation reciting "Kaddish" respond: "Amen."[45]

Mr. B's reflection on his response to his wife's plea for a child leads him back to Auschwitz in the novel's concluding pages:

> Auschwitz, I told my wife, struck me later as simply an elaboration of those virtues in which I have been indoctrinated since childhood. Yes, it all started then, in my childhood, that inexcusable process of breaking my spirit, my incessant urge for survival, I told my wife . . . Auschwitz, I told her, appears to me in the image of a father; yes, the two terms, Auschwitz and father, resonate the same echoes in me, I told my wife. And if the observation is that God is an exalted father, then God, too, is revealed to me in the image of Auschwitz, I told my wife. (*Kaddish*, 88)

Returning to the problematic statement "there is no explanation for Auschwitz," Mr. B shifts from, on the one hand, a declaration of indeterminacy, "I most probably must have said" to an enunciation of the simple past: "I told my wife. . ." Yet the simple past leads the reader to the same devastating conclusion of negation. For, "yes," Mr. B recounts, Auschwitz was present even before it was present, anticipated by his "incessant urge for survival," one of his childhood virtues. Mr. B moves from his childhood, through his troubled relationship with his father. The tense of the act of telling ("I told her") remains constant and is affirmed ("Yes, it all started then . . ."). The passage then undergoes a fleeting yet transformative shift: "Auschwitz, I told her, appears to me in the image of a father." Auschwitz slips to the present, as does the notion of fatherhood: it "*appears* . . . in the image of a father." The present tense of "appears" together with the indefinite article "a" spreads meaning across a vast expanse of space and time. Kertész may have solved his initial conundrum regarding the existence of Auschwitz by separating it from place and time—it always has and always will exist—but doing so, as he anticipates at the beginning of his narration, comes at the expense of his own survival. The title of this work, *Kaddish for an Unborn Child,* not only mourns what might have been—or, in Kertész's language, what must have probably been—but also mourns what no longer can be and what never was. That unborn child for which his book stands as a memorial is not only his son or daughter, the child who inspires the novel's ringing "No!"; that unborn child is the author/narrator himself. The "Kaddish" the narrator recites, which he identifies as "the true nature of my work," "is nothing else but digging, continued and continuous digging of the grave others had started for me in the clouds, the wind, in nothingness" (*Kaddish,* 94).

The unreadable aspect of the text like that illuminated with Rotgeber's diary, uncovered in Levi's, Delbo's, and Tedeschi's memoirs, and explicated in *Kaddish for a Child Not Born,* is not only a key feature of Holocaust literature but a defining one: reading the Holocaust should be understood in terms of the unreadable rather than the readable. In effect, if we think of Holocaust literature as revealing the inadequacy of older and current theories of reading, we can understand a dialectic of new kinds of readings emerging, one that requires a new theory of reading more generally. The first step in the dialectic is a historical one, coming to terms with the reading of what is unreadable. This first step involves identifying, valuing, and preserving that novel aspect of the text.

Applying the theoretical terms and ideas found in my introduction to survivor literature, I return to the eyewitness texts discussed here and ask if these and other eyewitness accounts of trauma and, specifically, of the Holocaust allow for the complex interaction between object, word, and reader that Bakhtin emphasizes in his *Dialogic Imagination* (1981). In his own estimation of his audience, Rotgeber indicates his dissent from this. In positioning themselves as their own readers, Levi, Delbo, Tedeschi, and Kertész's protagonist, Mr. B, a version of the author himself, believe that the construction of meaning as read—the making of sense that typically occurs as we read—is thrown into disarray by the cultural "system" in which the author writes. It is a system that makes "truth" unbelievable for the reader and thus a system that renders readers incapable of reading the world the author inhabits. Because, as the authors anticipate, their audiences will read these texts in a post-Holocaust world. The space of that world is one in which cultural and historical mediation between the language used to depict what happened to the writer and the language accessing this history for the reader stops short of meeting each other. The contextualization of writing and reading that must happen in order for a text to assume readability is simply not possible: the referentiality of the original moment cannot be recaptured and does not exist. To return to Bakhtin's language and ideas, there is no play, no back and forth, no reciprocity of verbal intentions.

The texts considered here are instances of many stories of trauma that *cannot* be read because they *will not* be read—this, after all, is the full meaning behind Mr. B's "No!" The system is not only disrupted because of authorial "authority" or the nature of narration. The text itself resists "dialogic play" and cultural interactions, past, present, and future. Rotgeber, Levi, Delbo, and Kertész all—remarkably—allow for the possibility of the act of reading, from the priming of the reader before reading commences to the physical placement of the eyes on the page to the words being pronounced and processed. However, it is specifically the meaning gleaned from the reading, the incompetency (Rotgeber's word), the incapacity (my word) of the reader to read and understand meaningfully, that they address. Why, as he sits in hiding, and why, decades after the atrocities of Auschwitz have been revealed, do Rotgeber and other eyewitness authors come together in their contemplation of audience?

The consideration these authors and many others devote to anticipating the responses of readers is akin to the question Cathy Caruth poses in her book *Unclaimed Experience* (1996), asking what it means for consciousness to survive a traumatic experience.[46] Caruth answers this question by stating that because the experience of trauma is an indirect one for consciousness—"the threat is recognized as such by the mind *one moment too late*"—the experience of trauma is "the repeated confrontation with the necessity and impossibility of grasping the threat to one's own life. . . . [S]urvival becomes for the human being . . . an endless testimony to the impossibility of living."[47] Caruth's understanding of the relationship between trauma and consciousness relates in specific ways to the projection made by memoirists and diarists of their readers' inability to read traumatic texts. An aspect of the trauma that Rotgeber experiences, one that he identifies in the opening passage of his diary, is tied to the prospect that any reader who picks up his diary and attempts to read it will not really be reading it. Caruth focuses on the "returning traumatic dream" that perplexes Freud in *Beyond the Pleasure Principle*, the "return of the event against the will of the one it inhabits."[48] The anticipation of audience and its implied repetition—every time their works are read, they will fail to be read—resonates with Caruth's understanding of survival in relation to consciousness: namely, it is the anticipated absence of readability that marks both trauma and survival—both of person and of text.

This conception of reading and readership derived from the texts of survivor-authors makes a number of assumptions, foremost among them that the reader, or the majority of readers, will themselves not be survivors. Rather, one underlying aspect of survivor memoir is both the need to persuade the reader that the writer experienced a traumatic and violent injustice and the sense that such an act of persuasion is utterly elusive. At the heart of this interaction is the moment when the text is read. In anticipating this action by their readers, eyewitness authors often record a sense of despair or futility. Part of this has been attributed to problems of representation—that is, with the limits of language obstructing the creation of an adequately representational text. And part resides in the act of reading about a traumatic moment that is inaccessible through reading; that is, unreadable. Elie Wiesel writes as he recounts the cattle car that carried him to Buchenwald how "strange" the process of writing remains. "Even while jotting down these words, the event seems incredible to me. I seem to be writing a horror novel—a novel that should not be read at night."[49]

In her work on Holocaust diaries, Alexandra Garbarini notes the regularity with which the authors express their inability to adequately record their experiences: "Our language has no words with which to express the calamity and disaster that has struck us"; "No, no pen, no writer will be able to describe what we are living through."; "We are so sad, so hopeless, and so ill that no pen can succeed in describing it"; "What I describe to you in this letter will not be one thousandth part of how it really was."[50] She also notes the impulse of these diarists to record their own dismay and sense of failure when reading their own words: "When, after writing, I read it over, it appears to me that everything [I write] is very naïve and absurd. . . . I will still record my thoughts, but I will not read them over immediately."[51] We see this reaction in many of the essays that populate Yizkor books: "I was the only one of my father Yitzhak Meir Piotrikowsky's children who survived the ordeal. My grief and pain are hard to describe. A pen is not rich enough to detail all the things I lived through during the Hitlerite occupation."[52] In her analysis of these diaries, Garbarini acknowledges that these diarists were "unable to avoid engaging in [a] self-reflexive process" of both writing and reading as eyewitnesses and they were "disturbed by the potential of their diaries to be distorting mirrors."[53]

The shift between writing and reading, however, is even more complex than Garbarini allows. Whether writing retrospectively or "in the moment," whether professional authors reflecting on their past or untrained writers recording the events around them, all authors adopt an entirely new position when they move from writing to reading, even when that transition involves their own work. When the writer reads his or her own text, he or she brings a sense of expectation to the text, willing the text to meet these expectations. In the case of literature of trauma more generally, and Holocaust literature specifically, not only is both the writing marked by a sense of urgency to record the experience accurately (a subjective term at best or at least empirically complicated), but the reading, too, is marked by a parallel sense of urgency: to read the record as it was intended to be written and not as it was actually written.

This kind of readability, however, is simply not available to most readers—a point readily acknowledged by almost all eyewitness authors. And it is this particular tension that marks the unreadable aspect of eyewitness or first-generation Holocaust texts. Charlotte Delbo notes that following the war:

> My discouragement in regard to books lasted a long time. Years. I could no longer read because I felt I knew already what was written in this book, and that I knew it in an altogether different way, a deeper, more trustworthy knowledge, manifest, irrefutable. . . . I also distanced myself from books because I could see through words. I saw the banality, conventionality, emptiness. Yes, I saw the skillfulness. But what does this one know that he's trying to impart? And why doesn't he say so? . . . I was no longer open to imagination, or explanation. This is the part of me that died in Auschwitz. This is what turned me into a ghost. What can still be of interest when falseness becomes apparent, when subtlety is gone, with no gradations of light and shade, nothing to guess at in people's eyes or in the pages of books? How can one continue living in a world stripped of mystery?[54]

Delbo here reflects on reading more generally, noting that Auschwitz has transformed and degraded her formerly favored role as a reader. Where once reading proved captivating because of the various unknowns any given text might hold in store, the knowledge and experience of Auschwitz has corrupted that sense of anticipation, that mystery, interrupting the necessary interaction between author, text, and reader that creates meaning. As authors of their experiences, survivors and eyewitnesses engage in a process of creation that they alone control; what has long gone unacknowledged is that as readers themselves and on behalf of other readers, however they might try to adopt a once familiar posture of inquiry and unknowing, the "feedback loop" that once sustained their own reading experience fails. It breaks down. The eyewitness author is both able to identify the non-experience of his or her reader—reading the unreadable with them—and, at the same time, reads from a position of indelible knowledge, one which renders, as Delbo notes, all texts readable. It is this disconnect that provokes a response such as that of Hinde Berlin who writes of being recognized by former neighbors and friends from her shtetl while in Auschwitz. They call to her. "I couldn't control myself then and started to yell to them, 'Where are the rest, where is Mordkhe, my brother?' More can't be written on paper, perhaps you will not believe any more; and there may not be a place left in your imagination for any more of this tale."[55] Similarly, Margarete Holländer writes in her diary that despite her wish "to describe accurately the *Aktion* [by the Germans]," she realizes upon reading her own words that she has failed: "I have barely portrayed one tenth of the atrocious experience."[56]

Theorist Ian Mackenzie notes that "if a reader does take the time to delve into potential meanings in a sentence, the final interpretation will never be the same as the initial one, even if the sentence defeats all subsequent hypotheses or constructions. . . . Because the past survives as memory, and leads to anticipations of the future, consciousness can never go through the same state twice."[57] Holocaust authors, most of whom are aware of the reader's presence, move from a position of knowledge tempered by the limits of language to a position of vulnerability tempered by the limits of reading. Indeed, since reading enables them to "see" the fallibility of their own text, they become witness repeatedly to the boundaries within the boundaries, the limits within the limits, of traumatic representation. Ultimately, it is these limits, these boundaries that mark the experience of textuality and reading in survivor literature, inscribing a place—deliberated upon and planned—for the experience and memory that cannot be written or read along with that which can.

# 3 • READING TO BELONG

## Second-Generation and the Audience of Self

Whenever I tried to read about [my family's history] in the books my father gave me or see it in the films he took me to, I could not take it in. The facts bounced like Ping-Pong balls inside my head, not only making no sense of their own but disordering whatever was already there.

—Helen Epstein, *Children of the Holocaust*

The presence and importance of unreadability in the sense of a direct relationship between the reader and the text becomes more intricate and convoluted in writings by second-generation Holocaust authors who often document their quest to discover or write a "readable" narrative of their parents' wartime experiences.[1] In the absence of this text, second-generation writers bear a more complex relation to even the idea of text than do eyewitnesses or other first-generation writers. Whereas eyewitness authors record their memories or at least try to put fragmented memories together and then read them, authors who identify themselves as "second-generation" writers search for a narrative structure that captures a complex interplay of living with the inherited memory that stems from the stories of their parents' survival and wartime experiences. They search for a text or archival collection, remnants of which will supply them with the missing images, memories, stories, and histories. Second-generation authors document their wish for a comprehensive narrative, one that can be both written and read. This act of searching combines often and quite naturally with the act of "reading around," or attempting to access, their parents' accounts. It is then, in a second step, recounted through narrative.

One difference between eyewitness and second-generation writers involves the ordering of their representational practices: more so than either eyewitness authors or still later (for example, third-generation) authors, the children of Holocaust survivors initiate their memoirs and stories with an examination of themselves as readers, a form of self-reflection and self-study that positions second-generation authors as recipients, heirs, and beneficiaries not only of their parents' stories and memories but of these stories in relation to their own personal histories and, in a broader gesture, toward literary narrative more generally. This assessment of their own reading practices ranges from including detailed and personal reading histories to analyzing their personal habits, responses, and analyses as readers before moving on to document their and their parents' experiences. Instead of moving from experience to authorship to readership in the uniform progression of eyewitness testimony, second-generation memoirists move from reading and the experience of reading to writing.

While identifying that the influence of reading is an important aspect for any author, the investment of second-generation writers in their readerly identity is amplified beyond that typically found in autobiographical works. Text and narrative provide a counterpart to the silences and gaps that many authors in the so-called Generation After grew up experiencing when the subject of the war was raised. Reading—and here I mean reading in the broadest terms of genre and interpretation—is both a means to approach their parents' experiences and at the same time, because these experiences elude the act of reading and are centered on textual silence, provides an escape from them. Second-generation authors attempt to read the silences and gaps of their parents' narratives—they reflect an all too familiar reality—as well as the language that is present. Reading provides second-generation writers with a sense of history, language, and order, a sense of rationality, that they can adhere to even as they realize that their own personal histories—which must include the lives of their parents and often the absence of grandparents and other relatives—are not readily explicable.

Most urgently, second-generation memoirists seek out the narratives and documentation that contribute to their parents' stories. For some of them, as in Helen Epstein's *Where She Came From* (2010), some textual presence is available. Epstein's mother gives her daughter, at her request, a densely written twelve-page document outlining the family's history that includes her wartime experiences. Similarly, in Ann Kirschner's book *Sala's Gift* (2007), the author's mother, after decades of silence, gives her daughter a cache of personal ephemera including dozens of letters written during the war and hidden until then. Likewise, after many years of silence, the suicide of his son prompts Henri Kichka to record his Holocaust experiences; his own text is then attached to his son's graphic memoir.

At times, however, no such transmission is on offer; there is no recorded testimony, no handwritten pages, no effort to textualize memory. In Lisa Appignanesi's memoir, *Losing the Dead* (1999), she and her daughter together ask her mother, a Holocaust survivor who has begun to talk frequently about the wartime years, to record her memories. They "present her with a bound book, full of glossy white pages, together with a series of questions about what we want to know about her life . . . what her house looked like, her school, her friends, the war years." But, while the mother/grandmother is more than willing to narrate her war experiences, "the book lies untouched, its pages still blank."[2] As Phyllis Lassner so aptly notes, this blankness enables Appignanesi not only to "fill in but also [to offer] interpretive frameworks to help her and readers find ways of picturing unfolding events and constantly shifting identities and relationships."[3] Paula Fass, in *Inheriting the Holocaust* (2011), asks pointedly and poignantly, "How do you write about them, people who were at once all important and always there, but never part of my life—people who had *no names?* [ . . . ] I was never even told my mother's [first] husband's name or that of my father's [first] wife."[4] Psychologist and painter Bracha Lichtenberg-Ettinger, the daughter of Holocaust survivors whose mixed media work reflects the reverberations of the Holocaust, notes that her "parents are proud of their silence. . . . But in this silence all was transmitted except the narrative. In silence nothing can be changed in the narrative which hides itself."[5]

In Art Spiegelman's *Maus* (1986), in which Spiegelman pictures and records his father's history and his own history through the use of animal characters and masks, the author dwells on the deeply felt absence of his mother and everything that was destroyed in connection to her. Spiegelman's mother was also a Holocaust survivor and committed suicide when he was twenty. Throughout Spiegelman's childhood she rewrote the diaries she had written and that were destroyed during the war. A good part of *Maus* is devoted to Spiegelman's search for these diaries, only to be told by his father—it is the climax of the first volume—that he has destroyed them.

Eva Hoffman, in her two beautifully written memoirs, the first focusing on her emigration to Vancouver from Cracow, the second on her identity as the child of two Polish Jews who survived the war through hiding with neighbors, repeatedly connects literary motifs to the Holocaust truths she faced as a child. In her mind, "the hypervivid moments summoned by my parents registered themselves as half awful reality, half wondrous fairy tale. A peasant's hut, holding the riddle of life or death; a snowy forest, which confounds the senses and sense of direction. A hayloft in which one sits, awaiting fate, while a stranger downstairs, who is really a good fairy in disguise, is fending off that fate by muttering invocations under her breath and bringing to the hiding place a bowl of soup."[6] In her earlier memoir, Hoffman compares her father's wartime stories—when he is finally able to recount them many years after they have transpired—as feeling to her "so far removed that they seem like fables again, James Bond adventures."[7]

For the children of Holocaust survivors, the importance of textuality lies in its very presence—its tangibility, its lasting quality, its comprehensive narrativity—that can withstand interrogation and examination in a way that typically is not available to them through their parents. The effort by second-generation authors to create a text documenting their own stories with their parents' histories is an attempt to acknowledge and define the gaps and silences that serve as the marker of the second generation. Significantly, second-generation literature consistently respects these boundaries and while a longing emerges to actually fill the empty spaces, those spaces are almost uniformly consigned over to the audience and, presumably, to the next generation of readers.

In certain respects, the relationship of the second-generation author to reading, writing, and memory imitates the self-reflexive posture of eyewitness authors (see chapter 2). Eyewitness authors initiate the contractual relationship between author and reader by identifying with both sides—as reader and writer—with the consequence that the self-same figure recognizes the limits of representation, on the one hand, and on the other hand, the limits of readability: the eyewitness acknowledges the constraints on both representation and legibility. The concept of unreadability shifts for members of the second generation, the children of survivors. These authors face a problem not present in the act of bearing witness or writing about witnessing, in part because they recognize that the text embodying the experience is a victim, bearing the marks of a trauma that renders it unreadable. Yet, unlike their parents, they stop short of being able to "see" the aspect of the text that is unreadable. The second generation is not just second in the sense of coming after the authoritative unreadability of eyewitness testimonials; it is also second in the sense of secondary, a position that is most recognizably not the document, the artifact, the object of study itself but, rather, a source that operates at a distance and further complicates the relationship between writer, reader, and text that is required by the act of reading.

Second-generation authors create a text that often centers on the missing text of their lives, so much so that their new text can be understood as an attempt to reformulate the missing text. Unlike their parents who recognize and are troubled, even traumatized, with each reading because it exposes the limitations of the act of reading, second-generation authors produce a reproduction that remains distinct from the original and yet attempts to create a "post-text," one that tries to fill in, without ever succeeding, the sense of lost text, of lost family history and narrative, that can be grasped only through imagined terms.

Eva Hoffman encapsulates just this difference when she writes about the "crucial distinction" separating "postwar children" from the parents who survived "wartime events": "Whereas adults who live through violence and atrocity can understand what happens to them as actuality—no matter how awful its terms—the generation after receives its first knowledge of the terrible events with only childish instruments of perception, and as a kind of fable."[8] This missing text—in Hoffman's term, the "fable"—serves a symbolic role, presenting in physical form the absence of a familial wholeness. The missing text serves another function as well. It is often one reason behind the creation of a text that can be read, one that tells an intertwined narrative between parent and child and through various means points to the cost of survival, its impact on the most central of relationships, and the role that trauma exerts years or even decades after it has been experienced.

Perhaps the most often invoked term recently bearing on second-generation authors is "postmemory." In her valuable work that examines the children of Holocaust survivors—the "generation of postmemory"—and their dependence on photographs as a means of transmission of traumatic memory, Marianne Hirsch defines "postmemory" as describing "the relationship of the second generation to powerful, often traumatic, experiences that preceded their births but that were nevertheless transmitted to them so deeply as to seem to constitute memories in their own right."[9] Postmemory, Hirsch continues, is a "*structure* of inter- and trans-generational transmission of traumatic knowledge and experience. It is a *consequence* of traumatic recall but . . . at a generational remove."[10] "Postmemory" is a term that understands the act of "remembering" by children of Holocaust survivors as real and authentic and yet as invoked by means of stories, pictures, images, and behaviors. Unlike actual memory, which is based on some understood version of one's own past, postmemory is informed by "imaginative investment, projection, and creation."[11]

Gary Weissman, in *Fantasies of Witnessing* (2004), rightly points out that while the term "postmemory" is valuable "for giving a name to the unique familial knowledge of the Holocaust that survivors' children attain by growing up with those who did live this history," once Hirsch extends it to include all post-Holocaust generations, the term loses much of its power.[12] The relationship and role of memory between what might be called the "third-generation" (that is, the post-second-generation) and the eyewitness changes significantly from that between the eyewitness and his or her children (see chapter 4). In connection to this relationship, however, the term "postmemory" is a key link to the idea of unreadability, mainly because of its sense of incompleteness. Building on Henri Raczymow's idea of *mémoire trouée*, or "memory shot through with holes," Hirsch identifies postmemory as fragmented and indirect, an understanding that helps locate unreadability in second-generation literature: "[Holocaust photographs] are the leftovers, the fragmentary sources and building blocks, shot through with holes, of the work of postmemory. They affirm the past's existence and, in their flat two-dimensionality, they signal its unbridgeable distance."[13]

Postmemories are the province of what Hirsch calls the "postgeneration," the generation of children born after the war. Other members of this distinctive community, the children of survivors, identify themselves using terms that similarly subordinate their identity or understanding as coming after—or in the margins of, or secondarily to—a point of origin: afterimages, secondary witnesses, children of Job.[14] Hoffman calls it the "hinge generation, in which the meanings of awful events can remain arrested and fixed at the point of trauma; or in which they can be transformed into new sets of relations with the world, and new understanding." The hinge generation for Hoffman is one in which "received, transferred knowledge of events is being transmuted into history, or into myth."[15] Other writers in this generation identify themselves or their place historically as the "children of Job" or as "afterimages." Alan Berger's work, both independently and with Naomi Berger, develops the idea of the "*presence of the absence*" as a quality that marks the voice and legacy of those belonging to the second generation.[16] Literary scholars Ernst van Alphen, Janet Handler Burstein, and Erin Heather McGlothlin consider the problems related to the inheritance of trauma and memory by examining second-generation texts that range from fiction to memoir to poetry and, in the case of McGlothlin and Berger, by including also the narratives of children of Nazi perpetrators.[17]

The term "second-generation" in relation to the Holocaust was coined in 1973 when four Montreal-based psychologists published the results of their research on children of survivors that they had been conducting over the previous decade.[18] That article, entitled "Some Second-Generation Effects of Survival of the Nazi Persecution," studied the "adverse physical and psychological effects" of Nazi concentration camp survivors on their "mid-teenage children."[19] The term "second-generation" has evolved and become more encompassing since its first more limited application. "Second-generation" no longer pertains exclusively to the children of concentration camp survivors but is more broadly applied to the children of all Holocaust survivors.[20] Furthermore, in contrast to the cool reception toward the research and findings in the late 1960s and early 1970s regarding the designation of this particular group, identification of this "second generation" now bears a distinct and recognized identity and even a sense of status that stems from being precisely the "hinge generation."[21]

The convoluted history of the "second generation" mirrors their own conflicted sense of identity, of a broadly shared experience that is, at the same time, mediated and indirect. The sense of memory as authentic but at the same time less than real; the sense of being connected and deeply protective of their parents but also separated from them, divided by the insurmountable gulf of Holocaust survival, all this and more informs the conception of text and reading in second-generation narrative. The central question here is thus twofold. First, how do second-generation authors in their own texts address, respond to, and incorporate aspects of the unreadable that are part of their parents' stories and histories? Second, insofar as second-generation authors are marked in specific traumatic ways by the Holocaust, do second-generation texts *also* contain aspects of the unreadable? The aim here is to explore the boundaries of unreadability and its relation in this second context to narrativity, textuality, and Holocaust memory.

## PICTURING UNREADABILITY: READING *MAUS* AND ITS SUCCESSORS

In Art Spiegelman's *Maus*, the narrator/author is regularly pictured in two modes: smoking and writing. The smoke and ashes of Art's father's story materialize in the ever-present cigarette (the brand is "Cremo Lights") and fuel each frame that Spiegelman draws. Given his fraught relationship with his father, writing is an act of conciliation and provocation, revelation and introspection, an act that works both as a form of personal private discourse and as a more public storytelling. As the frames progress, however, the reader becomes increasingly aware that what Spiegelman longs for, more than writing, drawing, or smoking, is to be reading, to be participating in precisely the narrative that he sets before us.

Two strains of reading emerge in *Maus*: the unreadable, presented by the diaries of Anja Spiegelman (Art's mother) that record her memories from the war, and the contested, namely, Spiegelman's own narrative, which emerges through his work as an interlocutor as he negotiates, demands, questions, and then receives the story of his father's past, linking it then to his own. These two modes of reading are joined by a repeated narrative technique: interruption. As Vladek Spiegelman (Art's father) recounts in his broken English, itself a form of interruption, the events before and during the war years, Art interrupts him to inquire after his mother and her history before his parents met: "About Mom—Did she have any boyfriends before she met you?" And when Anja is missing from Vladek's narrative, Art chimes in and redirects him: "What was Anja doing at around this time [when the family relocated to the newly formed ghetto]?" "Houseworks," Vladek responds, ". . . and knitting . . . reading . . . and she was writing always in her diary" (*Maus I*, 84).[22]

Art interrupts a conversation with Mala, Vladek's second wife, who is in the midst of recounting her own family's history in Auschwitz, to inquire about his mother's diaries: "Where are you going? You didn't drink your coffee," asks Mala. "I just thought of something. My father mentioned that Anja used to keep a diary, and I vaguely remember seeing them on his shelves in the den" (*Maus I*, 93). Interruptions abound in *Maus* and become a productive—at times violent—narrative tool for both Art and his father. Art regularly interrupts his father's narrative, asking him to narrate his story along chronological lines and in a more comprehensive form and, in so doing, vigorously inserts himself into his father's history, dictating its progress. Vladek also interrupts the narrative. He does this by returning insistently to his present-day woes—his problems with Mala, his son's smoking, his own health issues, and his need to catch his breath from all the cycling he does on his stationary bicycle—as well as by speaking in a fragmented, error-prone English. His interruptions help readers locate and differentiate his crippled postwar identity, with his glass eye, bad heart, and broken English, from his prewar identity, when he successfully provided for his family even in the most adverse of circumstances and when he was favorably compared to the movie star Rudolph Valentino.[23]

That Anja's presence makes itself felt through interruptions is significant—she, too, belongs to this family that both stifles and encourages expression. Significantly, the interruptions around Anja are not productive; they do not reveal,

FIGURE 1: Interruption through speech, action, and image.
Credit: Art Spiegelman, *Maus I: A Survivor's Tale: My Father Bleeds History* (New York: Pantheon Books, 1986), 84.

they do not redirect, they do not produce speech, drawing, or words.[24] The interruptions in which Anja's name surfaces are just that: moments in time where the narrative is suspended, where text and language are lost and unavailable, a blank that serves as the inscrutable story. They speak to an interrupted memory and an interrupted history, one that cannot be recovered or read. A powerful illustration of this can be found in the remaining frames of the scene in which Art inquires after his mother's activities while in the ghetto. His father's comment about Anja's diaries reminds Art that he used to see Polish notebooks lying around the house as a child. "Were those her diaries?" "Yes, and also no." Vladek explains. "Her diaries didn't survive from the war. What you saw she wrote after: her whole story from the start." Art exclaims over this discovery, wanting to locate them, to read them for his own book, the one he presents to us, his readers: "OHMIGOD! Where are they? I NEED those for this book!" (*Maus I*, 84) The next frame shows Vladek with his hand to his face, temporarily stalled on his stationary bike: "COFF! PLEASE, Artie, stop with the smoking. It makes me short with breath" (fig. 1).[25]

The smoke from Art's cigarette, itself an element of obfuscation leading to inscrutability, divides the frame in half, creating an interstitial space of white that separates father from son. "I think it's all your pedaling," Art responds as he stubs out his cigarette. Just for a moment, the activity that each of them continually engages in pauses. Art stops smoking. Vladek stops pedaling. The conversation breaks off with Vladek's coughing. When he recovers, Vladek does not respond to Art's question "Where are they?" Instead, he moves forward with his own: "Don't be so smart! . . . What I was telling you?" (*Maus I*, 84). He picks up the narrative thread from before the interruption involving Anja and her diaries and resumes his storytelling, an account that often omits Anja's presence.

What is revealed by these interruptions in the text is a doubling of both reading and the unreadable that I suggest here is specific to second-generation literature. There is, of course, the obvious—devastatingly so—missing text that Anja has labored over and that Art and we, the readers, learn about more than once. Ghostlike, the promise of Anja's written work follows Art around throughout his narrative, just as he pursues those same texts, repeatedly expressing his desire to recover them. His sense of urgency stems from a longing not only to read his mother's words but also to hold in his hands the tangible evidence of her story, for he wills that element of storytelling—its written history, its mythology (to return to Hoffman's word)—to be drawn into *Maus* along with his cigarette, his tape recorder, his pad, and his pen. As Nancy Miller notes, "the mother's story is doubly missing"—her "own self-narrative, her chance to refigure herself" as well as Art's version of it.[26]

In addition to the missing text that belongs to his mother, a second form of interruption asserts itself through the linguistic difficulties that mark Vladek's speech and distinguish it from his son's English. With its errors in prepositional and article use and the frequent reversal in his sentences of subject and object, Vladek's English—which marks both speaker and language as foreign—serves to fracture the text. Alan Rosen notes that "Vladek's broken English becomes the means by which Spiegelman articulates the incommensurability between past and present."[27] Spiegelman draws a definitive line between prewar and postwar, while Art's narrative attempts to make a whole history out of two parts. He incorporates moments of interruption—a pause in time, a space where storytelling is suspended, where text is unavailable, where language becomes distorted—that are themselves both events and memories of unreading.

A different but no less assertive form of interruption takes place in Martin Lemelman's graphic memoir *Mendel's Daughter* (2006), which documents the history of his mother, Gusta Lemelman. The memoir opens with the author, Martin, whose mother affectionately calls him Mattaleh, recalling a dream in which his mother, who had recently passed away, speaks to him, urging her son to listen to her: "'Sometimes your MEMORIES are not your OWN" (*Mendel's Daughter*, 4).[28] The next day Martin watches a video of his mother narrating her story that he has not thought of in years; this video becomes the text of his memoir. The introduction concludes with the only self-portrait of the author in the book, a rectangular frame that shows Martin's face, his eyes gazing distractedly beyond the reader, a serious expression on his face. He sits in front of a mirror that reflects the back of his head (fig. 2).

The reader effectively sees Martin's entire head, broken into two pieces, one facing backward, the other looking forward. Next to the self-portrait he has written, "This is her story. It's all TRUE" (*Mendel's Daughter*, 5). The juxtaposition of "her story" and his portrait, combined with the split views of his head, pictorially emphasizes the fractured nature of postmemory, the province of the second generation. Gusta's dream-words to her son, "Sometimes your MEMORIES are not your OWN," urge him to make her memories his, her story his.

FIGURE 2: His portrait and her story.
Credit: Martin Lemelman, *Mendel's Daughter* (New York: Free Press, 2006), 5.

Lemelman takes his mother's words to heart. The picture immediately following his self-portrait is an enlarged black-and-white photo of a baby with the caption: "My Nephew Eli, photographed June 15, 1938. My sister Jenny's only child" (*Mendel's Daughter*, 7). The narrator here suddenly shifts. Whereas in the introduction, Martin Lemelman introduces himself as the narrator, telling the true story of his mother, from the opening page of Part I and for the rest of the memoir his voice is sublimated by his mother's voice. The "my" in the caption refers to Gusta, and yet in the introduction the "my" is linked to "my mother"—it is the voice of the son. Linguistically, there is an elision of identity: *Both* Mattaleh and Gusta narrate the story. Pictorially, however, the photograph of nephew Eli, which takes up an entire page, interrupts the act of reading both text and drawings, imposing a real—yet simultaneously lost (we learn of Eli's death later in the book)—image that jolts the reader from the present to the past and back in another example of traumatic interruption (fig. 3).

The photographs in Lemelman's work disrupt the reader's progress in a number of significant ways. Most immediately, they draw our attention away from the printed word and the sketches to the face, the people, the clothes, the inscription. Either the photographs are enlarged to such an extent that they take up the entire page, or they are quite miniature, embedded, for example, within a sketch of a hand that is inside a frame (fig. 4). The text or captions accompanying these photographs are essential to preserving the identity and particularity of the image, but they become secondary to the image itself. In place of reading the text, the reader faces a fragment, one that, as Jill Bennett describes it, has "the capacity to address the spectator's own bodily memory."[29] Photographs interrupt the act of reading not only because they are visually arresting and distinct from the text as a whole but also because they evoke a more immediate and more visceral feeling in the reader.

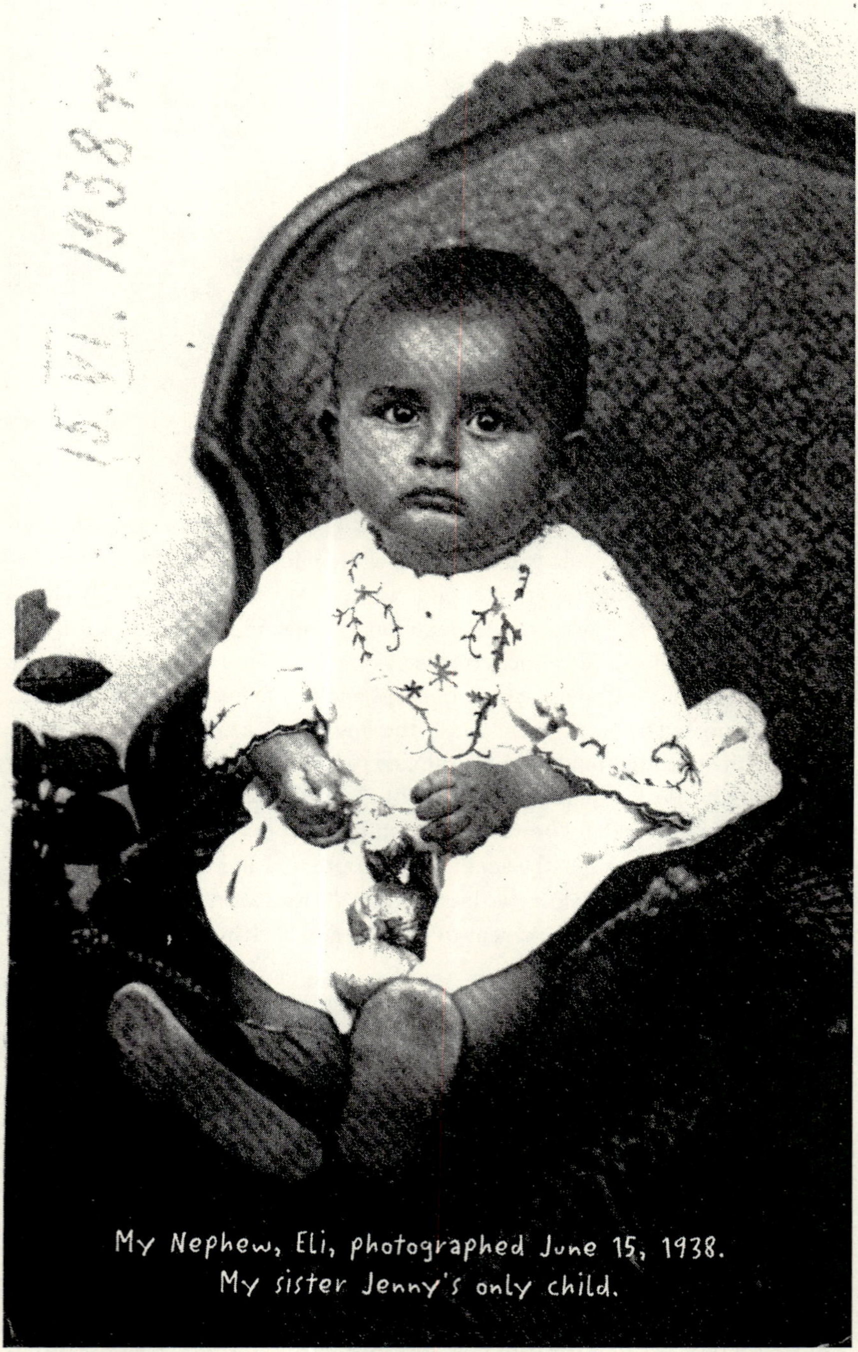


FIGURE 3: Narrating with his mother's voice.
Credit: Martin Lemelman, *Mendel's Daughter* (New York: Free Press, 2006), 7.

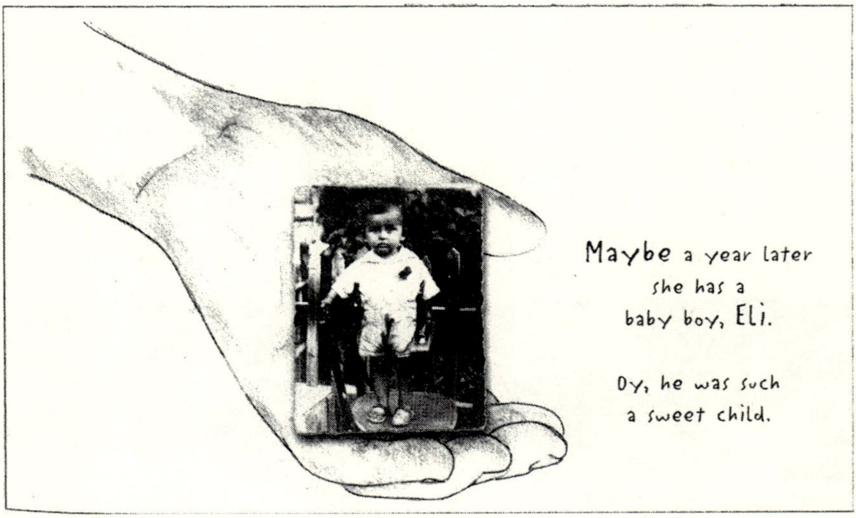


FIGURE 4: A photograph embedded in a drawing.
Credit: Martin Lemelman, *Mendel's Daughter* (New York: Free Press, 2006), 31.

In addition to photographs of family members, Lemelman regularly includes family and school photographs and other "real" artifacts throughout the memoir, including a picture of a piece of needlework (fig. 5), newspaper clippings, photocopied pictures of pages from the family *siddur* (the daily prayer book) that survived the war, and photocopied pictures of pages from a Yom Kippur *machzor* (a specially designated prayer book for that holiday). In the photographs of Hebrew texts, with a gesture replicating the reading of family photographs, the interruption is caused by the presence of printed Hebrew letters that, while comparable in size to those in the printed text, present a second language, that runs from right to left and thus against the direction of reading maintained for much of the book.

Marianne Hirsch notes that more than "oral or written narratives, photographic images that survive massive destruction and outlive their subjects and owners function as ghostly revenants from an irretrievably lost past world. They enable us, in the present, not only to see and to touch that past, but also to reanimate it by undoing the finality of the photographic 'take.' The retrospective irony of every photograph consists precisely in the simultaneity of this effort and the consciousness of its impossibility."[30] Hirsch notes that the "ghostly revenants" of photographs mark them as "very particular instruments of remembrance, since they are perched at the edge between memory and postmemory, and also, though differently, between memory and forgetting."[31] Borrowing a term from W. J. T. Mitchell, she identifies memory as an "imagetext," a word that she employs to identify its visual and verbal dimension.[32]

FIGURE 5: A photograph of one among very few surviving family heirlooms. Credit: Martin Lemelman, *Mendel's Daughter* (New York: Free Press, 2006), 19.

"Imagetext" takes on a different meaning in Lemelman's work. In a fascinating twist on Hirsch's understanding of photography, Lemelman not only inserts photographs of family members who perished in the Holocaust, clearly wanting to reanimate them, but also takes his own photographs of surviving family artifacts—in black-and-white and so matching those that predate his birth—and inserts them also into the text. The "ghostly revenants" of Holocaust photography in this case stand before a tangible, physical object. The three-dimensionality of that object combines with the two-dimensionality of the photograph, rendering the former more ghostly and the latter less so. Just as in the opening pages of the book the "my" of Martin's mother's voice is conflated with the "my" of the son, so too do photographs of past and present become mingled and of indeterminate origin.

In *Mendel's Daughter*, it is this affiliative response to the many artifacts pictured in the text that marks the boundaries of what is readable and separates it from the unreadable.[33] Readers recognize the highly fragmented nature of what they are viewing. For Lemelman, these fragments symbolize a fractured personal history. He embeds these pieces in a textual and pictorial narrative—indeed, his drawings have a lifelike quality—but the inclusion of his photographs and the interruption they both stand for and cause in the reading process, symbolize the disruption of his family narrative. Lemelman's incorporation of all kinds of photographic evidence works to recover the dead—parallel to his effort on a different track to historicize the living. Reading *Mendel's Daughter* requires the reader to differentiate between these two gestures, an effect that requires breaking away from Gusta's (and Mattaleh's) narrative in order to take stock of both present and past.

In contrast to Lemelman's inclusion of photographs spanning a range of time and holding various histories, both interpretively and as documents that have survived and traversed great distances, Michel Kichka's recently published *Deuxième génération* (*Second generation*; 2012) moves in precisely the opposite direction: all photographs that reflect his notion of family and self are redrawn in the artist's hand.[34] These include redrawings of photos of Michel and his three siblings during family vacations and as teenagers, all of them marked by a white margin or by a wavy scalloped edge around the image.[35] There are also redrawings of two "head-shots" of his paternal grandparents who perished in the Shoah, the only photographs that clearly come from a larger album, as is made clear by the triangular corners that are shown to keep them in place.[36] The photographs often overlap and are placed at angles to one another, distinguishing them from the frames that encapsulate Kichka's drawings, which are always drawn in relation to and conforming with the larger rectangle of the page. Positioning the photos in pairs or small groups underscores a sense of relationship—both in subject and time—between the sets.[37]

While redrawn photographs of figures that can be identified in Kichka's work are framed and positioned in relation to each other, these contrast with Kichka's redrawing of well-known historical Holocaust photographs where the identities of most of the subjects are unknown. Michel's father, Henri Kichka, is the only survivor of Auschwitz from his immediate family and collects books about the Holocaust but relates very little of his own experiences to his children. Michel reads many of these books, searching the photographs for his father and his paternal grandparents. He documents his reading by redrawing photographs and including—above, below, or in thought bubbles within the photograph—his reading of the image. So, for example, in the now-famous picture of the liberation at Buchenwald in which Elie Wiesel is identified as one of the concentration camp survivors lying on a crowded set of wooden bunk beds, Kichka's hands hold the newspaper page that contains his rendering of the photograph. As he scans the faces, looking for his father, he reviews each one: "That's not him . . ."; "Not him."; "Not him."; "Not him either" (fig. 6).[38]

FIGURE 6: Kichka searches for his father in a photo he both holds in his hands and has redrawn.
Credit: Michel Kichka, *Deuxième génération: Ce que je n'ai pas dit à mon père* [*Second generation: What I didn't tell my father*] (Paris: Dargaud, 2012), 6.

Floating in the open space to the right of the photo, Kichka notes that he searches for his father "as if he needed to see him to believe it." The child Michel suggests that being able to identify a familiar face within the alien landscape of, for example, Buchenwald, would help him to read and truly understand his father's history. In another well-known photograph, with a Nazi soldier pointing a rifle at a mother clutching her child, Kichka attempts to read the pictured woman as his grandmother, writing above his redrawing: "I searched for my grandmother."[39] In perhaps the best known and most widely reprinted Holocaust photograph, picturing a small Jewish boy in the Warsaw ghetto with his hands raised and a few feet behind him a German soldier with his gun trained on him, Kichka reproduces the photograph drawing himself as the boy. "I found that I resembled this boy," Kichka notes, applying his trademark freckles and round nose to the face under the cap (fig. 7).[40]

By inserting himself into the photograph, Michel attempts to read history as intimate, as personal. This is the first of many moments in which Kichka documents his child-self devising a series of memories, dreams, or fantasies that include him in his father's Holocaust history as an attempt to read and understand it. He wishes to create the postmemories of which his father's silence has deprived him. Ultimately, however, only the suicide of his younger brother, Charly, the premature death of a beloved sibling whose own difficult relationship with his survivor parents both inspires Kichka's father to tell his story in more detail and allows Michel to think about the implications of being his father's (other) son.

FIGURE 7: Kichka discovers himself as the boy in the photo "Warsaw Ghetto Boy." Credit: Michel Kichka, *Deuxième génération: Ce que je n'ai pas dit à mon père* [*Second generation: What I didn't tell my father*] (Paris: Dargaud, 2012), 8.

Lemelman interrupts his text through the insertion of photographs that halt the progress of reading because they are so visually different from his drawn pictures and text. The figures pictured in Lemelman's photographs are foreign to his larger narrative; they are marked by a troubling combination of lifelike quality filtered through the reader's knowledge of their deaths. They are figures who belong, along with pictures of their few treasured belongings, to a different, other world. Kichka's redrawing of familiar Holocaust photographs runs parallel to Lemelman's situating photographs that were taken after the war next to photographs taken before the war. Kichka redraws these photographs in attempting to read and understand the history they encompass; unlike his drawings that accompany his portrayal of himself, drawings almost always neatly framed by the familiar black thin line of a comic artist, the moments in which Kichka explores Holocaust history are not framed. Instead, the white background of the page on which they are printed become a part of the redrawn photograph, moving them from the past to the present—along with Michel's insertion of himself within them, either visually or through his "captions" that accompany the pictures. Reading these photographs produces anxiety, as Michel notes in redrawing face after face of concentration camp figures, a traumatic echo of the redrawn photographic portraits of his surviving grandparents. "I was afraid that I wouldn't recognize him," he notes on one side of the page; "I was afraid that I would recognize him," he notes on the other.[41] His redrawing of well-known

Holocaust photographs imposes the same burden of anxiety on his reader: we recognize the photograph and yet remain ignorant of the identities of those within them. Our reading, like Kichka's, stops because of these unknowns. They are and remain unreadable.

The alternating interruptions enacted by Art and Vladek come to a wrenching conclusion with Art's renewed search for Anja's diaries at the end of the first volume of *Maus*. In response to Vladek's description of his and Anja's separation in Auschwitz, Art comments: "This is where mom's diaries will be **especially** useful. They'll give me some idea of what she went through while you were apart." Vladek replies: "I can tell you . . . she went through the same what me: terrible!" Vladek attempts to substitute his words and his experiences for Anja's text. His error-prone English starts off accurately but concludes with a sense of missing agency. "The same what me" is a clause that omits the verb and confuses subject and object. Yet this grammatical imperfection "tells a story about limitations," one that is measured and documented by the next generation.[42] In the next frame Art rises: "It's getting cold. Why don't we go upstairs and see if we can find her notebooks." "No," answers Vladek, still sitting, "I looked already . . . it's just not to find anymore!" "Well," returns Art, "Let's check out the garage. You've got loads of stuff in there." Art's search is foiled. Vladek reminds himself of his own actions: "These notebooks, and other really nice things of mother . . . one time I had a very bad day and all of these things I destroyed." "You what?" exclaims Art. "After Anja died I had to make an order with everything. . . . These papers had too many memories. So I burned them," Vladek responds. "Christ! You save tons of worthless shit, and you . . . did you ever read any of them? . . . Can you remember what she wrote?" Art's father responds: "No. I looked in, but I don't remember. . . . Only I know that she said, 'I wish my son, when he grows up, he will be interested by this.' " Art ends the conversation, and the volume, by accusing his father of being a "murderer" (fig. 8).[43]

In *Maus*, the Holocaust is not fully readable for the non-survivor, an individual who is not an eyewitness, in part because the text embodying it is also a victim. This is not to say that if the text were available it would be readable; rather, one aspect of second-generation trauma that distinguishes it from survivor or eyewitness trauma is both its testimonial unreadability *and* its unavailability, the fact that it is both absent and interrupted. Spiegelman's quest for the text leads to the creation of another, secondary work that invests him in the process of remembering and reading: he aligns himself with his readers as a means of exploring the text that is unavailable for his own reading. This indirect picturing links up with Hirsch's notion of postmemory with the act of transmission in *Maus* connecting father and son and drawing them closer together (the book opens with an acknowledgment that the two had not seen each other in a long time). But it is important to remember that transmission comes with many forms of mediation, including, of course, the familiar, public "structures of fantasy and projection,"

FIGURE 8: Text is also a victim.
Credit: Art Spiegelman, *Maus I: A Survivor's Tale: My Father Bleeds History* (New York: Pantheon Books, 1986), 159.

the "shared archive of stories and images that inflect the broader transfer and availability of individual and familial remembrance," but also—and *especially*—the mediation effected by interruption, by absence and unavailability, the full stop that, however painful, delineates a border between postmemory and memory, between readable and unreadable, between first- and second-generation.[44]

Second-generation writers regularly express an urgent, "frustrated need to know about" the traumatic Holocaust past of their parents.[45] They long to read; and yet it is almost uniformly a need that goes unmet. Spiegelman deems his father partly complicit (his mother also shares in this) in rendering the text unavailable—and it is in this light that he accuses his father of being a murderer. For Vladek, the Holocaust survivor, reading the Holocaust diaries evokes "too many memories." For him, reading and narrating are valued differently from his son: narrating may be partially possible, but reading is impossible. Reading the diaries has compelled him to destroy them—this is his way of making order, thwarting his own attempt and that of future generations to read, turning the attempt to do so into an act that surveys absence.

Art's search for his dead mother's diary leads him "to make an order with everything" according to his own method, one in opposition to that of his father.[46] Spiegelman's drawing of frame after frame, his overlaying of present and past, his self-conscious self-representation of writing and drawing *Maus*, connect him not only to the compulsive "order making" of his father but also to the determined and repeated act of recording by his mother. Indeed, a second kind of reading emerges as a counterpart to the unavailable diaries written by his mother that Art seeks; this is his own presentation of *Maus* and, within it, the reading of "Prisoner on the Hell Planet," his previously published "case history," the comic within the comic that documents his mental breakdown following his mother's suicide.

The fraught nature of reading presents itself in a different light when Vladek discovers the comic strip published long before by Art that centers on Anja's suicide and his own subsequent breakdown. Art never showed his father that piece, and Mala, Vladek's second wife, conceals it from him, but Vladek somehow discovers and reads it. "Gee," Art says to Mala, "I'm surprised that Vladek READ this when he found it. He NEVER reads comics. . . . He doesn't even look at my work when I stick it under his nose." Mala responds: "But this isn't like other comics . . . I tell you, when Ruthie showed it to me, I thought I'd faint, I was so shocked. It was so . . . so personal! . . . But very accurate . . . objective. I spent a lot of time helping out here after Anja's funeral. It was just as you said."[47]

"Prisoner on the Hell Planet" introduces the contested nature of reading in *Maus* even before its opening page. Spiegelman's work as an author of comics underscores his desire to document his past in a way that is widely accessible. He *wants* his father to read his work, deliberately handing it to him for his perusal. The frames that compose *Maus,* which include maps, diagrams of hiding places, how-to instructions for a range of activities, clear and concise lines of text, and spare animal drawings, all point to his wish to document accurately and yet simply. The very genre of comics, with its history of "reading as child's play," gestures toward Spiegelman's desire to design a text that is emphatically readable. Its readability is a response—defiant, irreverent, direct—to his relationship to the "texts" of his parents' lives, the destroyed diaries of his mother and the narrative history of his father.

Spiegelman's wish both to read and be read is seconded by Bernice Eisenstein in her comics memoir *I Was a Child of Holocaust Survivors* (2006).[48] In a chapter titled "The Meaning of Books," Eisenstein not only recounts at great length her own reading habits but also notes the first time that she asked her father, an inveterate newspaper reader, to read a book that moved her. The text she volunteered was *The Book of Alfred Kantor,* a collection of Kantor's mainly re-created drawings of concentration camp scenes he witnessed and effectively memorized along with brief captions.[49] Eisenstein hopes that since "it impressed [her] so much, [it] might be of interest to him and that we could talk together about it." After looking briefly at a few drawings, however, her father "closed the book. 'Ich kenish . . . I can't look at this.' He got up and walked out of the room, leaving me upset with myself . . . and feeling sick with regret that I had opened up his pain. . . . In the quiet of the kitchen, I realized that I had needed my father to recognize the importance this book held for me, but once again that sorrowful time in his life pulled itself back out of reach, severing a connection between us."[50] Eisenstein's father responds both in his native Yiddish and, moments later, in English. He first tells himself, "Ich kenish," and then tells his daughter "I can't look at this." Eisenstein's inexact transliteration of the Yiddish—"kenish" is in fact two words, "kenn (or "ken") nisht" ("cannot")—marks her own inability to understand her father in the tongue that marks both his cultural inheritance and its devastation.

In another example of second-generation readership, Michel Kichka, in *Second Generation,* wants to talk to his father about Primo Levi's *Survival in*

FIGURE 9: Reading interrupted.
Credit: Michel Kichka, *Deuxième génération: Ce que je n'ai pas dit à mon père* [*Second generation: What I didn't tell my father*] (Paris: Dargaud, 2012), 81.

*Auschwitz* and Art Spiegelman's *Maus*—books that would surely help his father realize, Kichka notes, "that we were not the only family marked by the past."[51] Speaking to his father in his study, where copies of his Holocaust experiences loom large and number many, Henri Kichka responds coolly to his son's inquiry about Primo Levi: "It's well-written . . . but he didn't suffer as I did. Did you put a little milk in [my coffee]?" And *Maus*, Michel's father continues, with its depiction of Jews as mice, "made me uncomfortable. I closed the book after five pages! Did you put a little sugar in [my coffee]?"[52] Their conversation about the war and its impact specifically on the Kichka family is cut short, abbreviated by Henri's greater interest in preparing his drink (fig. 9).[53]

Like Spiegelman's wish to share a reading experience with his father, Eisenstein and Kichka understand that the symbolism behind a collective or mutual reading experience would narrow the distance between their generation and that of their parents. It is an impossible achievement, as Vladek Spiegelman, Henri Kichka, and Barek Eisenstein all reveal. The reader, in reading a text, engages in a creative process where each sentence is "transformed into the background for the next correlate and must therefore be modified."[54] The transformation is dependent on the reader and on the reader's own past. This moment of understanding fuels an expectation, one specific to individual readers, toward the next sentence or moment in the text. Reading, then, relies on a constant interaction between reader and text, one in which the reader's expectation or prediction of text and memory of what has already been read informs whatever will yet be read.

Vladek Spiegelman, Henri Kichka, and Barek Eisenstein resist this experience of reading because the creative process involved in reading goes against the absolute destructiveness of their histories as survivors. In contrast, in their attempt to read with their parents, Art, Michel, and Bernice want to capture a moment that feels to them like a natural one for a parent and child, one that looks forward and

FIGURE 10: Reading separates memory from experience.
Credit: Art Spiegelman, *Maus I: A Survivor's Tale: My Father Bleeds History* (New York: Pantheon Books, 1986), 103.

creates new and original meaning. In one highly compressed frame of "Prisoner on the Hell Planet," into which Spiegelman packs five images, one of them is of his mother reading to a young Art, tucked into bed, still dressed in the striped clothes of a concentration camp inmate (fig. 10).[55] But reading, with its highly involved interplay between memory and experience, becomes another means of separation between Holocaust survivors and their children.[56]

## BECOMING THE ARCHIVE: SECOND-GENERATION AND THE ACT OF COLLECTING

In his short story "The Library of Moloch," second-generation author Melvin Jules Bukiet writes about a Philadelphia-born professor-turned-librarian who becomes obsessed with recording and collecting video narratives of Holocaust survivors. It is the act of collecting, the accumulating of testimony and history, that drives him. The narrator pointedly and devastatingly connects the scholar-librarian's "insatiable" desire "to hear more and more" to the killers who "were driven to kill more and more."[57] One elderly survivor, recognizing the bloodthirsty prurient nature of the librarian's interest, proves a less forthcoming witness for his project and questions his motives. The librarian responds: "Well, like it or not, we are in the archival era. This library does not exist in order to examine experience. Here experience exists in order to be examined."[58]

The librarian-professor's response to the survivor encapsulates the complex relationship, both enabling and disabling, toward the act of archiving that is faced by second-generation authors—more than by contemporary Holocaust writers and also more than by eyewitnesses themselves. I shift here from considering the graphic works written and drawn by members of the second generation to analyzing the more traditional (and solely textual) memoirs written by many children of Holocaust survivors. The memoirs analyzed here serve as a representative sampling of many second-generation memoirs, most of them initiated in response to the death of one or both of the author's parents. The connection between death and archiving is an intimate one. It stems not only from the prospect of reanimating the dead through the reading, organizing, and donation of their papers and not only from the act of amassing a collection that often comes as part of a legal behest following the death of their original owner or creator. But the act of archiving, as one might glean from the title of Jacques Derrida's work *Archive Fever* (1996) and as Carolyn Steedman considers in her book *Dust* (2002), also invokes a pathology that emphasizes and connects the material existence—and its erasure—of both object and reader, text and archivist.[59] For the librarian in "The Library of Moloch," archiving indeed proves lethal as the films catch fire from one of his cigarettes, a moment that both connects him to the fires of Auschwitz (he survives) but also implicates him—his obsessive desire to collect testimony holds, at its heart, an interest in collecting, not in listening or remembering. The fire that destroys the video testimonies is in effect a reenactment: the librarian's self-interest has already proved devastating. Bukiet links his archivist-librarian to Art Spiegelman's depiction of his father: the testimony they have been charged to protect and memory itself both perish at their hands.

The peculiar and undertheorized relationship between second-generation writers and the role of archives is the focus of the remainder of this chapter. The librarian in Bukiet's story identifies a tension between examination and analysis or between reading and the act of experience. Archiving for the non-eyewitness, as the librarian demonstrates, relies on a tense combination of remembering and forgetting, what Derrida calls "anamnesis." Derrida notes that "the archive takes place at the place of originary and structural breakdown of . . . memory."[60] Archival events are typically recursive, both protected by the shelter of the archive and at the same time "*shelter[ed]* . . . from this memory which it shelters."[61] In its broadest sense, archived material relies on a documentary movement, enabled by the archivist, that in the act of archiving tends to shift in two overlapping but distinct directions: (1) private material is made public, and (2) the act of reading (public) archived materials often entails an encounter between two private histories, both the reader's and the private history described in the archived document.[62]

Texts written by second-generation authors complicate the relationship between private and public, between reading and memory, and between the unreadable and the unknowable. For second-generation authors, who often write in the wake of their parents' deaths, the breakdown of memory is literalized and personalized: the moment of forgetting, which is precisely what is archived, not only serves as cultural memory and institutional history but as the precious and tenuous link to a family history that, because of the trauma of World War II, remains largely unknown.[63] At the same time, second-generation authors are in the position of archiving an event the original version of which, as Agamben claims, is unarchivable, escaping "both memory and forgetting."[64] The unarchivability of testimony is closely connected to its unreadability. Just as the eyewitness, in reading his or her own testimony (see chapter 1), recognizes its unreadability for a non-eyewitness audience, an aspect that most readers can learn to identify, so too does eyewitness testimony resist the shelter of the archive, in its effort both to protect and to make disappear. "Testimony," writes Agamben, "thus guarantees not the factual truth of the statement safeguarded in the archive, but rather its unarchivability, its exteriority with respect to the archive."[65]

In contrast to the unarchivable aspects of their parents' histories, second-generation authors turn to the act of archiving and the institution of the archive, becoming themselves repositories. It is precisely this aspect that stimulates the production of the second-generation memoir. The unreadable and the unarchivable exist in second-generation memoirs; indeed, the foundation of these memoirs is built on the fragments of postmemory and parental eyewitness narrative and the in-between spaces or gaps that these do not cover. In contrast to the typical discursive element of archiving in which there is a "doubled movement of remembering and forgetting," a sense of pushing and pulling that ultimately neutralizes itself, second-generation memoir works at a less even pace, desperately trying to retrieve at-risk memory, both personal and historical.[66]

Rather than the doubling that occurs in other archival events, second-generation memoir as archive creates a doubling of the doubling, the creation of a veritable echo chamber—a shelter that resonates within and by itself. No sense-neutralization permeates second-generation memoir. Instead, a multiplication of urgencies and exigencies both propel it forward and hold it back: the memoirist must run just to stand still. The gravitational pull of forgetting, of not knowing and not being able to know, is inexorable.

In her fine work *Reluctant Witnesses* (2014), Arlene Stein not only applies herself as a scholar analyzing the documentary impulse of many children of survivors to "search for beginnings and endings, a continuous narrative of their parents' and grandparents' lives, a chain of events in a cause-effect relationship occurring in time and space, and for a coherent origin story of their own."[67] She also includes her own efforts to excavate and collect the fragmented history of her father. Reviewing the work of other second-generation memoirs, Stein notes that, while "survivors had memories of the worlds they had lost, their children did not. They had story fragments, and scattered objects upon which descendants had projected their fantasies."[68] The second-generation memoir is "part travelogue, part elegy"; part past, part present; part empty, part full; part real, part imagined.[69] In keeping with the notion that second-generation memoir doubles the doubling, Stein notes that in order to "put yourself in someone else's story," one must "put another person in yourself."[70]

The tools of the second-generation memoirist-archivist—tools such as remembering through speechlessness and through silence, remembering through interviews, remembering through the lucky discovery of a precious few documents—are feeble in the face of what they are trying to remember, document, and archive. The historian Paula Fass, the daughter of Holocaust survivors, notes that discovering the fact that her father had a wife and four children who did not survive the war and that her mother had a husband and son who did not survive the war led her first to become a historian and then, later in her career, to search for the archived records relating to these members of her family. "The details of who they were, how they were lost . . . have remained obscure and dangerous edges of a history I can never fully penetrate."[71] Typically, the act of archiving involves a gesture of depositing that is at the same time a relinquishing, a letting go of memory that marks the peculiar give and take of archiving. "The analysis of the archive," Foucault writes, "delimits us."[72] The second-generation memoir, however, is built from a combined source—of the limitations that come with the rare fragments available and of the absence of limits that accompanies the loss of the whole. In response, in their efforts to read the text of the eyewitness, second-generation authors become themselves the figure of the archive, on the precipice of reading and not reading, remembering and not remembering.[73]

Consider the letter, written on a torn page and in her father's hand, that Eva Hoffman finds among her parents' papers after their deaths. It was addressed to a man named Hryczko who, Hoffman is reminded only as she reads, is the son of the family who sheltered her parents during the war, thus helping to save their lives:

> The rough draft, written a year before my father's death, was an attempt to make contact after all those years. . . . It contained the suggestion that Hryczko's family should be placed in Yad Vashem's roll call of 'Righteous Gentiles.' It also told Hryczko something he apparently might not have known—how and when my father's brothers died. Both of them were killed when the war was in effect over, in crossfire between the receding German and the incoming Soviet armies. Among the familiar facts, there was a sentence I read with shock: "There was no one to help me," my father wrote. "I had to bury them myself."[74]

We read here about a complex exchange between generations, archival memory and the emotional response to reading testimony that remains external to the archive and yet internal to another, secondary text. Hoffman learns for the first time about her father burying his brothers and tries to imagine her father at that specific moment in time and place; she concludes this mental foray by recognizing that this moment of death and burial "plunged him into speechlessness" so profound that she "felt it as a child, within all his outbursts, a silence he did not fully break until his death."[75] Indeed, it is a silence she feels as she reads the letter, surprised at the revelations it contains and aware of the very limited purview she has of her father's history; the torn document she holds in her hands is emblematic of both the fragment that she is able to hold and read—that which has been archived—and that which she cannot.

At its foundation, the archive is a system of privilege built on its own enunciability, namely, its capacity to be read, cataloged, and identified.[76] Hoffman's father's silence defies this system; Hoffman's pressing need to serve as an interlocutor leads her to it. Not knowing if the letter's intended recipient, a man who would be her father's age, has ever received it, Hoffman returns to the village where her parents hid and—"half-torn piece of paper" in hand—goes to the "shabby little offices of the 'Town Council'" of Załośce. Here to the best of her ability Hoffman seeks to fill in the narrative where it has been abruptly condensed. Once in the town hall, some local people help her locate Hryczko who indeed had never received the letter. Hoffman then reads it to him aloud, in the presence of other local residents.

This is not the only public performance of the letter. The letter, not only as a document in itself but as a document read by the daughter of the survivor-author, goes on to acquire a talismanic presence, becoming "an iconic object" in the village. The "director of the council . . . makes me read it over and over again, to groups of young people she summons to her office for that purpose. She wants them to know, she says, something of their town's history."[77] From hidden to hidden; from found to found. This private letter, containing unknown facts and wishes, acquires a place in the public eye precisely where the initial and enabling act of hiding, of sheltering, occurred. The unarchivable remains, significantly, just that; but the archivable and the archived—the almost forgotten—are rescued, at least in part, salvaged by a member of the next generation, who becomes a part of the document she carries to its intended reader and then reads to the others who gather. The "hinge generation," a phrase Hoffman coins, is necessary for the archiving of Holocaust memory, recognizing the crucial and ongoing interactions between history and memory that are animated by the intimacy between parent and child.

As part of their role in archiving family and cultural history and memory, one that serves to heighten the tension between the private and the public, many second-generation narrative memoirs discuss at length the author's return to a parent's hometown and the visits paid to personal landmarks, such as homes and places of work, as well as to the local archives. These trips to recover some trace of the past are fraught and emotionally turbulent in no small part because of the normalcy associated with them for many other generations of immigrant children. Often called "roots tourism" or "heritage tourism," children, grandchildren, and still others return to their ancestral homes in a journey that uncovers and defines for them a sense of familial, cultural, and ethnic belonging.[78]

Belonging is, however, a far more complicated feature of any return visits to the "old country" performed by Holocaust survivors or their children. As Carol Ascher describes it, "both Vienna and Berlin [her parents' hometowns] lay on the dark side of a dreaded gravitational field that held me captive."[79] When Ascher does return to Vienna, she moves about the city in a "dreamlike state," feeling reunited with her estranged father who died years earlier and, at the same time, intensely self-conscious about her Jewish identity, an identity inextricably tied to her sense of herself as a child of a Viennese Holocaust survivor. Her research in various archives only heightens her contradictory sense of both belonging and estrangement. She uncovers her grandfather's military records from World War I, only to find his relative anonymity exposed by the "J" stamped on the file, the work of a Nazi bureaucrat decades after her grandfather's military service ended. Most troubling to Ascher is the discovery of her father's renunciation of Judaism, recorded in a "large, heavy, leather-bound *Geburtsbuch*, or birth boo[k]." Under his name and date of birth, under the date of his circumcision and his Hebrew name, is the date September 1924 and the entry "withdrawal from Judaism."[80] Ascher reacts with a combination of shame and defensiveness, in large part because she reads her father's withdrawal from Judaism as a rejection not only of the religion but also of her, his Jewish child—and this, in spite of the fact that his "withdrawal" occurs many years before her birth. She stakes out a piece of the city for herself, registering as a city resident, a gesture enabled by her status as a daughter of a Viennese Jew; yet, in her application she hides the fact that she is Jewish, declaring herself a Buddhist. And then, in a different turn, she is insulted when guards at the Israëlitische Kultusgemeinde question her status as a Jew. Ascher's experiences in the Austrian archives, both what she discovers and what her own actions and newly created records add to her family history, place her squarely in the echo chamber that is the province of the second generation. Each of her forays into the Austrian archives not only reveals new information about her family but also illuminates direct parallels in her own life, pointing to what she has become but, even more crucially, pulling her back to the story of her origins. The second-generation Holocaust author—as Ascher and others mentioned above illustrate—share in the subjectivity of the archives.

For second-generation authors, the archived papers inscribed with their family names are often the only surviving physical traces specific to the lives of parents, grandparents, and great-grandparents. Paula Fass writes that, in "trying to reconstruct specific events and the lives of the lost, I often have nothing more than a few bare details, details that I have refused to embellish even with the historical imagination that I have developed as an adult."[81] Helen Epstein notes that a "person whose family has remained in place inherits possessions—a hat, a cupboard, old diaries, a prayer or recipe book—that transmit personal history from one generation to the next." In contrast, the objects that would have been passed down to her were "confiscated and crammed into warehouses by the Nazis along with hundreds of thousands of other pieces of property belonging to Czech Jews."[82] In place of things, second-generation authors document their search for a single name that they can identify as their own among the many enormous volumes housed at the archive. Yet this search is fraught, as Ascher shows, not only with the certainty that not enough has been documented but also with the concern of what might be revealed by that which has been.

Further complicating and deepening the sense of dispossession is their awareness that the few items that can be traced to their parents and their families belong, both in present day and during the lives of their parents and grandparents, to a government and its institutions that at one time failed to protect its citizens even as it still shelters documents that enlarge their children's knowledge and sense of their family. Ascher notes that she "had expected a Jewish institution [the Israëlitische Kultusgemeinde] to be a haven of comfort in Vienna. . . . Yet . . . the heavily guarded insularity of Judaism at the Kultusgemeinde made me feel trapped inside someone else's ghetto."[83] In spite of feeling an intimate connection with the family documents she unearths, Ascher recognizes her foreign, outsider status within the archives. It is her position as such that at once enables her access to the archive yet deprives her of the very shelter it promises to grant.

This same sense of entrapment is heightened by another physical feature of archives, namely, their limited accessibility, a necessary feature in the institutionalization of documents, objects, and memory. Restrictions on who is allowed to read files and for how long forces readers and visitors to acknowledge the power structure in place. Archives are built and organized under a central authority that quite explicitly impedes access just as it has sifted through materials, determining if they are worthy of being archived. In second-generation memoir, the figure of the archivist who lends assistance to those looking for word of their family becomes almost a priestly figure, empowered to determine more or less relevant documentation. Often, as Appignanesi, Ascher, and others note, their quest is met with a sense of indifference on the part of archive employees—as a "distraction" from the primary task of archiving local Jewish history. "The living," writes Appignanesi in terms that echo Bukiet's librarian, "are patently a distraction."[84]

Second-generation memoirists enter the archives with a sense of both entitlement—they belong there and deserve to be reunited with the documents bearing their family name—and vulnerability, aware of the fraught history behind just this kind of precipitous belonging. In ways both analytically and symbolically meaningful, the power structure of the archives in relation to the second-generation reader-author imitates the structure in which they were raised, where the experiences and authority of their survivor parents imposes a longing for knowledge within a larger system that precludes just that. Derrida opens *Archive Fever* with a discussion of the etymology of the word "archive," which is rooted in the Greek *archeion*: "initially a house, a domicile, an address, the residence of the superior magistrates, the *archons*, those who commanded."[85] The archive is not just an institutional space but the site of authority and privilege, a place that serves to shelter, to hide, and to conceal. As a rule, archives are systems that determine not only what "can be said" but also how these statements are organized and who is allowed access to them.[86] Second-generation authors document their visits to the archives in part because these repeated events are a return home, with the combination of estrangement and intimacy that such visits dictate. It is precisely this conundrum that marks the conclusion of Appignanesi's *Losing the Dead*. When she returns to her home in London after a trip to Poland, the birthplace of her parents and where she was born shortly after the war, her Polish lawyer writes to notify her that no record "of Elzbieta Borensztejn (or Borensztajn)—that is, me—exists in the Łódź Registry archive."[87] With no evidence of her birth, Appignanesi wonders if she has really lived. Perhaps this same thought runs through all the archival research so carefully detailed and documented by the second generation.

Second-generation memoirists bequeath to the reader their own, not their parent's, understanding and postmemory of the Holocaust: an ambivalent, complex, and contested mix of past and present, participation and exclusion—the story that can be read and pictured, the one that draws from the archives, but also, and most deliberately, the story that cannot be accessed in these ways. Rotgeber, Kertész, and other eyewitness-authors project the limits of reading and suggest that the reader may not even recognize precisely these limitations. Second-generation memoirists read inherited memory, they read the void of unavailable text. Spiegelman aligns himself with the readers of his text by creating his own diaries, namely, the frames that compose *Maus*, a work that is eminently readable, its comic strip form making his text accessible to a wide array of readers. His work serves as a drastic and deliberate counterpart to the destroyed diaries that had been painstakingly written and rewritten by his mother. Similarly, in the purely textual memoir *Where She Came From*, Helen Epstein decides to construct her memoir based on the family histories recorded by seventeenth- and eighteenth-century Czech Jews, *megillot mishpachot*, that provide a multigenerational history. In contrast to those documents, written by and focused on men, Epstein opts to bring "three generations of increasingly secular women to life in an old Jewish literary form."[88] Nazism followed by communism made access to Czech archives exceedingly difficult, and yet Epstein succeeds in finding some documentation relating to all three generations, building on her discoveries with a wide range of historical sources, scholarly texts, archival materials, and personal interviews. *Where She Came From* succeeds as a postmodern *megillah mishpachah*, a family history that was once virtually forgotten.

In reviewing their growing up with inherited traumatic memory, second-generation authors initiate a process of reading and readability that acknowledges the absence of crucial text—with the absence itself integral to the traumatic memories—while at the same time creating a text that conforms with all measures of readability. A parallel process emerges in relation to the act of archiving: in deep ways, second-generation authors recognize the limits of the archive, all the while becoming a repository for family and cultural memory that is then set before us, bound and typed. "In the beginning . . . ," begins Hoffman's memoir, invoking the first words of Genesis, ". . . was the war."[89] Children of Holocaust survivors define their origins as a moment of loss, a place of speechlessness. Second-generation memoir marks these boundaries, writing about them and around them, because in the end these boundaries and what they encompass serve as a central component to second-generation memory and history.

# 4 • THE THIRD GENERATION'S HOLOCAUST

## The Story of Time and Place

> I had the vague notion that when I reached each house, each square that I had heard so much about, I would recognize it, it would produce emotion in me, a sense of the time, memories almost. As if I were not I, . . . not visiting, but revisiting.
>
> —Kate Cohen, *The Neppi Modona Diaries*

Second-generation authors are also readers of inherited memory, recognizing the presence of the unreadable through aligning themselves with their audience.[1] Part of the drive behind second-generation authors wanting to document their relationship with their parents is to read and touch the material presence offered by a text that they have been largely deprived of through a range of destructive and traumatic means. By their own recounting, second-generation memoirists acknowledge the push and pull of two incongruous forces: a desire to read—to handle, to contain—the experience of their eyewitness parents and, at the same time, a desire to understand the necessary silence or absence that informs that narrative. Second-generation authors document the legibility of postmemory, the fact that it can be both recorded and read; what second-generation memoir consistently and deliberately does *not* do is re-create or re-imagine eyewitness memory. The traumatic memory of their parents haunts second-generation authors as it eludes them, creating a cycle of perpetual unmet desire for what, ultimately, they place before us, their audience.

Third-generation Holocaust authors, in contrast, are a wide-ranging, categorically resistant group whose nonfiction narratives include imagined endings, rewritten histories, emotionally laden textual interactions, verbal and physical interplay, interviews with relatives and strangers who are Holocaust survivors, intense and well-documented historical and archival research, travel to distant places, and feelings for their subject matter that begin with a fascination bordering on obsession and often include a deeply personal brand of interest and investment. While the breadth of definition of the words "survivor" and "victim" has generated considerable debate, it has been accompanied by a sense of the identifiable.[2] The U.S. Holocaust Museum defines "Survivors and Victims" broadly as "any persons, Jewish or non-Jewish, who were displaced, persecuted, or discriminated against due to the racial, religious, ethnic, social, and political policies of the Nazis and their collaborators between 1933 and 1945."[3] In a report on Holocaust victim compensation, Dr. Jacob Ukeles defines a Jewish Nazi Victim as a "Jew who lived in a country at the time when it was under a Nazi regime; under Nazi occupation, or under the regime of Nazi collaborators or who fled to a country or region not under Nazi rule or occupation due to Nazi rule or Nazi occupation."[4] In a parallel report, demographer and statistician Sergio DellaPergola bases his report around the title "*Shoah survivor*" rather than "Nazi victim" and defines this as "*all those Jewish persons who are alive today and who at least for a brief period of time were submitted in their locations to a regime of duress and/or limitation of their full civil rights in relation to their Jewish background—whether by a Nazi foreign occupying power or by a local authority associated with the Nazis' endeavor—or had to flee elsewhere in order to avoid falling under the aforementioned situations.*"[5]

While DellaPergola's definition comes closest to that acknowledged by the U.S. Holocaust Museum, with its considerable reach among the public, it has generated pushback from academicians and (European) Holocaust survivors. Holocaust historian Yehuda Bauer, for instance, claims that "Holocaust survivors are only those people who were physically persecuted by the Nazis or their cohorts. This means people who lived in ghettos and concentration camps or compulsory labor frameworks, who hid or who joined the partisan ranks . . . these are not Holocaust survivors."[6] Further complicating the narrative behind demographics, even some individuals who meet the most stringent conditions of the term "survivor" or "victim" prefer to identify themselves otherwise, often in deference to those they believe truly belong to that category. For example, Dori Katz, born in Antwerp in 1939 and placed in hiding with a Belgian Catholic family at the age of three, remains uncomfortable with being called a survivor. In a talk she gave, Katz noted that for her the term "survivor" referred to her mother and her mother's friends (her father perished at Auschwitz), older people who "had lived, consciously, through the horrors of the Holocaust."[7]

The challenge of identifying Holocaust survivors involves a piecing together of time and place. Holocaust survivors are defined as being born before 1945 and living in a place subject to some aspect of Nazi rule.[8] The controversy and indeterminacy that accompanies the categorization of the terms "Holocaust survivors" and "Holocaust victims" is both amplified (the terms become broader and increasingly inchoate) and diminished (the pull of identification is more muted) for succeeding generations. The category "second-generation" in relation to the Holocaust, originally defined by one or both of their parents' survival of Nazi concentration camps, has since expanded to include the survival of the broader designation of Nazi persecution.

In its narrowest form, then, the third generation (often abbreviated now to 3G) refers to the grandchildren of one or more Holocaust survivors or victims, with those words themselves producing a range of definitions. Understood more broadly, the term "third-generation" applies to those who have inherited a family history that, two generations prior, was tragically affected by the Holocaust. This would include not only grandchildren but all third-generation descendants. At its most diffuse, the term "third-generation" might seem even more all-encompassing. While some members of the third generation write about a living relationship between themselves and their grandparents and members of their grandparents' generation, other third-generation writers often rely exclusively on textual and oral resources—family histories, archives, and interviews—as the basis of their exploration. In this sense, "third-generation" might apply to an untold number of people who, through a variety of means—the building of and participation in memorials, travel to sites of devastation, investigations into family and Jewish history—develop a connection to the trauma of the Holocaust, one made personal for them by their attention to the life of a single person or a single family.

These three variations behind the term "third-generation" reveal a defining trend: far more people claim some sense of personal link to the Holocaust now than in its immediate aftermath. Indeed, as second-generation author Jules Bukiet notes, the "weird thing" about the Holocaust is that, "contravening all physical laws, the waves [around it] do not diminish. They build upon each other, getting larger rather than smaller as history itself recedes. No other event of our time has attained this emblematic significance." Bukiet makes a case for the "special place" occupied by the second generation: "Whatever wisdom others bring to [the Holocaust] comes from the heart and head, but for us it's genetic. To be shabbily proprietary, we own it. Our parents owned it, and they gave it to us. . . . I'd like to tell everyone from the Bellows and the Ozicks to the Styrons and the Wilkomirskis, 'Bug off. Find your own bad news,' but no one can legislate artistic imperative, and perhaps no one should."[9] Bukiet's possessiveness is in itself tinged with irony: his "bad news" is not derived from direct experience but from a tense combination of inheritance and transmitted experience. Contained within the definition of "third-generation" are the very issues that Bukiet raises peremptorily in relation to those he feels intrude on second-generation territory: concerns of legitimacy, exclusivity, and belonging that illuminate and complicate the presence of precisely these matters as they relate to members of the second generation and eyewitnesses in texts written by authors who are at a still further remove, the third generation.

Beyond the identity of the writers themselves, another aspect challenging any definition of "third-generation" are the questions raised regarding the authenticity of a grandparent's connection with the Holocaust, namely, the need for some sort of validation of their designation as a Holocaust victim or survivor. It is an issue that resonates uncomfortably with the process of defining Jewish identity that was used and manipulated by the Third Reich. The Nuremberg Laws, implemented in 1935, "defined a Jew as a person with three or more Jewish grandparents, or a person with two Jewish grandparents who was either married to a 'Jew' or had belonged to a Jewish religious community as of the date the laws were implemented. A grandparent was by definition a 'Jew' if he or she had belonged to the Jewish community."[10] Bukiet may want to tell American-born Jewish authors with no immediate personal Holocaust legacy to "bug off" but would he make the same retort to his own children, nieces, or nephews—to his parents' grandchildren?

Essayist and short-story writer Erika Dreifus dwells on these and other problems of third-generation identification. Dreifus's grandfather, whom she classifies as a "refugee-survivor," fled Germany in 1937 (her grandmother left in 1938) and was then drafted into the American military in 1938. Dreifus identifies herself as "among the elders of the third generation," and as someone who has "not been able to fully separate from her grandparents' past." Dreifus, perhaps more than any other third-generation author, explicitly ponders her status and identity: "If my grandparents were not 'survivors,' then how can I have remained so affected? So tied to this territory? Has there been something toxic, wrong, inauthentic about my obsessions?"[11] Her willingness to reflect on her status, on her grandparents' introduction to the United States, and on both their and their family's—past, present, and future—losses and gains in coming when they did provides a lens to much of her writing. In contrast to the clarity that Bukiet brings to his understanding of the second generation, Dreifus investigates the challenges and complications of her self-designation, questioning her relationship to it and yet all the while adhering to an understanding of herself as a member of the third generation.

Dreifus's uneasiness stems from a requisite division of labor that is difficult to bridge: third-generation authors are necessarily self-referential at the same time that they write about a past that is in many ways deeply disconnected from them. In the second generation, many were born in their parents' native countries, raised in households where there was more than one primary language (and the accompanying accent that indicated foreign roots), where grandparents were often blank spaces on a family tree, where time-honored family treasures were scarce, and where the past was often hidden from view. Unlike the second generation, third-generation authors are far more likely to document their loving (if complicated) homes, their far-flung and often large families (for at least two generations), their inability to speak the native language of their ancestors, the material wealth of their middle-class or upper-middle-class status, and a desire to discover a history that has long gone uninvestigated. Third-generation stories, both fictional and nonfictional, emerge from a need to design a connective web intended to draw closer together the eyewitness (first) generation and the third generation. I argue here that this connective web is established both imaginatively, through a process that involves third-generation authors developing a version of testimony (I call it post-testimony) that attempts to uncover the unknown, and physically, through visiting and finding meaning in specific sites that played a role in their family's history.

For my purposes here—to investigate and develop a categorical understanding of third-generation memoir and to understand its relationship to earlier generations of Holocaust memoir—I locate the "third generation" somewhere in between the second and third definitions. My conceptualization of "third-generation" is founded less on the categorical principles of family background (a diffuse and many times challenging record to investigate) and more on the unifying textual qualities that define the work of many third-generation authors and serve arguably as the most accurate means by which to designate them. This has led to instances where the boundaries of third-generation memoir become blurred with those of second-generation writing and even with the writing of those who might not otherwise be considered in the line of inheritance at all.

Authors Erin Einhorn (*The Pages In Between* [2009]) and Daniel Rose (*Hiding Places* [2000]), both of whose parents survived the Third Reich, write texts that are narratively more in keeping with third-generation memoir. This makes sense as Einhorn's mother was hidden as an infant, and much of her memoir focuses on her grandparents' generation. Rose returns to Europe with his two young sons and, often through their eyes, narrates a family history that is far more preoccupied with the generation of his grandparents than with that of his parents.

Artist Edmund de Waal and author and poet Vikram Seth are two more authors who can unexpectedly be read as third-generation authors. De Waal's Jewish grandmother, who converted as an adult to Christianity, left Austria in the late 1920s but returned to facilitate her parents' departures. The family was one branch of a storied Jewish banking dynasty comparable to the Rothschild family and also owners of an important art collection, all of which was lost during the war, as documented in De Waal's *The Hare with Amber Eyes: A Hidden Inheritance* (2010). Seth's *Two Lives* (2006) investigates the improbable marriage and history of his Indian-born maternal great-uncle and his wife, Seth's great-aunt, a German Jewish refugee whose mother and sister perished in the Holocaust and whose histories Seth researches.

All this is to say that the designation "third generation" is fluid and complex, made up of Jews and non-Jews, some intimately connected to their family history and losses and some entirely ignorant of them. In a move that counters Bukiet's position, although applied to a different generation, I suggest that in determining who or what "counts" as third-generation—that is, as the inheritors of a specific Holocaust history—self-identification, which often comes through narrative explorations of family history, is sufficient. What I categorically reject in the assumption of these titles is the application of the word "survivor" to the second or third generation. Rather, I refer to second- and third-generation authors or texts in an effort to locate them in terms of time in relation to the Holocaust.[12]

## TEXTUAL MEMORY AND READING THE END

Perhaps the most notable quality of third-generation texts is the effort exhibited within them to render visible the unreadable narrative. This can at least in part be attributed to the historical distance between the Holocaust itself and the act of composition, a distance reflecting the fact that many third-generation authors have either limited or no direct relation to the Holocaust. The recovery of family memory, history, and trauma, then, occurs primarily through the experience of textuality, that is, through the act of reading. Members of the third generation rely heavily, often exclusively, on the condition of readability, ultimately producing readable texts that form a response to the same quality of reading that informs much of their historical understanding. Awareness of the unreadable, so present in the work of eyewitness and second-generation authors, is a response to living memory and postmemory, a response that recognizes, among other things, the physical proximity of trauma. This proximity is necessarily absent from third-generation writing, and yet many third-generation memoirists write lingering accounts of the trauma, torture, and death suffered by their relatives. This attempt, I suggest, reflects a wish to capture the sense of immediacy that permeates the texts of their parents and grandparents. Doing this ensures their presence—that is, the presence of the third-generation author—in historical traumatic memory. But precisely these descriptions, because of their graphic content, often obscure the fact and nature of unreadability, a claim I will return to. The impulse toward rendering traumatic history and memory readable, or more readable, is a function of time and sources; while not inevitable, it is predictable, a product of a keen desire to know and to know absolutely, coupled with a sense of remoteness that makes real knowing elusive. Given that the unreadable itself stems from a kind of unknowing, the continual striving toward readability is, counterintuitively, a loss, one that can be compared to the dimming of memory. Ultimately, eyewitness testimony recognizes the presence, role, and even importance of the unreadable; it, too, serves as a function of memory. Trying to "crack the code" of the unreadable, trying to penetrate it, while perhaps the most human of gestures and understandable in its intentions, fails to recognize the place and role of the unreadable in the history and aftermath of the Holocaust.

Third-generation authors invest a remarkable amount of time in recovering documents, artifacts, and places. Their works effectively document their role as readers of texts, illustrating through the act of recovering documents and the reading process the dynamic and essential interaction between text and reader.[13]

We, their audience, read about an experience of reading, a more mitigated and mediated process than the act of reading itself. The difference I find here is akin to the difference between watching a film oneself and learning about it as recounted by someone else, that is, the experience of reading (or viewing) is diluted and shaped differently from the experience in itself. The condition of readability is aided by the mediated relationship contained within third-generation memoirs. Indeed, I suggest that, in the absence of the events themselves, readability is an essential condition for representation. Readability enables historical facts and details to come to light, although not historical trauma. More notably, however, readability shifts the temperament of the text from reflecting backward to leaning forward. Through the readability of the text, the authors aim for both themselves and their readers not only to witness but to participate in the restorative powers of literature, a significant and important though unstated motivation behind third-generation memoir. The nature of this restoration is twofold. On the one hand, authors work to restore survivor memory and history with the belief that through doing so some element of the healing power of literature will exert itself, that is, the act of restoration mends a rift in time and place between the survivor's history and the contemporary reader or writer's understanding of it. On the other hand, however, this pull toward readability does not come easily. Unreadability stands as a form of memorialization, a recognition of the trauma that efforts toward readability hope to excise. An element of remembrance is deeply embedded in recognizing the unreadable, as survivor literature indicates over and over again. Thus, it is important to recognize that readability is an achievement, one that is both crucial and unavoidable.

Whereas first-generation eyewitness authors anticipate the unreadability of their text for their audience, and second-generation authors, in an attempt to gain access to—that is, read—their parents' stories, align themselves with their own audiences and identify themselves as thwarted readers, third-generation authors are typically left with only the artifacts of unreadability. In an effort to construct a meaningful narrative from such artifacts, third-generation authors engage in a kind of recovery that attempts not only to capture a historical narrative but also to tie this narrative to the present. More than anything else, third-generation Holocaust texts are intensely personal: the effort to overcome the unreadable means inscribing oneself as author into the story and representing that figure in relation to the primary artifact, the primary account, the primary eyewitness, that remains largely unavailable. In this way, the central concern of third-generation texts is a relationship to the unreadable that is founded on readability. This readability, however, comes at the expense of a form of memory deemed essential to the act of remembering, one that is so regularly referenced in literature written by Holocaust survivors and victims that it serves as an anchoring feature of Holocaust textuality, one that surveys past history and anticipates future readership.

Third-generation memoirs often extend their narratives back to generations earlier than those affected by World War II and often investigate the features and concerns of their relatives' daily lives, while a striking number of third-generation memoirs also reconstruct in great detail moments of terrible abuse, trauma, and death suffered by members of their family. These graphic and often blow-by-blow descriptions are frequently preceded by extensive historical and archival citations from which the description is derived. At the same time, the descriptions become an opportunity for the writer to insert himself into the text, creating a moment of proximity to historical trauma that would not otherwise exist.

In Daniel Mendelsohn's *The Lost* (2006), a book dedicated to discovering more about the lives and deaths of the author's grandfather's brother Shmiel, his wife, and their four daughters, Mendelsohn vividly reconstructs the murder of his cousin Ruchele. He does this only after a significant amount of research. By connecting with a Holocaust survivor—Jack Greene né Grunschlag from Bolechow, his family's ancestral home—Mendelsohn learns the correct names and birth order of his cousins (Ruchele was the third) and that "Ruchele perished on the twenty-ninth of October 1941," the same day that Greene's mother and brother also died.[14] More research produces information about Ruchele's schooling, her looks, her friends, her social activities, and information about her family. A trip to the archives at Yad Vashem yields the detailed testimony of Rebeka Mondschein, who reports what was told to her by a Jewish man, Ducio Schindler, who managed to escape the mass killing and witnessed the events while hiding in a tree. Mondschein's testimony, recorded in 1946 and cited in full by Mendelsohn, describes the first *Aktion* carried out by the Germans, one that killed approximately nine hundred Bolechower Jews, including Ruchele. Based on that testimony, Mendelsohn notes that "now it is possible to know what happened even if it is difficult to reconstruct with any certainty what happened to Ruchele."[15] He then continues, putting together the pieces of narrative he has gathered, which I cite here in its near entirety:

> She was picked up, most likely, sometime after noon on Tuesday, the twenty-eighth of October, as she walked the streets of her hometown with her girlfriends. She was then herded toward the Dom Katolicki, and there probably witnessed certain of the events described [in the Yad Vashem testimony]—although we must keep in mind that the Jews who were forced onto the floor of the D.K. that afternoon were told to keep their heads down, and that those who got up off the floor were often shot dead on the spot, so maybe it's better, instead of saying that Ruchele *witnessed* some of what happened, to say that she mostly *heard* shots, screams, shouts, taunts, the piano playing, the footfalls of the awkwardly dancing feet on the stage.
>
> It is possible (to go on) that the sixteen-year-old Ruchele was killed there [at the Dom Katolicki, the Catholic community center house where the Jews were

> first gathered], as we know some people were. It is, indeed, possible that she was the naked girl on the stage, with whom the rabbi, his eyes running blood, was forced to dance, or forced to lie on top of. I prefer not to think so. Then again, if she survived those [first] thirty-six hours, as some did not, we know that at around four o'clock on the afternoon of October 29, a Wednesday, after spending the previous day, night and morning in a state of terror that it would be foolish to try to imagine; after weeping with thirst and hunger and, undoubtedly, soiling herself with her own urine, for nobody can go a day and a half without relieving herself, she was then taken, exhausted, hungry, terrified, filthy with her own bodily fluids, something it is hard, perhaps even embarrassing to think about, a disgusting, deeply shaming experience for any adult, but a possibility I must consider, as I try to imagine what happened to her; she was taken to Taniawa—whether she walked the few kilometers or was put in a truck, it is impossible to know—and there, after waiting in even greater terror while watching group after group of her neighbors, people she'd seen around the little town her whole life long (well: sixteen years) line up on a plank and fall into the pit: after watching this, she took her inevitable turn, walked naked onto the plank—with what thoughts it is impossible to know, although it would be difficult not to imagine that she was thinking, in those last moments, of her mother and father and sisters, or home; but perhaps . . . perhaps for the most fleeting moment, she thought of Jakob Grunshlag, the boy whom she's dated for a year and a half, his dark hair and eager smile—and standing on the plank, or perhaps at the edge of the freshly dug pit, with the bodies beneath her and the cold October air above, waited. The cold October air: we know that she was naked by this point, and between the weather and the terror, surely she was shivering. Again and again, as she waited her turn—unless she was the first?—the sounds of machine-gun fire rang out. . . .
>
> So: the rattling bursts of gunfire, the cold, the shivering. At some point it was her turn she walked with the others onto the plank. Likely this plank had some give, perhaps it bounced a little as they lined up: an incongruously playful motion. Then another burst of fire. Did she hear it? Was the fervent activity of her mind at this moment such that she didn't really hear; or, by contrast, were her ears exquisitely attuned, waiting? We cannot know. We know only that her soft, sixteen-year-old body—which with any luck was lifeless at this point, although we know that some were still alive when they fell with a wet thud onto the warm and bleeding, excrement-smeared bodies of their fellow townsfolk—fell into the grave, and that is the last we see of her; although we have, of course, not really seen her at all.[16]

In her review of Mendelsohn's book, Ruth Franklin calls this among his "most moving episodes" because "he steps outside himself and allows his creative powers to take over." But Mendelsohn only partially "steps outside himself." The imagined end to Ruchele's life is punctuated by authorial asides—"it would be foolish to try to imagine" or "a possibility I must consider"—that closely position the first-person narration of the memoirist, Mendelsohn, to the subject of the narration, Ruchele—so much so, that their individual subjectivity is very nearly shared. Does, for example, the shaming experience that Mendelsohn mentions involve the imagining or the actuality of soiling oneself? According to this passage it involves both.

Part of Mendelsohn's challenge in *The Lost* is one of narrative construction. How does he tell the story that documents his own emotional discovery of his family's history and, at the same time, achieve his goal of effectively bringing his relatives back to life, documenting "how they had lived, who they were"? He does so in a move that is characteristic of third-generation narrative: by drawing near to his subject, by inserting himself into the narrative. Moreover, by positioning his own reading of Ruchele's final hours just a few pages after he cites the lengthy testimony of Mrs. Mondschein, Mendelsohn suggests that a relationship exists between the two accounts, that is, the testimony of Mrs. Mondschein, while identifying some people by name, leaves the identity of most of the Jews victimized and murdered in the first *Aktion* unknown. Mendelsohn's research deliberately fills in some of the missing knowledge about how Ruchele ended up in the Dom Katolicki, even as his narrative relies on conjecture and probability for much of its portrayal of her final hours. Furthermore, his role as a third-generation writer writing more than half a century after his cousin's murder moves him to dwell on details that he can determine and define, details that have (understandably) gone unnoticed previously, such as the cold October air and the bounce of the plank. These details are not peculiar to Ruchele or to her story; each of the hundreds of people murdered that day with Ruchele experienced the air and the plank. In this sense, Mendelsohn never fulfills his mission of discovering his cousin's particular story. Instead he contributes to the narrative detail that lends a quality of readability to her final moments.

In an interview with the French magazine *La Revue des Deux Mondes*, Mendelsohn explores the influence of Marcel Proust's *In Search of Lost Time* on *The Lost*, both on the title of the work but also in the shared preoccupation with the preservation and resuscitation of the past. Most immediately, Mendelsohn notes his effort to imitate Proust's style in two specific ways. On a more minute level, Mendelsohn wants to reproduce Proust's inclusion of multiple seemingly disparate elements in a single sentence. So, for example, in *The Lost* he writes about a day in 1942 when certain family members are murdered in Belzec while, on that same day, his eleven-year-old mother sets out on her regular route to school. "By threading both of these events into the same long sentence, I tried to achieve a kind of pointed juxtaposition which spoke to a larger theme of my book, which is what I think of as the ironies of 'unknowability.' How much of what is transpiring in the world, of what has happened in history, we simply can never know."[17] On a more macro level, Mendelsohn is captivated by Proust's ability to create revelation and meaning through a method that initially introduces the reader to a seemingly trivial piece of information, only to have it take root and bloom in deep and unexpected ways hundreds of pages later. In writing *The Lost*, Mendelsohn notes that he is intent on re-creating in his writing "some of the emotional intensity" he experienced in his research. "In other words," he notes, he wants "to make it emotional for the *reader*." He introduces an element early on in the work, so "the reader would be able to 'recognize'" it later on and "share in my [Mendelsohn's] shock." Strategically, Mendelsohn explains, the "information needs to be given early enough, but not *so* early that it can have been forgotten by the time it comes into play."[18]

I raise these reflections because they illuminate the degree to which Mendelsohn wants the reader to share in his experience as a self-declared mediator between past and present, if not physically then emotionally, a move dramatically different from survivor or second-generation narratives where a motif of difference and not belonging establishes a crucial and irrecoverable space between reader and author. In contrast, Mendelsohn's creation of the past is accomplished through intimacy. He deliberately invites the reader to identify with himself and with other "characters" in an effort to remember and perhaps better understand the history of his family's past. Unlike eyewitness narrative, which purposefully excludes the reader, Mendelsohn wants to create an affiliative experience—between himself and the reader—through narrative. In a deep sense Mendelsohn and other third-generation memoirists return us to the familiar exercise of reading, one that involves dialogic interactions, predictive understanding, and emplotment.

Third-generation authors, and Mendelsohn powerfully illustrates this, use their research and writing to create a sense of relevance and connection to the traumatic history of their ancestors, inscribing themselves as authors into the story. Although what they produce is not testimony, third-generation memoirists do write a specific form of post-testimonial representation that marks a relationship to historical trauma. Sidra Ezrahi notes that testimonial and imaginative literature representing the Holocaust can be loosely grouped into two major clusters, the fundamental distinction appearing either in their "static" or in their "dynamic appropriation of history and its moral and social legacies." "The static or absolutist approach," writes Ezrahi, "locates a non-negotiable self in an unyielding place whose sign is Auschwitz; the dynamic or relativist position approaches the representation of the memory of that place as a construction of strategies for an ongoing renegotiation of that historical reality."[19]

Written in 1995, before third-generation literature became a recognizable body of work, Ezrahi's identification of these two approaches has been sustained in the years since—we see a convergence of the polarity she identifies. Third-generation literature unquestionably establishes "Auschwitz as the ultimate point of reference" but also, at the same time, willfully and consciously reconstructs and renegotiates traumatic history through an often uneasy combination of testimony, historical research, and imaginative investment.[20] This is not so much the creation of a third category but, rather, a narrowing of the distance between the polarities Ezrahi introduces. As time passes and Holocaust literature relies increasingly on artifacts and textuality (conditions that value and promote readability), texts about these texts and readings of these readings turn in the same direction.

Mendelsohn's efforts to reclaim the lives of his six family members are based on his desire to rescue them "from generalities, symbols, abbreviations."[21] In the absence of any other marker that points to their deaths, Mendelsohn constructs a narrative that takes into account as much as he could gather about their lives and deaths, including his own narrative impulses. *The Lost* illustrates the influences—cultural, literary, and emotional—to which testimony and historical findings are subject as they are made available and as they become further removed and distanced from their primary source. In sum, *The Lost,* like many (if not most) third-generation memoirs, centers on a retelling of a moment or series of moments that are composite memories, testimonials, and historical entries, generated from a range of different sources. Through this retelling, a narrative emerges that bears all the signs of a complete story: it is narratable, readable, tragic, and organized. Yet as a story, it neglects, obscures, and obviates specific individuated historical and traumatic memory—precisely Mendelsohn's intention in researching the lives and deaths of his relatives.[22] Mendelsohn's conclusion, in which his desire to turn around and look back at Bolechow through the car's rear window—a desire fueled by the "impossible wish" that "nothing will be left behind"—is foiled. As he and his fellow travelers drive off, "we all start talking at once, telling the remarkable story of what we had found and where we had walked."[23] The story of the past is a story of the present; what is lost is what remains behind, hidden from view, and so in some sense preserved.

While a less epic narrative than that found in Mendelsohn's *The Lost,* Vikram Seth's *Two Lives* (2005) presents another rich example of third-generation memoir. Seth's double biography tells the history of his maternal great-uncle Shanti Uncle, an Indian-born British émigré, and his wife, Aunty Henny, a German Jew who managed to flee Germany in the late 1930s. Seth lived with his great-aunt and great-uncle when he first moved to England as a sixteen-year-old; he presents the Holocaust from a different perspective from that found in *The Lost.* Unlike Mendelsohn's work, which connects in ways both essential (through his use of the Bible) and less substantial (for example, his family's celebration of Hanukah), Seth's research into his great-aunt Henny's history and family lacks some of the sense of global connectedness on which Mendelsohn relies. Yet many of Seth's narrative gestures follow lines found in *The Lost* and reflect the author's personal investment in his subjects, all of whom are beloved family members. So, for example, while researching the fate of Aunty Henny's sister and mother in the archives at Yad Vashem, Seth discovers their names on two separate transport manifests, noting not only his discovery of their names but also the disconcerting blank spaces following their names that might have yielded more printed information about their fate, and yet, through their emptiness, symbolically yield all.

As he reads the documentation regarding Lola Caro, Aunty Henny's sister, Seth writes that "something happened that has never happened to me before or since. My right knee began trembling rapidly and violently. There was nothing I could do to stop it. Suddenly I heard a voice behind me address me in English with a very strong German accent. . . . The very accent embodied sickness and evil, and I turned round in a fury to face—just an alarmed young man, a German schoolboy, about seventeen years old."[24] It is not so much this response that is unique; surely all readers have experienced powerful physical and emotional responses to certain texts. What distinguishes this moment of reading from others is the fact that Seth records it, illuminating his role as a reader, his interaction with the text—and with a German, with all its incumbent meaning—to his own readers. Our interaction with the text, while dependent on his for providing us with a reading subject, further modifies his reading experience into our own. The story of his aunt's family and their tragic murder now includes his presence, his response to his reading and discoveries. Similar to Mendelsohn's inserting personal interjections in *The Lost*, Seth redirects the subjectivity of the memoir, expanding it in this particular moment to include the author and availing his memoir of a certain degree of readability.

As with many third-generation memoirs, Seth chooses to dwell on the indeterminate final moments of his aunt's family. Of her sister Lola, who most likely perished in the gas chambers of Auschwitz, Seth traces her probable steps, using the testimony of survivors and other historical documents to guide him:

> Lola would have been taken to Block 25, where she and many other women would have waited for death. . . . [They] would have been herded out and made to march, five abreast, to the gates of the crematorium yard. . . . Along a grey path amid green grass she would have walked to the grey railings that led down a dozen steps to an underground undressing-room, a vast space with supporting pillars and benches and pegs. Here she would have been ordered to take off her clothes and shoes and to remember the number of her peg so that she could retrieve what was hers after the so-called disinfection and bath. The oak doors beyond would have been opened, and the SS personnel would have urged, and finally forced, the people to enter the huge underground "disinfection room," in fact the gas chamber. Here too there were pillars from concrete floor to ceiling, but these pillars were hollow and perforated. Lola would have been crammed in with the others, up to two thousand or more. The oak doors would have been closed and secured, and the light dimmed or turned off. What thoughts went through her head in these last few minutes of her life it is presumptuous to imagine, but it is difficult to doubt that among them must have been thoughts of Henny, Heinz [her brother] and her mother.[25]

After describing in excruciating detail the implementation of Zyklon-B, Seth continues his portrait of Lola's death:

> Lola's naked body, grotesquely contorted, possibly broken-boned, her face blue and unrecognisable and bleeding from mouth and nose, her legs streaked with shit and blood, would, after hosing-down, have been dragged out of the room, possible with a noose and grappling hook, to a large lift that would have taken her together with the many others up to the ground floor of the building. Here, in the furnace room, a trolley would have moved her body along to continue the procedure. Any gold teeth she might have had would have been broken out of her mouth with pliers.... Her hair, shorn off earlier, would have had various uses, from the manufacture of felt to insulation to submariners' socks. Her bones, if any fragments remained, would later have been ground to powder. This, together with any ashes that had not been dispersed through the chimney as smoke, would eventually have been dumped into the River Sola.[26]

The combination of sources in Seth's retelling of Lola Caro's final hours comes through most clearly in his repeated use of the modal verb "would," which occurs in nearly every sentence of a lengthy description of violence, death, and destruction. The use of "would" speaks to Seth's care in not making assumptions about events of which he has no conclusive knowledge and yet his determination to paint a scene that relies on a combination of primary and secondary sources, inference, implication, and imagination. Seth's repeated use of "would" parallels Mendelsohn's frequent asides, which appear between dashes or as questions. In each case, the author's voice—hesitant yet dogged, uncertain yet decided—gains a sense of place and even authority (whether mistakenly or not is another matter). The third-generation author becomes a part and indeed a marker of the post-testimonial, integrating the present—and himself—with historical trauma.

What happens as we read this and other mediated personal histories of trauma? What, precisely, are we as readers bearing witness to? As this historical trauma is mediated over time and through narrative it at least attempts to describe, imagine, and represent one small piece of the Holocaust, an event that has time and again been described as unimaginable, unrepresentable, indescribable. In certain ways Seth (and Mendelsohn and other third-generation authors) respects the unapproachable nature of the Holocaust. His use of the verb "would" insists on an indirect look, a sideways glance, at what may have happened to his aunt's family; the "would" acknowledges the author's imaginative limits and conveys them to his reader. That said, the word "would" stands pallid, thin, and barely noticed, even in its repetition, next to the language of violence and horror that is also implemented in the passage. The importance of "would" stems less from its meaning and more for the function it serves the reader: "would" points to the necessarily disjointed nature of this description. It is not only that "would" creates an indirect point of contact between the reader and the subject but that "would" creates a series of discrete and fragmented images. In recounting in wrenching and minute detail, which they gather from historical sources as well as their own sense of narrative, the moments leading up to the murders of their family members Seth and Mendelsohn work toward a representation of the Holocaust: they represent a version of the past that is clearly filtered through the present. It is one that falls deliberately short of purely historical claims, filling in gaps and spaces with imaginative inference. Reading these moments of invention is difficult not only because of the violence they reference but because the attempt to make legible, to illuminate—to make readable—a past that is widely accepted as unreadable (for this is what the "would" implies) is itself an act of violence, one that has moral repercussions that are both beneficial and harmful.

Like Seth and Mendelsohn, David Laskin in his third-generation memoir *The Family* (2013) constructs out of a combination of survivor testimony, memoir, and imaginative inference a scene of devastation—the murder of thousands of Lithuanian Jews in the forests of Ponar, one of whom is Shepseleh (a Yiddish diminutive for Shabtai), the author's grandfather's first cousin. Laskin sets up his own depiction of Shepseleh's death by first citing from Richard Rhodes's *Masters of Death* (2002). He then describes Shepseleh's death:

> Shepseleh was not one for making trouble. He took his place with the others in the trench. He waited for his pick and shovel to be issued. But no work tools were in eviden[c]e. Instead the men with the carbines ordered all of them to take off their shoes, jackets, and shirts. Jackets and shoes were to be piled on the side of the trench. Shirts were to be wrapped around their heads and faces. Anyone who was slow or reluctant got slammed with a truncheon or the butt of a rifle. The orders were loud, clear, quick but incomprehensible. Shepseleh was told to grasp the naked waist of the man in front of him. A pair of wet trembling hands grasped his waist from behind. Shepseleh and nine other men were marched like that out of the trench. The ten of them stood in a blind human chain at the lip of a pit intended for fuel tanks. The air exploded, bullets ripped into flesh, and Shepseleh fell into the pit. The witnesses differ on exactly how the firing was done. One said there were ten Lithuanian auxiliaries armed with rifles or handguns—one for each victim in the batch. Another swore the killing was done by one man with a light machine gun. When Shepseleh's body fell into the pit, it landed on a pile of warm bodies. Some of them were still alive. A guard stationed above the pit used his pistol to finish off anyone who was moving.[27]

It is a smooth and commanding recounting, without the authorial interpolations of Mendelsohn or the verbal modality that shifts the reader's attention in Seth's work. But Laskin's voice comes through in an endnote to this passage in which he makes the following remarks: "I used Rhodes's vivid and carefully documented account as the basis for what I imagine were the circumstances of Shepselesh's death, though the exact details will never be known. The idea that he was rounded up early in the occupation and killed at Ponar is speculative—but Tsipora Alperovich, who was in the ghetto, said during our interviews in Tel Aviv that this was his fate (though she did not see him snatched)."[28] Laskin, too, acknowledges his own role as a reader and writer of his family members' histories, even if he does this at the relative distance of an endnote. While his presence is less noticeable in the reading and recounting of Shepseleh's death, his note illustrates both his own sense of caution in establishing the scene set in Ponar as definitive and his role as narrator of a scene that presents readers with readable violence.

What Mendelsohn's, Seth's, and Laskin's works make clear is an insistent need for the authors to position themselves in connection to the eyewitness, either as readers of testimony or as producers of post-testimony, thus yielding a version of historical events that is infused with personal and imaginative possibility. First-generation Holocaust texts are directly informed by memory while the immediate experience of the absence of direct memory but the presence of postmemory is documented by children of survivors. It is this direct relationship to traumatic events that disrupts the "pre-relationship" between reader and the text, guiding texts toward unreadability (see chapter 2). Eyewitness authors acknowledge and contemplate the unreadability of their own texts; for them, it is an indisputable textual quality that goes hand in hand with traumatic memory and representation. Second-generation authors acknowledge unreadability through different means: the absence of a text they continually seek and that the seeking itself makes present. The voice that emerges in third-generation texts, in contrast, is one that holds on to texts and artifacts—"things"—as opposed to experienced memory or postmemory.

This elevation of the physical is particularly pronounced in Edmund de Waal's *The Hare with Amber Eyes* (2010), a memoir of the author's grandparents and great-grandparents, Austrian Jews who were part of a European banking dynasty and owners of a significant and valuable art collection. De Waal's great-grandparents manage to escape Austria and eventually make their way to England, where they join de Waal's grandmother.[29] The memoir documents the history of 264 netsuke (small but valuable Japanese carvings), the sole surviving objects from the author's great-grandparents' vast collection. De Waal's focus on objectivity is fed by his own artistic identity as a potter; he is known for the many uniform vessels that he exhibits, some clustered together and some spaced apart, in different-sized vitrines. The notion of presence and absence, and of the liminal spaces where viewers or readers are not sure about either state, is an intrinsic component of de Waal's exhibits, and the role of objects is also central to his memoir.

The one moment of violence where de Waal imaginatively elaborates a scene of Holocaust memory is the looting by the Gestapo of the Palais Ephrussi, the grand home of his great-grandparents and grandparents. The Nazis pick objects up, rifle through drawers, engage in a "convulsive disordering" that is "barely looting; it is a stretching of the muscles, a cracking of the knuckles, a loosening up." The crescendo comes when three of these uniformed intruders sweep everything off a Louis XVI desk, a wedding gift to de Waal's great-grandparents from long ago, and then pick it up to "send it crashing over the handrail until, with a sound of splintering wood and gilt and marquetry, it hits the stone flags of the courtyard below." The desk "takes a long time to fall. The sounds ricochet off the glass roof."[30] The trauma exposed in this scene cannot compare to the scenes of mass death and its aftermath that are narrated in other third-generation memoirs. And the reader feels the greater accessibility, the heightened readability of this passage. Nevertheless, the violence captured through this reimagining, emphasized by the narrator's use of the present tense, as if some part of him has in fact witnessed or experienced the crimes he describes, forcefully brings together the past and the present. *The Hare with Amber Eyes* is a book centered on the physicality of objects—de Waal speaks with reverence and love of the tactile nature of art. But for him art and language are "one thing."[31] The destruction of the sort described in *The Hare with Amber Eyes* signifies destruction on a far grander scale.

Through this focus on things, third-generation literature attempts—and often succeeds—in achieving a specific kind of intimacy in relation to eyewitness testimony, an intimacy that positions the narrator as virtually omniscient, almost always present. Unreadability is still, however, a feature of third-generation memoir. It emerges in the asides, modalities, endnotes, and self-declarations by which third-generation authors (rightly) hedge their bets about the terrible scenes of violence and trauma they detail. But the nature of unreadability makes a historical shift in third-generation texts. No longer a quality the presence of which announces the memory of trauma and that is itself a form of memory and memorialization worth preserving in its wholeness, unreadability in third-generation memoir becomes marginalized and encroached upon. Third-generation authors dwell on moments of violence precisely because these are the moments where the relationship between the reader and the unreadable is most evident. And so it becomes the moment most vulnerable to interception, translation, and modification. In eyewitness and second-generation Holocaust memoir, the unreadable is an important narrative aspect—a methodologically sound reference point; in third-generation memoir, however, the unreadable is regarded differently. Its place in the text is subject to the approaches and interpretations that come with reading. In this way unreadability in Holocaust texts written sixty or seventy years after the events of the Holocaust itself concentrates on objectivity, recognizing the durability of surviving artifacts, even if what is constructed around them—the Holocaust narrative—is less a historical recounting and more an investigation into possible memory, imagined as intimate and personal. The dialogic nature of reading proposed by Bakhtin becomes in these iterations largely fictional, an attempt to recover readability that publicizes a desire for intimacy brought on by experience and the memory of experience.

Does effective narration depend on readability? One effect of the firsthand experience of trauma in a writer or reader is the recognition that the readable and the unreadable are not of equal but of opposing measure. To the contrary: the unreadable asserts a greater power, blocking access to read meaning except on the rare and often painful occasions where it momentarily lifts, revealing a glimpse of text that can be—should be—read. Thinking of the readable as but a small, even insignificant, portion of narrative lends a different sense of comprehension and experience to the process of reading as a whole.[32] One primary focus of third-generation memoir, however, is on the process of constructing narrative. This, in itself, is an appeal to audience, a petition to readership. The shift in third-generation memoir is that it identifies readability as central to understanding the trauma of the Holocaust. The recognition of third-generation authors that even their most concerted effort leaves an aspect of the trauma of the Holocaust unreadable suggests that even if they tie readability to the production of meaning, the presence of the unreadable carries on, significantly and inevitably.

## THE SPACE OF MEMORY IN PRESENT TIME

In second-generation memoirs, the authors often document their return "home," a trip taken to the native country of their parents with the intention to visit sites that informed their memories of their lives before and during the war. These sites range from former family homes, workplaces, synagogues, and the homes of friends that their parents frequented before the war to the hiding places, labor camps, concentration camps, and jail cells where loved ones spent the war. Their return to these places of origins is emotionally and movingly described, and yet, it is their journeys to the local archives, a different form of institutional connectivity in relation to their parents' lives, that more often make an impression in these visits than the actual sites where their parents lived and suffered (see chapter 3). "Like a child learning to read," writes Lisa Appignanesi of a foray into the Polish archives:

> I work my way slowly through the list of B's, my index finger marking the route along the thin sheets of poorly typed and mimeographed paper. When I come across a Borensztejn, Aron [her father], a shiver goes through me. With it comes the realization that I had assumed this foray into archives was a ritual I felt I should undertake, but one attended by the certainty that no tangible discovery would be made. Now that my father's name perversely leaps out at me, I am at a loss. Despite my middle age, the child inside me, like all omnipotent infants, has had difficulty in believing that my parents really did lead a life which pre-dated me—a life outside of story and family myth. But here in front of me, on this rickety table in an old Warsaw building, is the historical proof.[33]

Appignanesi's textual encounter in the archives is deeply personal and intimate, illuminating a return to childhood. As she goes through the alphabet, she searches for a name that is both familiar—it belongs to her as well—and foreign, a combination writ large that reflects the inevitable push and pull behind the accessible and the inaccessible, the readable and the unreadable. Her response to reading her father's name resonates physically and emotionally as she works to reconcile the jarring collision of past and present taking place in a rundown Warsaw room.

As evidenced in *Losing the Dead*, visits to the authors' parents' native countries in second-generation memoirs tend to focus less on places of memory (like the homes where their parents lived) and more on records that document some aspect of their parents' lives. This reflects the draw of narrative for second-generation authors, an allure that is as present in their propensity to read as it is in their desire not only to record the story of their family's history but, through reading, to engulf it. Certainly the idea of place is significant to the second-generation memoir: Carol Ascher notes that although she visited her father's apartment building once in order to photograph it, she "resisted" going again because doing so would "only reveal their [her father and grandmother's] terrible absence."[34] Yet, as Ascher demonstrates, the symbolism behind "place" becomes subject to specific and important shifts. Unable to access or return to her father's actual home, Ascher's repeated visits to the archives stand in its stead. Reading in the archives is an intimate act and becomes the mode of interaction where family is recognized and held near by way of a certain arrangement of letters on the page.

It is this intimacy that compels Ascher, Appignanesi, and other second-generation authors to return—repeatedly—to the archival institutions where they are able to dwell in family history. The sense of home offered by the archives is compounded for many children of Holocaust survivors by the vast destruction of World War II and the subsequent decades of construction and urban expansion. Many buildings and homes that still exist have been changed beyond recognition; others have simply disappeared. Consequently, visits to places familiar to their parents are often limited to the traumatic spaces they occupied during wartime. While descriptions of these visits are emotionally exacting, there is also a sense that these particular spaces do little to reveal the longer history of their parents and their parents' families; the archives become, in contrast, a refuge.

The meaning behind physical space—its history and its presence—shifts between second- and third-generation memoir. The archive remains an essential tool for the production of third-generation memoir as it is for second-generation memoir, but the meaning behind physical space and place grows in symbolism as well as in practicality, becoming a marker of historical and personal identification—locate-ability even—and a key link between earlier history and contemporary research. In *The Hare with Amber Eyes*, de Waal asks: "How can I write about this time? I read memoirs . . . look at photographs . . . read the Vienna newspapers

... but I realise that I can't do this from London, from a library. So I go back to Vienna, to the Palais [the home where his grandmother was raised]."[35] While identifying specific buildings and homes as well as archived family documents becomes increasingly difficult over time, third-generation memoir centers on the search for the physical, devoting itself as much to the process of discovery as to the object itself. The construction of a narrative is deeply connected in third-generation memoir to physical objects or structures that once marked place and home. In contrast to second-generation memoirists, who attempt to reclaim the painful loss of family artifacts ranging from family history to family heirlooms through reading and writing, third-generation memoirists reflect on walking the same streets as their ancestors did, occupying their spaces, handling objects they may have used, and otherwise quite literally trying to touch the lives of those that preceded them by many decades. Second-generation memoirists are content with a visit to the past lives of their parents, one that is often filled with misgivings and that is unquestionably temporary. Third-generation writers, however, want to move into these same spaces in their effort to recapture the past.

In Mendelsohn's *The Lost*, the search for place becomes central both to the narrative and to the method by which the narrative is told. Mendelsohn, a classicist, uses place as an organizing function to weave together the story of origins as it appears in Genesis, beginning with the Tree of Knowledge in the Garden of Eden, with the micro-history of his family, whose origins were tied to the Polish town of Bolechow. Early in *The Lost*, Mendelsohn recalls hearing his grandfather and then later his mother say, "*I know only they were hiding in a kessle*."[36] Adjusting for his grandfather's accent, Mendelsohn figures that his grandfather means his relatives were hidden in a local "castle." The discovery that their native town of Bolechow "had been at one time owned by an aristocratic Polish landowner" confirms in Mendelsohn's mind that, "clearly," his uncle and his family "had managed to find a hiding place in the great residence of the noble family who'd once owned their town, and it was there that they were discovered after [being] betrayed."[37] In short, Mendelsohn constructs a brief but comprehensive narrative about his family in which the castle is an identifiable landmark, one that Mendelsohn latches on to, in part because it invokes his memory of his grandfather and in part because in the limited information he has regarding his family, this one tangible detail—a description of place—centers and grounds his search. At the close of conversation after conversation with local Bolechowers, Mendelsohn inquires about the existence of a local castle, a line of inquiry included mostly as a parenthetical comment in *The Lost*: "(Was there a castle nearby? I'd asked everyone we met, remembering what I'd overheard my grandfather saying, ages ago; and the inevitable answer came again, as I always knew it would, that there was no castle, no place to hide)."[38]

Mendelsohn finally does track down the yard, belonging to a modest home, where his great-uncle Shmiel and one of his daughters were killed. He asks the current owners if there is a cellar of some sort, and as they pull away the living room rug and raise a trap door, it occurs to Mendelsohn that his grandfather had been talking about "a *kestl*, a *kestl*, not a *castle*." That is, his grandfather was using the Yiddish word for "box" and not an English word that was slightly distorted by a Polish accent:

> All those years ago I had listened to my grandfather talk, the one time he had offered me information about Shmiel's death, and I listening to those plush vowels and thickened consonants, had heard what I'd wanted to hear, a story like a fairy tale, a tragic drama complete with a nobleman and a castle. . . . It had taken me all this, the years and the miles, had required that I come back and see the place with my own eyes before the fact, the material reality, allowed me to understand the words at last. They'd been hiding in a terribly small and enclosed space, a space that someone, somewhere, must have once described as being like a kind of box, a *kestl*, and now I was standing in the box, and now I knew it all.[39]

For Mendelsohn, as for other third-generation writers, place is a point of access in the wide featureless expanse of unknown memory. Indeed, this need to define and identify historical place is the motivation behind Daniel Rose's *Hiding Places*, a memoir that documents the author's travels with his two young sons to meet Holocaust survivors from his mother's side of the family living in Belgium and to discover and visit the various hiding places that enabled them to survive. Rose speaks of his and his sons' needs to "collect a memory greater than the three of us and see ourselves in a new light."[40] The act of collecting memory depends not only on communal experience but on communal experience grounded in certain spaces that members of their family had been in, among them a hidden synagogue, a hotel room, and finally, a small concentration camp near Rivesaltes, in the south of France, where the twin daughters of Rose's cousin perished. Discovering the grounds of the camp just as the sun set, the unlikely threesome find themselves stuck in the middle of a military training exercise. Before being rescued by friendly members of the French armed forces, Rose and his sons feel that they are looking out on a Holocaust landscape, "a Nazi dystopia of rubble and rats."[41] Reflecting on that climactic experience, Rose writes that it "could have been traumatic for the boys. But it's had the opposite effect. It lanced the boil. They faced it down and it purged them and maybe they'll be the better people for it. Something I never expected from that place."[42] Discovering and connecting to place not only defines the past but lends a sense of form to the future.

The feature of Holocaust postmemory that so directly informs the relationship between the second generation and their parents' Holocaust experiences bears little meaning for the third generation.[43] Instead, the place of memory becomes a physical point where time appears to be compressed, thus allowing the writer to connect the past with the present. This link enables third-generation memoirists to write comprehensively a personal story that, before their generation, had been largely unknown. It is this absence of knowledge that third-generation memoirists wrestle with: in an effort to draw near to events that elude them on so many fronts, they challenge the notion of the unknowable—and with it the unreadable. This feature of third-generation memoir makes it markedly different from other kinds of Holocaust memoir. In the generations between Daniel Mendelsohn and his grandfather, no one in the family really knew, definitively, the story behind the deaths of Shmiel and his family. Fragments, rumors, interrupted stories—these were, for two generations, the makeup of the family's history. Mendelsohn's goal is to fill in the silences, to answer the questions, to lend breadth and space to six family members who had all but vanished. Visiting Auschwitz, he is struck by the "dreadful irony" that "the sheer scope of the crime" as memorialized at Auschwitz is "paradoxically asserted at the expense of any sense of individual life."[44] As he stands in the hiding place that once sheltered his family members, Mendelsohn declares: "now I knew it all." His story becomes an essential part of the family record, lending it shape and features, a point of origin and a resting place. Mendelsohn touches the bark of the "ancient apple tree" in front of which his great-uncle and cousin were murdered and recognizes the power of confronting "the thing and not the idea of it."[45] He concludes his family's history as he introduced it, through relating place to time, recording his experience of discovery and wrapping it around the story itself.

Mendelsohn faults himself for not being a better listener to his grandfather's voice and the information he relayed. But it is entirely possible that if Mendelsohn *had* understood his grandfather's account perfectly, realizing that his relatives hid in a box and not a castle, the anonymity of that description, the fact that there are so many hiding places that match this description, he might have resigned himself to knowing without seeing instead of both seeing and understanding. And then, of course, we have to wonder how many mishearings and misreadings have not been corrected—because they are unknown, and not only in this family memoir—but instead have been incorporated into the larger tapestry of a narrative, becoming a part of the retelling and the re-retelling and, in a parallel movement, becoming a part of every reading, for this and future generations. Mendelsohn's work contains within it a difficult, although not unfamiliar, contradiction. The place of memory is intensely personal: like Appignanesi in her archive, Mendelsohn reacts physically—he "simply sank down and . . . started to cry"—at the discovery of the home where his family was hidden and betrayed. At the same time, the place of memory is universal—Mendelsohn links his search for his family's origins to the ultimate story of origins, Genesis. From the opening pages of *The Lost*, where Mendelsohn expresses a wish, as he introduces the opening story of Genesis, to "linger for a moment by this strange Tree," to its conclusion where he touches the ancient bark of the apple tree in front of which his great-uncle and cousin were shot, Mendelsohn shifts between place and Place, between hewing to his self-described inquiry—"to learn about only six of six million"—and enlarging its scope many times beyond.[46] Third-generation memoirists, of whom Mendelsohn is one, are deeply uncomfortable with the position of being the unreadable. While eyewitness memoir documents the inevitability of such an audience, and while second-generation memoir recognizes both the presence and the limits of the unreadable, in certain respects defining it, third-generation memoir tries to make up for lost time, place, and history with a reconstruction of a new version of the whole.

Another third-generation memoir in which place holds a central role is Erin Einhorn's *The Pages In Between* (2008).[47] While Mendelsohn, who writes about his grandfather's brother and his family, fits squarely into the definition of third-generation, Einhorn's identity is more complicated. Her grandfather Beresh Frydrych escaped from a train that was "most likely en route to Auschwitz" and returned to the Będzin ghetto in order to place his only child, Irena (born in 1942), with a Polish woman, Honorata Skowronska, with whom he had had some business dealings.[48] The child's identity remained a secret until after the war when, in 1945, Einhorn's grandfather, having survived Auschwitz and Buchenwald, returns to Będzin to collect his daughter, eventually bringing her to the United States. While Skowronska and Frydrych had some correspondence in the years after the war, the last personal letter contained in the file that Frydrych saved was dated 1962.

In her work reflecting on the Holocaust and her own experience of it as a young child, Susan Suleiman introduces the concept of the "1.5 generation," which she defines as "child survivors of the Holocaust, too young to have had an adult understanding of what was happening to them, but old enough to have *been there* during the Nazi persecution of Jews."[49] Can we—should we—then define the children of child survivors as the 2.5 generation? Although a case can be made for it, I have chosen here not to make that distinction for the simple reason that Einhorn's book explores the war experiences of her grandparents and her mother. Indeed, like Mendelsohn, Einhorn covers a total of five generations of her family, starting from records that predate World War II by decades and then, finally, bringing the reader up to date by introducing us to herself and her brother. Furthermore, Einhorn's descriptions and her narrative identity align themselves with third-generation memoirists, even if certain moments in the text (for example, her interview with her mother) are more characteristic of second-generation memoir.

Einhorn's story is complicated by current events, personal and political, and a multilayered family history, much of which is unknown. A journalist by profession, Einhorn commits herself to writing a book about her family's history, and in particular to re-acquainting herself with the family that hid her mother and so changed the course of her family's history. She recognizes that the family mythology about her grandfather's survival of the Holocaust was in fact a mystery, "a series of clues [Einhorn] needed to decipher."[50] Shortly after embarking on her project, Einhorn learns that her mother has been diagnosed with cancer; a few weeks into what was to be Einhorn's extended stay in Krakow, her mother dies. In mourning and adrift, Einhorn is unsure if she has the wherewithal to continue the project. When she returns to Poland, however, she gradually immerses herself in a study of family history that becomes remarkably personal; *The Pages In Between* becomes a project about family, a means for Einhorn to draw closer to her mother, someone who rarely spoke of her own history. In responding to Einhorn's questions of her past, her mother would often say "that she had been young, that she didn't remember."[51] *The Pages In Between* also becomes a reflection on the relationship between historical events that seem incomprehensibly remote and their localized, very personal, contemporary outcome. In a move that is less self-conscious than with Mendelsohn's *The Lost*, but certainly a prominent feature, Einhorn fixes on place—specifically, 20 Małachowskiego Street, Będzin, her family's home since the 1930s—as a means to tell a story that spans more than seven decades and directly involves four generations of her family.

Before her mother's death, Einhorn travels from Krakow, her base, to Będzin, the city of her mother's birth and her grandparents' home since the 1930s. A local historian helps her locate her family's address, a small apartment building that her grandfather, after the war, had allocated the management of—collecting rent, paying taxes, handling upkeep—to Honorata Skowronska, the Polish woman who cared for and hid Einhorn's mother. Mrs. Skowronska died in the intervening years, but Einhorn meets her son, a man who promptly recalls Einhorn's mother as his little sister; his family members all ask to be reunited with her. Einhorn's next visit with the Skowronska family takes place months later, after she has returned from Detroit following her mother's funeral. Reluctant to tell them about her mother's death, Einhorn keeps this information from them, effectively creating a scenario where, when she enters the home that housed and protected her mother as an infant, her mother's life still endures, even after her death. The focus of her visits to her family's holdings in Będzin slowly shift from a fact-gathering mission relating to her family's history to a need to resolve the problem of property ownership regarding the (current) Skowronski family home, a building so intimately tied to her own that, when Einhorn first sees it, she "felt suddenly winded."[52]

Recognizing this emotional response in her memoir about her Jewish Italian cousins who survived the war by hiding, Kate Cohen notes that she photographed each place mentioned in her cousin's journals, "looking for each one because of some other need."[53] As if the need for solidity and presence, the there-ness of the object, grows in each successive generation, third-generation authors seek markers with a sense of permanence about them, a sense of having existed before, during, and after the war, and continuing into the future. In many ways these physical places become symbols for the books they inspire that are also constructed around the past and are brought into the present. Indeed, the impulse of third-generation memoirists not only to document the more immediate history of their families—after all, uncovering the family's lives during the Holocaust is typically the motivating factor behind the memoir—but to uncover its history going back for generation after generation gestures toward a desire to institutionalize history and narrative in a way that reflects the memoirists' pointed concentration on place and the objectivity of the past.

The documents Einhorn uncovers in family and city archives that relate to her family excite her imagination, but it is the tangible solidity of her mother's former home and her grandfather's former property that register a physical reaction. As Einhorn's Polish lawyer explains to her, she is fortunate that the property was not nationalized, becoming publicly used and owned like many estates that had been owned by Jews. Unlike these buildings, the Einhorn family home always remained privately owned because Einhorn's grandfather had legally granted Honorata Skowronska the authority to manage the building. The documentation Frydrych gave Skowronska in 1945 enabled her to live on the premises and collect rent from the other tenants in the building and also required her to pay the property taxes. The deed itself, however, still listed Einhorn's great-grandparents as the owners of the building. Since Honorata Skowronska's death, the tenants of the building refused to pay rent, claiming that their obligation did not legally pass to Skowronska's son, although the Polish government still held the Skowronski family liable for the property's taxes.

By knocking on the door of her family's long-held property, Einhorn crosses the threshold into this dense tangle of past and present obligations. The building itself, according to Einhorn's description, remains distinct from the others on the block, as if in its construction, years before the war, there was a premonition of its unique role. A "wide three-story town house of pinkish brick, covered with a layer of grime, [it was] the only building on the block that wasn't flush with the sidewalk. It sat, strangely, twenty feet back from the street beyond a square of grassless lawn, a large, thick tree, and a jarringly ugly aluminum shack. The house seemed almost to be hiding."[54] The Skowronskis request Einhorn's help to officially make them the building's owners, thus relieving them of paying taxes without receiving any rental income. Einhorn retains a Polish lawyer and wades into the intricacies of Polish real estate law, a system that, her lawyer tells her, defies all logic and one in which Einhorn would have to prove that her great-grandparents, named on the deed of the building, two Będzin Jews who perished in the Holocaust, were no longer alive. She would then have to prove that their many descendants who also died during the Holocaust or since were no longer alive; she would then also have to get unanimous written consent from all living descendants of her great-grandparents to pass the building that had been in their family since the early 1930s, the building that once provided refuge for her mother and marked the family's status as wealthy business owners, on to the Polish family who had been living in it for more than half a century.

The story behind the family residence belonging to the Frydrych family, which serves as the center for Einhorn's investigation, echoes the story depicted in Rutu Modan's graphic novel *The Property* (2013), another example of third-generation narrative in which grandmother Regina Segal, whose son has recently died, returns to her native Poland with her son's daughter, her granddaughter Mica Segal.[55] Regina fled Poland unmarried and pregnant, just before the war broke out. Ostensibly, Regina has asked for Mica's help in reclaiming her family's former apartment. Her main motivation, however, is to reunite with her former sweetheart who, unknown to anyone in her family, is the father of her recently deceased son and currently lives in and owns her family's former apartment. In *The Property*, which Modan reveals is based in part on her family's history, the apartment—31 Nasza Street—becomes a place where past and present meet.

As Regina travels to the apartment for the first time, she looks out the taxi window and sees the area as it once was: peddlers selling wares; mothers and children walking through the streets; an elderly Jewish man making his way home, leaning on a cane. Framed by the taxi window, these views of the past appear to her (and the reader) as sepia, while the car's interior—the passengers and the driver—are all in their original and varied colors. The tension fueling the narrative rests on the misperception by both Mica and Roman (Regina's former lover) that Regina has come to reclaim her apartment after these many years. Ultimately, however, her mission is only to inform her son's father of their child's death. Mica, gradually becoming aware that she has accompanied her grandmother on a fool's errand, realizes only at the end of the narrative that the current resident of her family's former apartment is, in fact, her father's father. This knowledge stops her in her tracks, causing her eyes to widen and bringing her up short.

While place is at the heart of Mendelsohn's and Einhorn's works, Modan suggests here that memory need not be limited to that. This is best represented by Mica's daily excursions in Poland, which are marked by an uneasiness between past and present that borders on the comic. For example, in response to witnessing a reenactment of Nazi soldiers deporting Polish students dressed up as Jews, Mica exclaims: "What the fuck . . ."[56] And when her grandmother sends her to an invented address, claiming it is the family's property, Mica is, somewhat diffidently, gratified to think that the Hilton hotel that has been built there may now be in the family. Modan repeatedly and forcefully brings together past and present through the combination of colors and spaces—both within the architecture of rooms and the apartment and also within a single frame of her artwork (here I refer to the basic structure, typically a rectangle, that guides the organization of graphic literature). In an interview about *The Property*, Modan states that one of the book's main themes is "the pathetic and doomed-to-failure ways that people are trying to remember the past, or to bring it back, or correct it after the fact. I mock it but at the same time I identify with the effort. It's tragic that the past is something that we cannot hold onto. Life is unfairly linear."[57] Unlike Mendelsohn's transformative experience in locating the *kessle*, and unlike Einhorn, who maintains contact with the Skowronski family and helps them with their real estate problems even after she leaves Poland, Modan's conclusion to *The Property* is unsentimental and forward-looking, with Regina and Mica on an airplane returning to Israel to resume their lives—along with a group of Israeli teenagers who have been to Poland to see the (Holocaust) sites.

Einhorn balances her deepening involvement with the status of her family's historical home by investigating her family's history in local archives. She traces her family's history through their birth records and through their business holdings, noting finally that her great-grandparents' economic success meant that they would "one day upgrade to a bigger house at 20 Małachowskiego Street that . . . they would continue to own even sixty years after their deaths."[58] Their home becomes her home. "It was not a sentimental home," Einhorn writes, "but a real home where leaks needed fixing, occupants required attention, and people wanted feeding and care."[59] She takes care in her visits to

> take in the place, to try to wonder how it must have looked then, when the name on the bell outside said Frydrych, not Skowronski. . . . I wondered if any of the furnishings were here before the war, used by my family. Maybe the lace curtains over the two big windows were ours. The shiny brown cube of smooth ceramic that dominated one corner of the room was clearly here from the beginning. On winter nights, someone in my family might have opened the small iron door on the side of the cube, filled it with coal, and lit a fire inside to keep the apartment warm.[60]

In *The Lost,* Mendelsohn references Aeneas's famous response, as he gazes at a painting depicting the destruction of Trojan War hanging on a temple wall in Carthage: "*sunt lacrimae rerum,* 'There are tears in things.' "[61] As Einhorn views her surroundings inside her family's former home, her description imbues that place of shelter with life and history. The house on Małachowskiego Street, with its name on the outside and a warm center at its core, becomes "an enlargement of the body . . . its windows and doors, crude versions of the senses."[62] By locating the place of her family's past, Einhorn, like Mendelsohn, hopes to become a part of it, absorbing its knowledge and decades of experiences simply by stepping into its interior.

Indeed, Einhorn's involvement in the real estate woes of the family who helped her mother is part of her sustained conversation with them about a longer family history. Members of the Skowronski family have their own versions of her family's experiences during the Holocaust, stories that differ from the family lore Einhorn's grandfather has told many times over many years. For example, the details surrounding the death of Einhorn's grandmother remained largely unknown. She was deported with her husband; he managed to escape from the train and return to Będzin temporarily. The story long circulated within the Frydrych family told how Frydrych was unable to convince his wife to leap from the train with him; she was never seen again. But Honorata Skowronska passes on a different recollection, told to her by Frydrych on his return to Będzin: "My grandfather told her that he and his wife had jumped together from the train and that his wife had been shot, that he had watched her crumple when she hit the ground. He told Honorata that he didn't start running when he hit the woods. Instead, he turned back, hoping to save his wife, but found she was already dead." To her credit, Einhorn accepts both stories as possible, wondering about the motivations behind them: perhaps he had chosen "to pass down a less painful version to his daughter"; perhaps he lied to Honorata, "thinking she'd take better care of a child whose mother was already dead"; or perhaps this version "had been reconstructed in his mind as a protection against so wrenching a memory." Einhorn understands that only by taking all these versions together would she see "some glimmer of truth," thus recognizing a relationship between the unknowable and the unreadable, a relationship that emerges most definitively only when Einhorn reenters the place that is integral to her mother's survival and her grandfather's history.[63]

The third-generation works studied above—*The Pages In Between, The Property*, and *The Lost*—are all accounts motivated by the explicit mission of truth-seeking or truth-knowing in the limited framework of a single family, of gaining access to the narrative of history and trauma that occurred two generations prior, and of personalizing this narrative, making it the author's own. This may seem a relatively straightforward motivation, but it differs from the writings of the eyewitness generation who often recognized—both despairingly and with understanding—that many of their readers will not be able to read in any meaningful or comprehensive way the narratives documenting their Holocaust experiences. Third-generation work also differs from second-generation memoir, where the authors identify that which they cannot access and that remains illegible and unreadable. In contrast, third-generation memoir is centered on the role of the author, a figure who becomes imperative to the telling of the story, to uncovering parts of the family history heretofore unknown.

In so doing, the third-generation memoirist stretches family history—backward in time through the discovery of documents but also forward into the future with the construction of a story that includes the present with implications beyond that. One way this expansiveness happens is through the use of the word "my." While neither Mendelsohn nor Einhorn add emphasis to their usage of "my," throughout their works it is a word—proprietary, possessive, claiming, and reclaiming—that both authors return to repeatedly. Mendelsohn calls the six people whose histories he is searching "my dead"[64] and talks about "his" house in Bolechow. When he interviews a survivor who was once the best friend of Shmiel and Ester's eldest daughter, Frydka, he shows her "his" picture: "That is Frydka Jager. . . . That's my mother's cousin. She looked at me, not smiling, and [says,] Yes I know, she was my girlfriend, with just the barest, proprietary emphasis on the word 'my.' "[65] Einhorn candidly admits that her "search had always been about me and not about [her mother]."[66] Mendelsohn and Einhorn actively make themselves a part of their reconstruction of family history. Unlike eyewitness and second-generation accounts of the Holocaust, third-generation Holocaust memoir splits subjectivity and reinvests it in author, history, and story. The act of transmission both documented and enacted by third-generation memoir is imperfect because it is a collaborative effort marked by a chorus of voices—not so much "my" as "ours"—that both preserve memory and put it at risk.

Part and parcel of third-generation memoirists' writing and rewriting their family's histories, an activity requiring them to immerse themselves in wide-ranging acts of reading, is the fundamental notion that this history can be accessed, read, and recorded. And this is the most significant shift between eyewitness and second-generation writing, on the one hand, and third-generation narrative, on the other. Third-generation authors intimate through their narratives that knowledge of the traumatic past *can* be read—and, indeed, *should* be read. Third-generation memoirists insistently make themselves a part of the historical record, documenting themselves as readers and as subjects for other and future readers. It is a position that places them at odds with the writers who are located historically and experientially closer to the Holocaust, even as it attempts to define these relationships more intimately. Yet the concept of unreadability may be an idea limited to living memory and postmemory, an idea that runs against the grain of third-generation memoir, writing that is primarily based on the residue of memory: objects, papers, and place, all in relation to the self.

# PART II PUSHED TO THE EDGES
## The Holocaust in American Fiction

# 5 • AMERICAN FICTION AND THE ACT OF GENOCIDE

> I'd give anything to be accessible. I am hurt when I'm told that I can't be read; I want to be read.... It seems to me that sometimes a text judges its reader rather than the reverse.
>
> —"An Interview with Cynthia Ozick"

Paradoxically, the more time that separates the Holocaust from the present, and so the less available the Holocaust is in terms of eyewitness testimony, the more accessible it becomes to readers and writers of Holocaust fiction and the more it becomes historically normalized.[1] Whereas eyewitness authors overtly acknowledge the impossibility of reading their texts in the truest sense of the word—a consequence of reaching the limits of language and representation—contemporary authors, often in an effort to shorten the distance between themselves and the historical event at hand, create a version of the Holocaust that is increasingly available as subject matter for the imagination. The absence of direct memory or postmemory, then, correlates to the diminished explicit presence of the unreadable, which in turn actually works to distance the text from eyewitness literature even as it attempts to draw near. Not recognizing or marginalizing the unreadable bears important consequences not only on how we read the Holocaust (and even more broadly, any document of trauma) but also on how we remember, an intrinsic characteristic of any act of reading.[2] Third-generation memoir regularly tries to resolve the "problem" of unreadability through the creation of post-testimony, an imagined version of the events surrounding the experiences and often the murder of a relative in the Holocaust. In this way third-generation Holocaust memoir can often be more easily and more deeply connected to fiction than to memoir, because it engages so attentively to an imagined presence—namely, that of the author—and set of relationships.

With the trajectory that moves readers from history to a historical-fictive hybrid in mind, I turn to considering the role of unreadability in imaginative works around the Holocaust. The notion of unreadability as it applies to fiction that incorporates or references the Holocaust is complicated, deepened by the history of anxiety attached to the act of fictionalizing an event widely deemed inaccessible to the imagination. Lawrence Langer, in reflecting on a visit to Auschwitz in 1964, writes that the "existence of Dachau and Auschwitz as historical phenomena has altered not only our conception of reality, but its very nature. . . . The challenge to the literary imagination is to find a way of making this fundamental truth accessible."[3] Langer implies (I believe rightly) that time plays a role in the representation and reading of all Holocaust literature, memoir, fiction, and everything in between. In a similar vein, Alvin Rosenfeld argues that the "human imagination after Auschwitz is simply not the same as it was before."[4]

Moving one step further and considering the moral imperative in association with fictional representation around the Holocaust, Sara Horowitz claims that "fiction of the Holocaust inhabits a space beyond conventional categories, mixing *témoignages* [witnessing] with invention. . . . At the heart of Holocaust narrative resides an essential contradiction: an impossibility to express the experience, coupled with a psychological and moral obligation to do so."[5] Berel Lang alternatively argues that "wherever it appears, literary representation imposes artifice," and in the case of the Nazi genocide against the Jews, artifice "draws attention away from the subject itself." To "aestheticize," Lang argues further, "is to falsify or misrepresent the subject."[6] While these scholars focus on the tension between the attempts or failures of representation within and around Holocaust fiction, here I examine how this tension is experienced and interpreted through the act of reading.

Many scholars who catalog and investigate Holocaust fiction position at the heart of their inquiries texts that center on and around the Holocaust—whether this work interprets fiction developed around the survivor experience or whether the focus tends toward fictional works written shortly after the Holocaust ended with the understanding, in both cases, that in terms of Holocaust content these works present a more sustained lens through which to delineate conclusions about the nature of a genre still in its nascent stage. Yet many of these scholars also acknowledge the significance of fiction in which the Holocaust is *not* central to the work in question but, rather, remains in the background. This is a point that holds, I believe, a great deal of significance in general, and even more when considering the role that the Holocaust plays in American fiction, since the very absence of geographic proximity already pushes this particular vein of Holocaust literature away from its center in Europe and arguably Israel. The position of the Holocaust in the background of American fiction can initially be understood as symbolizing some combination of geographic and cultural remoteness from what was happening in Europe in addition to representing a sense of uncertainty regarding the method of accessing through writing—and therefore through reading—the enormity of the event. I will now focus primarily on American Holocaust fiction in general and what I deem is its ensuing counterpart, the position of the Holocaust as both background or marginal, a position that I read as a defining feature of much Holocaust literature other than that in which the first-, second-, or third-generation voice is central.

In spite of the many critical misgivings around Holocaust fiction, misgivings that are largely fed by the distance generated between the fictive subject and the history behind it, literature—and even more specifically, the creation of imaginative literature or fiction—that depicts, includes, or relies on the Holocaust continues to grow apace.[7] Beginning as early as the 1960s and continuing until today, scholars have taken up the tasks of identifying, classifying, and analyzing what has become, over the period of more than five decades of Holocaust literary production, a substantial and often interlocking body of literature that involves a wide range of genres, nationalities, and interpretations of the relationship between "historical fact and imaginative truth."[8]

At the core of their inquiries is a basic recognition that a text identified as belonging to the genre of "Holocaust literature" needs to position the Holocaust in ways that are both primary and necessary to the text itself and yet also as an essential part of a larger literary movement. The list of works that can be identified as Holocaust fiction (let alone Holocaust literature, as Robert Eaglestone acknowledges) is so vast as to be nearly unmanageable. Indeed, Eaglestone notes that "one might be tempted to ask . . . what it means when a novel or poem written after 1945 in Europe or America *did not* engage with the issue."[9] Yet, in spite of its overwhelming presence, Rosenfeld makes the point, persuasively, that Holocaust literature is more than "a loosely arranged collection of novels, poems, essays, and plays about a *subject*." Rather, Holocaust literature "is an attempt to express a new order of consciousness, a recognizable shift in being," one that is revealed through "shards and fragments . . . that together add up to something larger than the tragic sense implies."[10] In turn, Eaglestone notes that "Holocaust fiction is a temporal, not a content, label, and it names not only texts, but a way of reading: a genre. It is to be read with a specific range of questions, responses, demands, and issues in mind."[11] Far from a single canonical text or author dominating the genre, the closest readers come to "glimpsing . . . wholeness is to assemble some of the shattered pieces."[12] The texts most commonly examined in these critical studies of Holocaust literature include Elie Wiesel's *Night, Anne Frank: The Diary of a Young Girl,* and Primo Levi's *Survival in Auschwitz*—as well as a wide array of Holocaust fiction and poetry from Saul Bellow's *Mr. Sammler's Planet* to Andre Scwhwarz-Bart's *The Last of the Just,* from Nelly Sachs's *O the Chimneys* to *Selected Poems* by Dan Pagis, and many in between.

In spite of remaining in the background of so many American novels, the role of the Holocaust as somehow peripheral to a story is itself a telling position, one that bears significant implications for how the Holocaust was and continues to be represented by American authors and how it is understood and read by readers. The background position of the Holocaust in many American novels is strikingly symbolic—the reader only glimpses specific signs and referents, thus literalizing the "shards and fragments" on which the genre of Holocaust literature is built and further destabilizing a text that is already written from an unsteady position. The Holocaust as background serves to place it at the margins of the text and the story, making it largely inaccessible and unreadable. It is a locus that places the Holocaust in an uneasy literary tension: its background role limits it through the implied sense that, even as a small piece of the Holocaust is on view, much is hidden under the surface. At the same time, this background position limits the narrative, placing an extraordinary, even impossible, burden on the story as a whole because the enormity and severity of a Holocaust background threatens to encroach and swallow whole the narrative in which it technically plays only a minimal role. And then, yet again, including the Holocaust as background or as a brief reference point can serve to represent "the extremities of dehumanization."[13] Thus the marginalization of the Holocaust in fiction is also a way of indicating its extreme nature.

As Israeli novelist Aharon Appelfeld notes about his decision, in his own fiction, to write about the Holocaust indirectly: "It's just impossible to deal directly with the nakedness of the deaths. It's like looking at the naked sun on a clear summer day. You couldn't stand the temperature. You can never understand the meaning of the Holocaust. You can just come to the edges of it. If you wrote about it directly, you'd end up trivializing it."[14] Appelfeld here not only considers the writer but also the reader of Holocaust fiction. Just as limiting oneself to "the edges" of representation works, counterintuitively, to ensure the wholeness (or as much of it as is possible) of its representation through the absence of direct acknowledgment, so too does the act of reading "the edges." While there are surely differences between "backgrounding" the Holocaust and representing it indirectly, the gesture of deliberately holding the Holocaust at a narrative distance is strikingly central to the reading and integrity of many novels.

It is clear, however, that the critical assessments of many scholars and writers focus on a particular brand of Holocaust fiction, namely, works that hold the Holocaust if not at their center certainly as relevant on their works' periphery. In fact, a great number of imaginative literary works employ the Holocaust by placing it in the background rather than otherwise, a move that not only rarely elicits the kind of controversy that accompanies "real" Holocaust novels but also one that rarely elicits any kind of commentary at all. While it is surely possible that many of the novels that locate the Holocaust on the periphery do not warrant close examination, it seems to me important to recognize that moving the Holocaust to the background of an imaginative work repositions the subject in the reader's mind, too. Even more so than with imaginative writing that places the Holocaust at the center, texts that hold the Holocaust *away* from the core of the story not only need to be interrogated on similar grounds but complicate, in deep ways, how readers read, remember, and think about the subject. These stories on the one hand can be read and understood as all the more susceptible to—quite literally—marginalizing the Holocaust, making it both in place and in meaning something other and less than it is and, on the other, maintaining a distance from a subject that has been, can and will never be, fully comprehended or read with a sense of totality.

In important ways the issues raised by Langer, Rosenfeld, Eaglestone, and others as they work to introduce and define a new genre of literary significance has produced new challenges as more time elapses between the events themselves and their representation in both writing and reading. In *Voicing the Void* (1997), Sara Horowitz acknowledges that the effect of time can be productive. She notes that, for "survivor writing, a literature of testimony develops that encompasses not only autobiography but fictional autobiography and imaginative literature, as well as poetry. The actual experiences of the writer, whether represented or transfigured in the work itself, anchor and validate the writing."[15] Horowitz considers the effect of time in relation to the act of literary composition around the Holocaust. I explored this phenomenon in relation to third-generation memoir earlier, where authors clearly identify their role as readers and, in large part because of their temporal distance from the events they write about, steadily work to insert themselves into that history. Eyewitness authors anticipate this response to their texts; this awareness fuels their often plainly stated declaration that a text of their history can neither be written nor read. At stake in the act of reading and subsequent identification and the insertion of the self into the history is, as Debarati Sanyal notes, "the intractable violence" found in "unwriting" the one history in order to "weave" ourselves into a reimagined one, thus participating "in this confusion of proximity with intimacy."[16]

In the decades immediately following the end of World War II, the Holocaust was kept at arm's length, recognized as inaccessible in eyewitness literature, and simply unavailable more generally. The process toward normalization, which has taken place over decades, has extended many of these limits of representation. Still, I would argue, the limits around unreadability remain—necessarily—very much in place, even if the responsibility of readers and the role of readability vary and even if the relationship between text and reader becomes increasingly ambiguous. One reason behind the perception of changing values is that the explicit quality of unreadability—accompanied as it so often is by an awareness of unwriteability, a recognition often recorded by eyewitnesses, namely, that writing a record of their Holocaust experiences will never truly represent them—that in eyewitness literature becomes less explicit in successive generations.

Standing in stark relief to literature written by survivors, and far outnumbering them, are Holocaust texts that do not originate in the author's memory but that, rather, are largely imaginative stories inspired by historical representation. While a general consensus among scholars and readers supports the idea that any Holocaust text written without the authority of the eyewitness is significantly diminished simply by the absence of direct knowledge or memory imbuing the work, there is a range of views around the inherent value—moral, artistic, didactic—that these imaginative works convey. I will turn to these views shortly, but before doing so I examine the diminution itself, for it is this quality of Holocaust fiction that is at the heart of this chapter.

The most evident traces of reduction come with the recognition of authorship and, with it, the understanding that there exist types of memory other than survivor memory. The first shift in this representation of the Holocaust appears with second-generation writers, who relate their understanding of the event through accounts shared by survivor parents, the eyewitness generation. The second generation expresses what Geoffrey Hartman calls "the trauma of memory turning in the void" because they face a different challenge: to confront the Holocaust, an event that continues to affect them profoundly, at one remove.[17] Themes found in literature written by second-generation Holocaust writers often address questions of longing and belonging that signal the special location of the second generation: the events of the Holocaust remain pressing but the representation is less immediately proximate, more abstract.

Holocaust fiction written in the last two decades exhibits a still broader range of themes and is written by authors who, like the authors of third-generation memoir, are both personally and thematically difficult to quantify. This range itself may reflect the longer time frame and its correspondingly broader "emotional frame" that separates a new generation of writers from the actual events of the Holocaust that they choose to represent. These writers mark a second transition—or another remove—from the eyewitness, and also a further reduction. The first transition from eyewitness to a recounting by the witness now becomes, as the Holocaust enters history, an *indirect* relation to the original eyewitness. While these authors are typically called third-generation Holocaust writers, they do not necessarily serve as logical successors to the second-generation Holocaust writers. This is because (as with third-generation memoir) included within this definition of authors with an indirect relation to survivors are both authors who, while not having any immediate personal connection to the Holocaust, have memories of World War II and its repercussions and aftermath and also authors who have neither inheritance nor even a distant memory of World War II.

Of the authors discussed in the next two chapters, Nicole Krauss and Aryeh Lev Stollman are more regularly identified as third-generation, while Cynthia Ozick, Philip Roth, and Chaim Potok bear a more ambiguous, and yet also indirect, relationship to the Holocaust. These authors, whose own lives overlap with World War II, are removed from a direct inheritance of eyewitness—and yet, as I claim in relation to Holocaust memoir, their writing very much bears the markers of post-Holocaust literature. In particular (and as I illustrate below), this is most immediately demonstrated through the vexed relationship their writing bears to its own subject. This is perhaps most obvious with Ozick, who has documented her own resistance to writing fiction around the Holocaust and then, of course, cannot resist crossing her own boundaries.

As with Holocaust memoir, Holocaust fiction builds a hierarchy of post-Holocaust authorship that inadvertently documents the reduction of authority associated with the eyewitness and the generation of the eyewitness rather than, as it is often construed, that authority's construction.[18] All texts that reside outside the province of direct memory necessarily rely on other literary devices for representing the Holocaust event. These devices emphasize the distance between what is recorded and what is *not* remembered, even as they often position themselves, as Horowitz notes is the case with literature written by survivors, as tools to "anchor and validate" the text. In no way do these texts supplant eyewitness literature; to the contrary, the literature of second- and third-generation authors self-consciously stands in the shadow of "document and history."

Ultimately, literature of the Holocaust that is not grounded in direct memory is connected—to varying degrees and in an assortment of ways—to fiction. Whereas imaginative literature written by survivors can be understood as validated by its testimonial aspect, imaginative literature (that is, fiction) written by those with no immediate connection to the Holocaust has no such anchor and bears no such weight. While for first- and second-generation Holocaust writers the historical experience "conveys" a sense of immediacy and impact, the third-generation writer views these events as an indirect part of the narrative, one balanced by other, also significant, histories. Michael Chabon's *The Amazing Adventures of Kavalier & Clay* (2000) links the theme of physical salvation, escaping Nazi Europe, to the escapist nature found in art, comics, and magic. Indeed, precisely the position of these novels—at the apex of invention yet relying on a historical representation that is itself difficult, arguably impossible, to capture—works to convey the inherent instability of third-generation texts. It is an instability that plays out in the text's critical reception, affecting readers of the text. It is also an instability that has larger repercussions for understanding the work in a wider literary context, as suggested by the comparison of these texts to the "shards and fragments" of Rosenfeld's description of a genre comprised of Holocaust works.

Then, too, the sense of reduction comes from the text itself. "No Jewish writer of today," claims Lothar Kahn in 1969, "has written a book without the memory of Auschwitz propelling him to issue warnings."[19] While Kahn's bold statement encompasses Jewish writers from around the world, his primary focus becomes American Jewish authors, who he acknowledges largely refrained from using their fiction to reflect the atrocities occurring in Europe. Kahn's point, echoed by Sidra DeKoven Ezrahi in her study *By Words Alone*, notes the importance and influence of geographic distance on the imagination: "The American writer . . . had no direct contact with the life and death struggles of the victims of Nazism.

Nevertheless, an event of such enormity, which clearly carried far-reaching implications for the future of the Jewish people in particular and of mankind in general, could not be passed over in silence, even by Jewish writers in America who only a few years before were endorsing universalistic causes and may have been indifferent to or even contemptuous of their Jewish origins."[20]

Ezrahi thoughtfully accounts for the resistance or reluctance of American Jewish writers of the 1940s to address, in one way or another, the role or aftermath of Nazi atrocities in their work. While acknowledging the "personal bond" felt by nearly every Jewish American author to "an ancestral home or family in war-torn Europe," Ezrahi makes the case that the absence of direct experience, "as well as a paralyzing sense of the enormity of the unexplored event, impeded—and actually shaped—the assimilation of the Holocaust into American, and particularly into American-Jewish, literature."[21] Ezrahi then continues to trace the arc of the Holocaust in American fiction from the 1940s through the 1970s, beginning with the limited references of anti-Semitism in America, moving toward "growing documentation by survivors" in the 1950s, recognizing the role of the Eichmann trial in the 1960s in influencing poets, novelists, and nonfiction writers, and concluding with the "realistic fiction written by American-Jewish writers in the sixties and seventies," including the later poetry of Sylvia Plath, Arthur Cohen's *In the Days of Simon Stern* (1973), and Susan Fromberg Schaeffer's *Anya* (1974), among others.[22] Peter Novick and Philip Roth, largely in agreement with Ezrahi's conception of American Holocaust fiction's gradually gaining a greater foothold in the landscape of American fiction, acknowledge that while some literary recognition of the Holocaust was present by the end of the 1950s in the United States, it was of a fluid shifting nature, "hidden, submerged, emerging, disappearing, unforgotten."[23]

Whereas Ezrahi sees the role of the Holocaust in Jewish American fiction as becoming increasingly prominent over the decades, Emily Miller Budick's more recent overview understands the majority of American Holocaust fiction as belonging to one of two groups: those fictions "that deal explicitly with the survivor experience," of which Jewish American authors wrote only a "handful of more popular, epic novels that appeared in the decades immediately following the war," and "fictions that are Holocaust-inflected rather than about the Holocaust per se."[24] In this second category Budick counts the vast majority of American Holocaust novels, including the work of authors such as Edward Wallant, Saul Bellow, I. B. Singer, Rebecca Goldstein, Cynthia Ozick, Allegra Goodman, Melvin Bukiet, Lev Raphael, Nathan Englander, and Thane Rosenbaum.

My own understanding of the history of the Holocaust in American fiction resists the clean differentiating lines that Budick proposes. Holocaust content, I would argue, can be powerfully present and definitive even if its presence shines through generational reference or more distant-seeming symbolism. In this sense, I share the views of Lillian Kremer who, like Ezrahi, suggests that authors who have not themselves experienced the Holocaust in "ghettos, camps, and killing centers" cannot be denied "the privilege of writing about the Holocaust. Authority is not limited to those with personal suffering."[25] Many of the authors whom Budick lists—and there are many others who are not listed—write both more and less directly about the Holocaust. Our difference in understanding may well be one of definition: what qualifies as a Holocaust novel? Budick's understanding of "explicit" Holocaust fiction is one that limits fictional narrative to the eyewitness experience—an interesting, and at times troubling, comingling of fictional and historical.

Ezrahi and Kremer, in recognizing the proliferation of Holocaust literature as more time passes, willingly make that category available to a range of narrative explorations. In keeping with my own understanding of the term "third-generation" (which I think of as at its most useful when taken to refer to a set of textual conditions rather than strictly as an authorial marker), I propose here that Holocaust fiction can be and should be broadly understood. In spite of their differing definitions of Holocaust literature, both Ezrahi and Budick implicitly recognize the importance and widespread practice of employing the Holocaust as the backdrop to any number of American Holocaust novels.

In this chapter I investigate this position of implied marginality in relation to the concept of unreadability. Thus I turn to a close examination of five texts, whose authors both write about the Holocaust from a place of indirect knowledge (my definition of third-generation) and limit the Holocaust to a background role in their fiction. My focus here is on American Holocaust fiction both for the practical reason of containing what would otherwise be an unmanageably large survey and because of the sense that, through both time and space, third-generation American Holocaust literature occupies, by definition, a position that is widely acknowledged as, if not peripheral, at least significantly less privileged than the post-Holocaust literature originating in other countries, particularly Europe and Israel. As such, the texts I examine serve as representative examples of how readability and unreadability take on a revised meaning in particular settings. This chapter considers works that take place during the wartime period and its immediate aftermath: Chaim Potok's *The Chosen* (1967), Cynthia Ozick's short fiction and her novel *Foreign Bodies* (2010), and Philip Roth's *Nemesis* (2010). The following chapter considers the contemporary voices and reflections in Nicole Krauss's *The History of Love* (2006) and Aryeh Lev Stollman's *The Far Euphrates* (1998). Taken together, these formalist critiques convey a larger shift in contemporary American Holocaust fiction that allows for—even demands—a recognition of a new definition of Holocaust literature and a rethinking of the relationship between memory and reading—and between memory and "unreading."

## THE ROLE OF HISTORY IN POTOK'S EARLY FICTION

Chaim Potok comments that "there's a dark side to man. We are a killer species. There's no question about that. As a novelist, you have to cope honestly with that killer side.... The dark side is man's powerful ability to destroy and create at the expense of other people."[26] Born in 1929, Potok was not much older than the two protagonists of his novel *The Chosen*, Danny Saunders and Reuven Malter, who come of age in the years immediately following the Holocaust. The Holocaust plays a complicated role in Potok's works: the idea that a "novelist" must "cope honestly" with aggression produces a tension between narrative plot and historical relevance. At times the historical backdrop of his novels threatens to outweigh the fictive impact; at times, however, the thematic message resonates with historical memory and the two work to complement each other. This uneasy balance is most readily evident in Potok's novels that contain a specifically religious theme because these novels include the Holocaust as the backdrop to other kinds of violence set in the foreground. So, for example, *Davita's Harp* (1985), which is set between 1936 and 1942, primarily involves the fight against fascism and the Spanish Civil War and, secondarily, involves the destruction of European Jewry. In *My Name Is Asher Lev* (1972), the shadow of the Holocaust is carried by the background figures of Jacob Kahn, the artist who teaches Asher Lev, and Jacob's wife, Tanya, whose aesthetic and religious outlook have been informed by the death of family members in Nazi Germany. In *The Gift of Asher Lev* (1990), Asher's wife is a Holocaust survivor, and her history and the loss of her family inspire their return to his family's home.

Potok's first two novels—*The Chosen* (1967) and its sequel, *The Promise* (1969)—set the pattern for later novels in terms of representing the Holocaust and negotiating its place in a fictional setting. The novels are set in the late 1930s and 1940s; *The Chosen* takes place during the years of World War II and *The Promise*, set during its aftermath, serves as a historical and fictional continuation. Reflecting on the background role the Holocaust has consistently played in his fiction, Potok acknowledges that he has been "very hesitant to write a novel about the Holocaust because I don't know how to handle that material. I wasn't involved with it in terms of my own flesh.... I don't know whether I can get the distance needed to handle it aesthetically."[27] Potok's personal distance from the Holocaust, in which he defines himself as neither first- nor second-generation, does not translate into aesthetic distance. Positioning the Holocaust at the margins of narrative becomes for Potok a strategy, a method of recognizing and literalizing his belief that all Jewish writers, and American Jewish writers in particular, write "from the framework of the Holocaust, with the blood of the Holocaust always somewhere in the background" of their consciousness.[28] In much of Potok's fiction, this translates to incorporating the Holocaust into the background of the narrative structure or plot.

Here I focus on *The Chosen,* Potok's most popular novel, which was nominated for the National Book Award and has been reprinted more than a dozen times; it was made into a motion picture in 1981 in response to that popularity. Additionally, the book spent thirty-eight weeks on the *New York Times* bestseller list.[29] While scholarly interest in and recognition of Potok's work has been more limited than for work by Roth or Ozick, the number of readers attracted by *The Chosen* is largely due to the novel's use of history, both cultural and that involving the Holocaust. Potok's simultaneous willingness and reluctance to reference the Holocaust reflects his use of what I call historical violence—capturing a nonfictive and destructive period in a narrative work. Historical violence for Potok contrasts with other kinds of violence that are more central to these novels; I have labeled these "actual violence" and "imagined violence." Historical violence serves Potok so he can acknowledge a sense of distance to the subject of the Holocaust but, at the same time, allow a presence that is closely managed. The term "actual violence" describes a physical and real act of harm inflicted on one of the characters. In this sense actual violence is limited and circumscribed, especially in contrast to historical violence on the scale of World War II. Imagined violence is more psychological in nature and reflects particular acts of aggression or hostility that are no less tangible and no less real. For example, they take place within oneself and resist expression and counterbalance the confined pain inflicted by actual violence and the distance of the experience described in historical violence. Whereas actual violence demands a corporeal presence, imagined violence involves a painful sense of absence, often through repression and a lack of recognition or awareness from others. This notion of balance is central to Potok's fiction. Potok believes in "man's powerful ability to destroy and create."[30] The actual violence and imagined violence in his novels reflect this sense of giving and taking. The violence suffered by a single person's injury, such as Reuven's eye injury in the opening scene of *The Chosen,* is countered by some productive and beneficial consequence, the value of which more than makes up for the initial pain and aggression. Imagined violence is more difficult to confront and transform, in part because it is less manageable and less controllable. Actual violence and imagined violence in *The Chosen* are necessary and (even as they encompass the destructive) productive; they lead to the empowerment and growth of characters.

Potok's carefully balanced world, however, is thrown off-kilter with his background depiction of historical violence. This partly comes from the enormity of violence in historical events like World War II and the Holocaust, the two reference points he most commonly uses and which resist the background role assigned to them. While not all historical fact risks the larger narrative, by applying historical fact as charged as the Holocaust to a novel, Potok jeopardizes the balance he achieves in the fictive aspects of *The Chosen* and creates a tension between the historical violence itself and a story using violence to further its message of empowerment. Emerging from this imbalance is a repositioning of the readers' experience of background and foreground: while *The Chosen* is set in New York and World War II is clearly established as existing only in the margins of the novel, its presence disturbs the equilibrium of the novel to such a degree that it effectively relocates the backgrounded historical violence, moving it toward the center of the novel.

The struggle between moments of violence and the fruitful consequences that emerge from them fuels the relationship between Danny Saunders and Reuven Malter as seen in the opening scenes of *The Chosen*, when the two first meet as opponents in a viciously competitive baseball game. Reuven's teammate describes their "very Orthodox" opponents as "murderers" and "wild" (*The Chosen*, 8).[31] Reuven is understandably skeptical of such a harsh description, but after Danny Saunders, clearly the leader and the most athletic of the other team, tells him "flatly, without a trace of expression in his voice," that "we're going to kill you apikorsim [heretic] this afternoon" (*The Chosen*, 18), Reuven's view of the game shifts—"the game stopped being merely a game and became a war" (*The Chosen*, 24). As Edward Abramson acknowledges in his study of Chaim Potok, the "dramatic beginning to the novel turns a baseball game into a holy war"; his description echoes Reuven's own initially joking depiction of the competition (*The Chosen*, 9).[32] Certainly the "holy war" in which Orthodox Jews open to Western culture, as represented by Reuven and his school, are pitted against Hasidic Jews like Danny, who view such worldliness as detrimental to Jewish tradition, creates one key metaphor of conflict within the novel.

Contributing to this image of conflict portrayed on the baseball field are images and language involving World War II. Indeed, the narrator relates that "Danny and [Reuven] probably would never have met . . . had it not been for America's entry into the Second World War and the desire this bred on the part of some English teachers in the Jewish parochial schools to show the gentile world that yeshiva students were as physically fit, despite their long hours of study, as any other American student" (*The Chosen*, 5). Furthermore, Reuven's coach—about whom he wonders why he "wasn't in the army"—constantly uses war expressions, urging one member of his team to throw "like a sharpshooter," another to "keep our side of this war fighting," and emphasizing, in the name of sportsmanship, that he wants "live soldiers, not dead heroes" (*The Chosen*, 17). The "holy war" prominently featured in the foreground of *The Chosen* in its opening tableau establishes a metaphorical link to the fighting of World War II, a war that is located to the shadows of the novel through implication and opaque references only to become more explicit as the novel progresses.[33] In concert with the sense of imbalance caused by using the Holocaust as a historical reference point, this metaphorical relationship suggests that, even as the Holocaust is located in the background, it plays a central role in terms of meaning and import.

A number of critics point out that the holy war being fought in this scene by Danny and Reuven is one that resonates with the tension found between Hasidim and *Mitnagdim* and, although more obliquely, between ultra-Orthodox practice and interpretation of Halacha, Jewish law, and a more liberal understanding of it.[34] While this is certainly true, another less readily acknowledged historical aspect of this "holy war" is in fact the *disconnect* between it and the war going on simultaneously behind it. As Reuven and Danny struggle to achieve physical and spiritual dominance in their baseball game, Hitler renders moot any distinction between the practices of the ultra-Orthodox, the modern Orthodox, and any other interpretation of Jewish ritual, even the most secular. European Jewry in its entirety is in the process of being destroyed, with little differentiation made between Jews wearing long black jackets and sidelocks and those who are fully integrated into a larger social context. The tension between Reuven's and Danny's communities reflects a European Jewish history that stretches back several centuries. The ongoing destruction of the Holocaust, even relegated to the background, compresses time and place, bringing together practices, cultures, and even geographies, namely, European and American.

Potok himself inadvertently addresses the problem of defining and locating the Holocaust in his work of Jewish history entitled *Wanderings*: "The Jew sees all his contemporary history refracted through the ocean of blood that is the Holocaust."[35] The historical relevance of the struggle between various Jewish communities is changed—diminished? distorted? It remains difficult to assess the change itself—in both perception and meaning when viewed through the lens of later history, specifically the Holocaust. The implication here is that narrative history, like that provided by Reuven and Danny, is also transformed by the Holocaust. In Potok's novels, however, the Holocaust remains, as Kremer notes, "always in the background of his fictional universe."[36] Its constancy resonates with the importance Potok ascribes to it, but its role in the novels is problematic: a powerful and transformative influence that is referred to only in passing. As the author himself implies, however, such an event cannot be—indeed, emphatically resists being—limited. The "holy war" between Reuven and Danny and the larger cultural struggle it symbolizes are central to the plot and yet get swallowed up by the historical backdrop. One consequence of this encroachment is that it repositions the Holocaust as something other than background or marginal, even if, in terms of its narrative presence, the Holocaust itself never serves as the primary subject of the novel.

As the baseball game unfolds, the single-mindedness of Danny's team becomes increasingly evident and repellent. The "war" between the two boys reaches a climax with Reuven pitching Danny two curve balls that he misses; on the third pitch, Danny hits the ball directly at Reuven. "It . . . smashed into the upper rim of the left lens of my glasses, glanced off my forehead, and knocked me down" (*The Chosen*, 29). With shards of glass in his eye, it remains uncertain whether he will lose sight in one eye. One question that the opening tableau in *The Chosen* raises is whether the Holocaust and the baseball game, and the metaphor for which it stands, can be comfortably—or even uncomfortably—integrated. The answer, I would argue, returns us to the role and purpose of actual versus historical violence. After undergoing surgery, Reuven receives two regular visitors. The first is his father, who advises him to treat Danny Saunders compassionately and also to keep abreast of current events by listening to the radio:

> "When a person comes to talk to you, you should be patient and listen. Especially if he has hurt you in any way. Now, we will not talk anymore tonight about Reb Saunders' son. This is an important day in the history of the world. It is the beginning of the end for Hitler and his madmen. Did you hear the announcer on the boat describing the invasion?" . . .
>
> I wondered what that beach must look like now, and I could see it filled with broken vehicles and dead soldiers. (*The Chosen*, 64–65)

The second regular visitor is Danny, who pays Reuven a visit after his father leaves and asks:

> "Do you know what I don't understand about that ball game? I don't understand why I wanted to kill you. . . . I wanted to walk over to you and open your head with my bat. . . . It was the wildest feeling . . . I've never felt that way before."
>
> I looked at him, and suddenly I had the feeling that everything around me was out of focus. There was Danny Saunders, sitting on my bed in the hospital dressed in his Hasidic-style clothes and talking about wanting to kill me because I had pitched him some curve balls. He was dressed like a Hasid, but he didn't sound like one. Also, yesterday I had hated him; now we were calling each other by our first names. (*The Chosen*, 66–67)

The ends to two wars are described in these passages, the first involving the "holy war" between Reuven and Danny and the second involving the downfall of Hitler. The two sit uneasily together—in part for reasons already mentioned, the magnitude of the latter diminishes the meaning of the former, and in part because of the unspoken impossibility of applying the lesson that fuels Reuven and Danny's reconciliation and friendship to the perpetrators of World War II. The notion of repentance and forgiveness, so central to Jewish ideology and endorsed actively by Mr. Malter and more passively by Reb Saunders, makes the friendship between Danny and Reuven possible, even necessary. Reuven initially rejects Danny's apology but then, after listening to his father, apologizes for his response. Ultimately, he recognizes the truth in his father's words, that a truly intimate friendship becomes the only way to observe the concept of *mechila*, forgiveness, an aspect of Jewish culture that works not only to unite the two boys and their fathers, and to bring them closer together through friendship, but also erases some of the differences between them. By reconciling the Hasid and the Mitnaged to one another, Potok eases some of the historic and tension-producing differences that led to their confrontation in the first place. Their reconciliation serves as a bridge between two communities with a history of animosity and brings them closer together; Mr. Malter reinforces this closeness by telling his son that "true friends are like two bodies with one soul," and this is what he should become with Danny Saunders.

In the face of the destruction of World War II, the symbol provided by Danny and Reuven's friendship takes on near impossible dimensions. Can the world be considered whole again knowing of "the ocean of blood that is the Holocaust"? The idea of forgiveness that Reuven's father suggests should conclude the battle with Danny Saunders, can also—troublingly—be applied to the other war to which he refers. This stands out as one of the problems with so closely integrating the actual violence that is central to the narrative of *The Chosen* with the historical violence that, though marginal to the novel, remains so central in the consciousness of both readers and characters. One way of resolving the tension that emerges here is by understanding it as a commentary on the limits of forgiveness. Forgiveness must be both sought and granted, as we see in the mutual apologies—and their acceptance—between Reuven and Danny. In other words, the damage incurred through actual violence, where the injury is locatable and limited, is an example of a forgivable offense. In contrast, the sheer enormity of the injury inflicted by the Holocaust renders asking for forgiveness—and granting it—equally implausible, verging on the absurd. Forgiveness is possible, as Danny and Reuven illustrate, only when the wrong is both quantifiable and, consequently, identifiable. This extends not only to the action itself but to those who put the actions into effect.

The language of forgiveness becomes an essential tool in establishing the friendship between Danny and Reuven and in healing the moment of rupture or actual violence that threatened to separate them permanently from each other. The historical violence of the Holocaust as presented by Potok, in sharp contrast to the actual violence and imagined violence that ground his fiction, resists representation, both in language and in concept. This cannot be said of all historical violence found in Potok's novels (remember, for instance, Reuven's imagination picturing the beach in Normandy "filled with broken vehicles and dead soldiers") but has special resonance with the Holocaust, because it is an event that all characters acknowledge with a sense of intimacy and transference: the Holocaust happened to "my people," as Reuven puts it, or "our people," as Reb Saunders states. The Holocaust is a historical event marked by its actuality: Jews in Europe were murdered; Jews everywhere suffer.

Because the response to the Holocaust in *The Chosen* positions it beyond the limits of forgiveness, it locates it too beyond the scope of language and, with it, beyond the scope of readability:

> It was when my father read to me an account of what had happened at Theresienstadt, where the Germans had imprisoned and murdered European Jews of culture and learning, that I saw him break down and weep like a child.
>
> I didn't know what to say. I saw him lie back on his pillows and cover his face with his hands. Then he asked me to leave him alone, and I walked out and left him there, crying, and went to my room.
>
> I just couldn't grasp it. The numbers of Jews slaughtered had gone from one million to three million to four million, and almost every article we read said that the last count was still incomplete, the final number would probably reach six million. I couldn't begin to imagine six million of my people murdered. I lay in my bed and asked myself what sense it made. It didn't make any sense at all. My mind couldn't hold on to it, to the death of six million people. (*The Chosen*, 189–190)

News of the Holocaust makes each father figure respond against his character. One of the defining differences between Mr. Malter and Reb Saunders, differences that filter down to their children, can be found in their relationship to language. Mr. Malter, a teacher and scholar who writes controversial interpretations of religious texts, is his son's most intimate confidant and emerges finally as a public speaker and advocate on behalf of founding a Jewish state. In contrast, Reb Saunders "reads a lot, but he never writes. He says that words distort what a person really feels in his heart. He doesn't like to talk too much, either. . . . [H]e wishes everyone could talk in silence" (*The Chosen*, 72). Here Mr. Malter, rarely at a loss for words or explanation, is unable to help his son understand the loss inflicted by the Holocaust. Indeed, his own language no longer serves him; he reads aloud and responds with tears and silence. Reb Saunders, in contrast, meets with Danny and Reuven and talks "of the Jewish world in Europe, of the people he had known who were now probably dead, of the brutality of the world. . . . His body swayed slowly back and forth, and he talked in a quiet singsong, calling up memories of his youth in Russia and telling us of the Jewish communities of Poland, Lithuania, Russia, Germany, and Hungary—all gone now into heaps of bones and ashes" (*The Chosen*, 190). In spite of believing that language misrepresents one's emotional state, Reb Saunders is moved to recall and share his past with his children.

The friendship between Reuven and Danny that symbolically draws together two disparate communities and is initiated by an act of actual violence is echoed in the mutual abandonment of their fathers' regular practices that informs their response to historical violence, the Holocaust. This twin response comes in the face of mounting disagreement over the founding of the State of Israel, which

Mr. Malter sees as a way of giving meaning to the death of European Jewry and which Reb Saunders, because such a state would be secular, views as sacrilegious. In spite of these profound disagreements, which threaten the relationship between Reuven and Danny as well as pitting their fathers against one another, the fathers and sons draw near each other in the language each uses when talking about the Holocaust. In the passage cited above, Reuven struggles to imagine "six million of my people murdered." His father, a short time later, in legitimating the establishment of the State of Israel, exclaims that earlier "the world closed its doors, and six million Jews were slaughtered" (*The Chosen*, 196). In decrying the founding of a secular Jewish state, Reb Saunders asks: "For this six million of our people were slaughtered?" (*The Chosen*, 198). In explaining his father's tears and depression, Danny tells Reuven: "Six million Jews have died. . . . He's—I think he's thinking of them. He's suffering for them" (*The Chosen*, 199). The deep differences that divide the Malters from the Saunderses is never reflected in their response to the Holocaust, in which all convey a sense of loss that can barely be contained or defined. The mutuality of this response illuminates a sense that the Holocaust is, in fact, for Jews a unifying event, one that happened in some way or another to them all. The reconciliation symbolized by Danny and Reuven's friendship cannot, of course, be attributed to the Holocaust. What can be attributed to it, however, is an erasure of previously intractable opposition. And in this sense, as presented by Potok in *The Chosen*, the historical violence presented by the Holocaust is somewhat mitigated.

Kremer acknowledges Potok's "reluctance to use graphic description of torture or direct or dramatic references to the concentrationary universe."[37] Most references made to the Holocaust in *The Chosen* reiterate the number of Jews murdered and so emphasize the size of the loss for the world Jewish community. Through the scale of this devastation, Potok reinforces one message in his novel, namely, that including the Holocaust in a narrative work demands special consideration in terms of presentation. But the problem remains: in a fictional narrative can the Holocaust simply stand for itself? Potok uses the numbers of the Holocaust, rather than the stories of the Holocaust, as a means to illuminate its enormity. Furthermore, by refusing to fictionalize aspects of the Holocaust, Potok aligns himself with survivor-writers such as Borowski and Wiesel whose work is punctuated with the sense of disbelief at what they experienced.[38] The repetition of the death count of the Holocaust by various characters carries with it a ritualistic quality of prayer and unites them, even in the face of their fictional differences. Finally, historical truth—a truth that embodies violence—brings them together. As important as this union is in contributing to the metaphor of "combat" in the novel, it still leaves readers with the problem of integrating the backdrop of the Holocaust with the foreground of the narrative and maintaining a certain tension between them. The war between "righteousness and sinfulness" and its resolution take on a different meaning when applied to Reuven and Danny's relationship than when applied to the Holocaust. Ultimately, we as readers must recognize that actual and historical violence sit uneasily together, which is not to say they cannot—or should not—coexist but, rather (as Potok implies), that they need good reason to be positioned thusly.

As tentatively and gingerly as Potok may handle the Holocaust and as carefully as he distinguishes between its aftermath and the time and place of its occurrence, finally it plays an uneven role in *The Chosen*. Silence and rumors soften its impact in driving forward a fictional account, as does its background role. But ultimately the Holocaust is used to serve specific functions. One function involves depicting the event itself—writing about the Holocaust, and writing carefully about it, using language to describe its impact on characters and silence to impart its unspeakable nature are attempts to "penetrate" and so better represent it. Another function places the Holocaust in a position subordinate to the narrative as a way of fueling it. Another possibility allows the positioning of the Holocaust to place pressure on other aspects of the narrative. The latter two roles conceive of the Holocaust as itself part of a larger text, a larger story. In many ways, one could argue, this makes sense: the Holocaust is a part of a larger history and its piece in that narrative structure can be borrowed and transplanted to fictional narrative. The problem with doing this, however, is that once the Holocaust becomes part of the fabric of a novel, it becomes subject to ideas outside itself, subject to excess and limitation, subject to the skill and motivation of the author, in short, subject to storytelling. No longer standing simply for itself, the Holocaust needs to be balanced with the larger message or theme of the novel. With *The Chosen*, the Holocaust is imperfectly balanced between oppositional forces—dark and light, silence and communication, friendship and enmity, rage and love. While Potok's caution in positioning and leaning on the Holocaust suggests his own uneasiness in doing this, an uneasiness that is itself a significant part of the story, finally he commits himself to the challenge—and the accompanying problems—of subjecting the Holocaust to a larger fiction.

Potok claims, rightly I think, that "nobody knows yet how to handle the Holocaust as a motif in Western art."[39] His response of not knowing how to handle the Holocaust in his novels does not entail avoiding it altogether. To the contrary, in his fiction Potok refuses to be silent on the matter of the Holocaust, even if his means of accessing it is through the silence of his characters. On the one hand, he preserves its historical truth; on the other hand, however, involving the Holocaust in a larger fiction throws history, plot, and character into disarray. The power of silence when applied to the Holocaust means one thing; the power of silence between people is another. Potok, in conversation, acknowledges the crucial distinctions between actual, cultural, ontological, and theological silences. In his fiction, however, these layers are often too closely associated with each other to be distinguished. The consequence is that readers are left wondering about the redemptive value of all the kinds of violence Potok introduces. Yes, actual and imagined violence can be—and in *The Chosen* are—redeemed. Can we make the same assertion for the Holocaust? Potok claims we can try to do so, that this is the "redemptive power of art. The artist, in strange fashion, redeems the horror of reality through the power of his or her art."[40] This may be true with many horrors of reality, some of which are described—and redeemed—in the course of his novels, horrors such as war, self-mutilation, and physical violence. But what Potok takes to be the unspeakable and indescribable nature of the Holocaust places it outside art altogether, and consequently, outside its redemptive power as well.

## CYNTHIA OZICK AND THE CONFLICT OF LANGUAGE

The American author Cynthia Ozick insists that depictions of the Holocaust "ought to remain exclusively attached to document and history," yet at the same time she repeatedly recognizes that even if she does not "want to tamper or invent or imagine . . . I have done it. I can't not do it. It comes. It invades."[41] In a later interview, Ozick reiterates both the strength of her intellectual position—"I'm against writing Holocaust fiction: that is, imagining those atrocities"—and the will exerted by art: "And yet, for some reason, I keep writing Holocaust fiction. It is something that has happened to me; I can't help it. If I had been there and not here I would be dead, which is something I can never forget."[42] A marked tension underscores Ozick's role as author: she employs the Holocaust with purpose and control and, simultaneously, with a sense of helplessness. Born in New York City in 1928, Ozick reluctantly admits that the lure of writing, and writing about the Holocaust, overcomes her misgivings of doing precisely this. Like Potok's reluctance to aestheticize the Holocaust, Ozick also recognizes the combined push and pull of its historical claim—the distance she has to it through her lack of intimate connection and the proximity it holds for her otherwise, one that serves, inescapably, as a filter to the vast majority of her fiction.[43] In effect, Ozick uses the Holocaust in her fiction in precisely the way she decries. Her position of unmitigated longing and willfulness combined with a reluctance bordering on dread is one she seems anxious for the reader to occupy with her: readers of Holocaust fiction, Ozick intimates, should feel compelled to read such stories, unable *not* to do so, and at the same time reluctant, resistant, pained; their compulsion to read and process the narrative balanced and sometimes stymied by an unwillingness (perhaps morally informed, perhaps emotionally) to bear witness as reader. As John Sutherland notes, Ozick is, "particularly on matters Jewish, a ferocious polemicist."[44]

In matters relating to the Holocaust, however, Ozick herself concedes some degree of defeat around her own point of view. The place and role of the Holocaust in many of Ozick's fictional stories reflect her ambivalence about creating a fictional web about a subject that should be held apart from precisely these initiatives. While Ozick's most deliberate story about the Holocaust is "The Shawl," a story that takes place en route to and within a Nazi concentration camp, most of her other fictional works include references to the Holocaust in the background of the story. Ozick's language in both cases is a tense combination of symbolic and literal, so much so that it seems as if a meta-dialogue is often being conducted in her stories: on the one hand, the protection offered by symbolic language on behalf of the reader serves to blanket and even stifle our understanding of the Holocaust, and on the other hand, the spare language of brute physicality is uncomfortable, even unbearable, to read. Reflecting her ambivalence about attaching the Holocaust to storytelling, Ozick often and insistently positions it in the background of her fiction—its presence, as with that of language, heightened as much by what is not there as by what is.

One effect of Ozick's effort to use language and imagery that both shock and shelter is to identify and confront barriers between the subject matter and the reader. In *The Space of Literature,* Maurice Blanchot writes that "the reader's reality, his personality, his immodesty, his stubborn insistence upon remaining himself in the face of what he reads" most threaten the act of reading about the Holocaust.[45] Ozick's shifting narrative strategies between language of symbolism and language of the physical body, the language of literality, acknowledges the challenge of representation and the Holocaust and, at the same time, the connection between that challenge and reaching the reader. For Ozick, referencing the Holocaust comes with a desire to displace the reader, to move him or her out of the complacency that typically accompanies the act of opening a book or turning a page. The danger, it seems clear, is in losing control over the relationship between the reader and the subject and, instead of rendering the reader productively uncomfortable, arresting his or her progress as a reader and letting the text go unread.

Like the character Feingold's voice in her short story "Levitation" (1982) when he keeps repeating the word "Holocaust," Ozick's language regarding the Holocaust is "less a human word than an animal's cry; a crow's. Caw caw."[46] It is sharp and penetrating and sticks uncomfortably in the throat. Here the echo of the word "Holocaust" illustrates both meaning (it is a "human word") and meaninglessness (one that is more like an "animal's cry"), a juxtaposition that Ozick returns to repeatedly in describing the Holocaust. Earlier in the story, the narrator describes Feingold's non-Jewish wife, Lucy (she is the daughter of a Presbyterian minister), listening to a Jewish war refugee who presents himself at the Feingolds' party. "The refugee was telling a story. 'I witnessed it,' he said, 'I am the witness.' " The narrator's voice, attentive toward Lucy, then summarizes the refugee's story into a series of triptychs: "Horror; sadism; corpses. . . . A gray scene, a scrubby hill, a ravine. Germans in helmets, with shining tar-black belts, wearing gloves. A ragged bundle of Jews at the lip of the ravine—an old grandmother, a child or two, a couple in their forties" ("Levitation," 14). Ozick uses the word "triptych" to describe the layout of the Feingolds' apartment, with its "wide center hall," the dining room opening to the left and the living room to the right (only Jews have congregated here). The narrative construction of the refugee's testimony, as it is echoed and—importantly—reduced by the narrator to a bare series of words, imitates the physical layout of the apartment in which it is told. These sentence fragments, carved out of the "refugee's whisper" and hung together in loosely formed families, leave Lucy "feel[ing] nothing," the same feeling she had after seeing "all the movies. . . . That same bulldozer shoveling those same sticks of skeletons, that same little boy in a cap with twisted mouth and his hands in the air" ("Levitation," 14). To counter the unreadability of the witness's testimony, Lucy positions his images as a backdrop for her own visualization: "As if—Lucy took the image from the elusive wind that was his voice in its whisper—as if hundreds and hundreds of Crucifixions were all happened at once. She visualized a hillside with multitudes of crosses, and bodies dropping down from big bloody nails. Every Jew was Jesus. That was the only way Lucy could get hold of it" ("Levitation," 14). The witness's testimony prompts Lucy to interpret and apply his images into a landscape that she can "get hold of," a landscape of crucifixion that is punctuated by "big bloody nails," "bodies," and "crosses." It is a landscape she has faced since her childhood, one filtered through the lens of Christianity that emphasizes and interprets the physical as leading to the salvational, an interpretation that separates her physically and interpretively from others in the room.

Lucy's response, and the only way she *can* read the Holocaust, is through a historic and primal anti-Semitism. In the story's concluding moments, "Lucy decides it is possible to become jaded by atrocity. She is bored by the shootings and the gas and the camps, and she is not ashamed to admit this. They are as tiresome as prayer. Repetition diminishes conviction; she is thinking of her father leading the same hymns week after week. If you said the same prayer over and over again, wouldn't your brain turn out to be no better than a prayer wheel?" ("Levitation," 19). Reading and re-reading, watching "all the films" with their repetitive images, hearing stories that invoke the same words—"shootings," "gas," "camps"—all diminish their meaning. "Levitation" concludes with the living room containing Feingold, the refugee, and the other Jews breaking away from the rest of the apartment and floating upward and away, growing smaller and dimmer with each passing moment: "Their words are specks. All the Jews are in the air" ("Levitation," 20).

In *Between Witness and Testimony* (2012), Michael Bernard-Donals and Richard Glejzer position Ozick as standing "between the two dicta of Holocaust fiction, to present an image of the suffering and the horrors of the Final Solution as a memorial that guards against historical and cultural amnesia, and to respectfully remain silent in the face of the experiences that only survivors can speak of."[47] I would counter, however, that these "two dicta" both stem from the same source: a recognition of the importance of unreadability. Lucy's reimagining of the refugee's testimony from "Horror; sadism; corpses" to "crosses," "bodies," and "nails"—her boredom with seeing the iconographic imagery of the Holocaust ("same bulldozer shoveling those same sticks of skeletons, that same little boy") and with hearing or reading the telltale words—speaks to the need to preserve unreadability, to recognize that their words are but specks, moments of (attempted) transmission on a blank page that is unreadable. The repetition of the few words and images that are available, whether through hearing, reading, or viewing, serves to illuminate the negative space in which they are recorded, emphasizing all we cannot hear, read, or view. The true problem of not recognizing or acknowledging the unreadable, as Lucy demonstrates, is being satisfied with understanding the enormity of the Nazi Holocaust with these few words and scenes, stubbornly reading them as fully descriptive and emblematic of readability. Lucy's boredom stems from her ignorance of what comprises real reading—and real knowledge. For Ozick, the language of imagery and the language of silence are both necessary, even as they work in opposition to each other. By recognizing precisely this tension, where words deteriorate into sounds ("Caw, caw"), and where read meaning places the unreadable in unwavering relief, Ozick offers the reader a "speck" of language that helps them acknowledge all that they cannot read.

A similar presentation of language occurs in Ozick's most recent novel, *Foreign Bodies* (2011), which, like "Levitation," takes place in the decade following World War II—the year is 1952. The novel is narrated by Bea Nightingale (anglicized from the family's original surname, Nachtigall), a divorced, middle-aged, Jewish, high school English teacher who lives on the Upper West Side in New York City and whose family has been in the United States for several generations. Charged by her brother to go to Paris to discover the whereabouts of his son, Julian, and to convince him to return to the United States, Bea meets her young nephew's companion, Lili, whom she describes to her sister-in-law as "a displaced person—you know what that means, a displaced person?" (*Foreign Bodies*, 95).[48] Tellingly, the question is never followed by an answer or a definition. The title *Foreign Bodies* refers not only to the physical displacement of Nachtigall family members moving around Europe and Lili's travels to America. The displacement also reflects the resistance that language imposes on trauma, physically and psychically. That is, displacement occurs both in terms of representation and in terms of reading, in the making of narrative and in its processing. In the novel, the foreign body is not limited to one's own self but also to the pronouncement and understanding of oneself.

Nowhere is this better illustrated than in the depictions of Lili's wound, which she managed to survive even as similar injuries proved fatal to nearly her entire family. Described as the "ugly hole in her arm (she covered it over) from a failed shot" (*Foreign Bodies*, 104), it is a "second mouth, misplaced—lipless, speechless" (*Foreign Bodies*, 227). Lili's scar has "bulging depth and pucker, like a toothless mouth that has swallowed a bone. It meant what it meant. It told too much; there was nothing to say" (*Foreign Bodies*, 128). In another iteration of the presentation of Holocaust violence and a recognition of the need to also preserve a quality of inaccessibility around it, Lili covers up "the hideous hole" (*Foreign Bodies*, 104) during the day, remains largely silent regarding the murder of her family, and yet all of those who interact with her know that the wound is "always there" (*Foreign Bodies*, 128). Here Ozick combines in quick succession the language of the grotesque (a bodily and literal description of the deformity) with the language of symbolism. As in "Levitation," Ozick suggests that neither the physical nor the allegorical by itself suffices in conveying the devastation of the Holocaust. That is not to suggest, however, that the sum is greater than its parts and that, by taking together the two modes of usage both through representation and through reading, it is made accessible. To the contrary: such a combination emphasizes the scant reach of language—"words are specks." Ultimately, the power of Ozick's skilled use of language comes through her ability to illuminate the vast area of traumatic experience that words cannot access or penetrate.

In *Foreign Bodies* (more so than in "Levitation"), Ozick addresses the place and impact of the Holocaust in American life and connects that, too, with language. As with the refugee in "Levitation," certain details about Lili are fixed, secured by the fact that various characters repeat and reiterate them: she is in her mid-thirties but looks and sounds far older; her parents, husband, and three-year-old son were killed, shot during the war; she is from Bucharest, the daughter of a linguist and a university professor; a deep scar on her arm serves as the physical marker of the trauma she has borne. Lili's history is told in pieces, with gaps in the narrative deliberately left unfilled. At times these gaps are more recognizable to the reader than to the character being addressed in the novel. For example, when Lili and Julian first meet in a Paris café, she urges him to "go home." He claims he can't because he has no home: "'Getting born in a place,' he retorted, 'doesn't make it your home, not if they don't treat you like you're an actual person.'" Lili's response is matched by that of the reader, pushing back at Julian's false sense of knowledge: "'You speak better than you know,' she said" (*Foreign Bodies*, 104). At times, however, these gaps in narrative reveal meaning that is limited to those within the novel. When Bea first meets Lili and inquires about her intentions regarding her young nephew, Lili responds: "'I had once a husband. I had once a son.' Up rose her chin, a warning, a wall. She would go no further with this. 'Today I have Julian.'" Bea registers her response silently: "A husband, a son. People like that, one of those. There was no innocence in this woman" (*Foreign Bodies*, 74).

Lili's stilted use of the past perfect is both expressive—it indicates that something happened before a specific time and action in the past—and guarded: the physical gesture of her chin rising in warning and deflection matches the grammatical impediment that her words plant. Between her past and present husband (she and Julian have secretly married) is a lapse in time, space, place, and life. Bea is both able to identify Lili—she is "one of those" and "a displaced person"—and yet at the same time unable to capture any real sense of her history or its lasting impact. This comes through even more clearly in the rather antiseptic letter Bea sends her brother once she learns of Julian and Lili's impending return to the United States:

> What moves him to return appears to be his attachment to the young woman you already know of—it won't do anymore to say "girlfriend," and I discovered belatedly that it was never the right word to begin with. I have had two or three rather scanty encounters with this person. My impression is one of uncommon gravity and endurance—nothing lighthearted or frivolous. I have learned very little of her background, beyond that she is the daughter of an educated Bucharest family, and apparently has some literary skills in several European languages, though her English is stilted and in certain aspects insufficient. She is older than Julian, I would think somewhere between eight and a dozen years. She is a widow and has lost a child—I gather she was interned with her family during the war and somehow ended in Paris with hundreds of other such uprooted people. (*Foreign Bodies*, 185)

Bea resists using definitive and descriptive language to describe Lili, preferring instead language of negation: instead of calling her Julian's wife, she notes that Lili is not his girlfriend; Lili is neither "lighthearted" nor "frivolous" and speaks "insufficient" English. Lili's presence, then, points to absence, an aspect that is conveyed most effectively through Bea's acknowledgment that "the right word" to describe Lili, both in terms of what she means to Julian and in summation of her past and presence, simply is not available.

Bea's brother Marvin describes Lili in far cruder terms:

> I'm not about to have some little old grandma with broken English creep into my family. . . . I don't want to set eyes on the woman. I know what's coming, I've seen the films like everybody else, and I can't have one of those, not in my own family. All that's blood under the bridge, it's not my business, and I don't intend to invite it in. . . . I'll contribute all they want to those organizations, whatever they are, same as I give to the Red Cross and such, and more if they think I owe it to 'em for solidarity's sake . . . solidarity! But I don't want any of those people in my house. . . . I don't want to see her—I don't want to smell her—and I don't want to see my son, the damn fool. . . . Bucharest, where the hell is that, Romania, Bulgaria, who cares? He's gone back three generations into the past, the boy's digging up skeletons—. (*Foreign Bodies*, 197)

Lili, Marvin bluntly suggests, is part of both a near past and a more distant past from which he has worked hard to dissociate. In terms of his own family, Marvin married a non-Jewish woman, Margaret Breckinridge—her "blood was satisfyingly blue" (*Foreign Bodies*, 14)—who helps further separate him from his immigrant grandfather whose accented English inspires Marvin's lifelong contempt toward those like him. If Bea's description of Lili focuses more on what she is not, Marvin's description pulls the other way, creating an image of Lili as "old," "broken," and bad-smelling, from a country that is utterly insignificant, and with a history that is familiar, unspecial, even banal.

The split in style between the two siblings, with Bea opting for the language of negation and Marvin employing more brutelike forceful terms reflects again, albeit in more subdued tones, Ozick's approach to describing the Holocaust and its aftermath, here from the perspective of distance and privilege. Both Marvin and Bea mark Lili with a sense of degraded otherness as "one of those." Indeed, even though the action in the book takes place in 1952, in many ways Ozick traces a familiar generational picture of the response of American Jews to the Holocaust. Author Shlomo Katz, writing in 1940, notes that "only the slimmest of cultural and psychic ties bind him to the Jews of Poland."[49] Whereas both Marvin and Bea pull away from Lili, content not to know, not to name, not to read or learn of the event she stands for, the next generation—Julian and his sister, Iris—act on a desire to draw closer to this history, this "knowledge of death" (*Foreign Bodies*, 129).

Their process of discovery is uneasy and necessarily incomplete. It is filled with blunders and punctuated by a tense combination of incomprehensible speech, such as the "savage syllables and crazed chatterings" (*Foreign Bodies*, 127) that comprise the language of Lili's dreams about her past, waking up all those around her. In contrast to these wild moments of shouted incomprehensibility are the enforced silences that "Iris must never penetrate. She was not to ask about the dead husband and the dead child. Julian had given her all she was to know—that the husband was called Eugen, that the child, three years old, was called Mikhail, and that was enough, that was all" (*Foreign Bodies*, 128). The differences in language and approach between the four members of the Nachtigall family are, in fact, founded on common ground, namely, their distance from the Holocaust. In spite of their varying motivations and responses to Lili, it is their not knowing, their not experiencing, that links them. Through language both brutish and barely visible, through positioning the Holocaust as a background that is ever-present and yet never at the center, Ozick takes measure of a post-Holocaust world. It is defined by an absence, Ozick suggests, as with Lili's wound that is always there, a bulging history of loss that is at once too much to know and impossible to hide.

## SHADOW BOXING: READING THE JEWISH BODY IN ROTH'S *NEMESIS*

Philip Roth's novel *Nemesis* (2010), a deeply evocative and wrenching story, is narrated by a polio survivor, Arnie Mesnikoff, who is a virtually invisible figure until the novel's final chapters. Arnie casts back to the summer of 1944 in Newark,

New Jersey, when he and other kids in the "city's southwestern corner, in the Jewish Weequahic section" looked toward their local hero, the twenty-three-year-old Mr. Bucky Cantor, a sincere and diligent playground director whose physical presence—steady and firm—seemed strong enough to stand between the children, whose rule-bound games he enforced and guided, and the virus, whose origins and destructive path were undetermined and mysterious and threatened the community.[50] Bucky, who takes special pride in his diving and javelin-throwing skills, quits his playground job just days before the mayor, in response to a growing number of polio cases, shuts down all public gathering places. He heads to the Poconos to join his fiancée, Marcia Steinberg, at Indian Hill, "a camp for Jewish boys and girls" (*Nemesis*, 31) as the waterfront director. Soon after his arrival, a number of campers and staff, including Bucky himself, come down with polio. Believing himself the carrier of the infection, Bucky essentially never recovers. He loses most of the function and strength of one arm and one leg, breaks off his engagement, finds a job as a civil servant, and exiles himself from his former life. Decades later he is recognized by Arnie Mesnikoff who, while disabled from his bout with the disease, has married, raised a family, and not only come to terms with the changes polio wreaked on his body but has used the disease to fuel a successful career as an architect specializing in disabled accessibility. In contrast to Arnie's acceptance of his body's limitations, Bucky stands in self-imposed isolation. His firm muscularity has melted away—his hand feels like "soft fruit"; he remains solitary, stricken, and guilt-ridden (*Nemesis*, 271).

Two problems of identity emerge in *Nemesis*. The first of these addresses a common assumption regarding Roth's writing, namely, that it is Jewish fiction. What makes it so? Roth resists the classification of both himself and his fiction as "Jewish." "I'm not crazy about being described as a Jewish American writer," he says in a film interview. "I don't write Jewish, I write American. Most of my work takes place here. I am an American."[51] The intimation here is that "Jewish American" imposes conditions and boundaries on Roth's fiction that limit scope, meaning, and impact, either in how his fiction is read and understood or in how it is conceived and written. Born in 1933 and a second-generation American, Roth's understanding of himself as such in large part fuels many of the issues of identity that are raised in his novels.

To Roth's apparent chagrin, however, his identity as a Jewish American writer of Jewish American texts persists. As opposed to the process of identification surrounding the question of *who* is Jewish, a problem with a thorny history and ongoing debate, the larger question behind it is what it means for a work of contemporary American fiction, written for a wide-ranging audience, to be identified as Jewish. Roth's own Jewishness is a matter of course and, as we see in *Nemesis*, many of his characters bear identifiably Jewish names: Myron Kopferman, Herbie Steinmark, Joey Rosenfield, Bernie Lewy, Irv Schlanger, Paul Lippman, Leo Feinswog, Kenny Blumenfeld, Bill Blomback. Living up to any number of stereotypes is Marcia Steinberg's father, a doctor, well-off, and with a nose that is described as "curved like a scimitar at the top but bent flat at the tip, and with the bone of the bridge cut like a diamond—in short, a nose out of a folktale, the sort of sizable, convoluted, intricately turned nose that, for many centuries, confronted though they have been by every imaginable hardship, the Jews had never stopped making" (*Nemesis*, 100).

Is the identification of the author and the deployment of Jewish names and physical attributes enough to determine the identity of a novel? By way of an answer, Roth asks readers to think about the relationship between various personal—as well as national and religious—identities throughout *Nemesis*. Roth himself initiates a discussion around this issue before the novel even begins. In an unusual move for Roth, the novel contains an Acknowledgments page that recognizes textual influences: *The Throws Manual*; *Teaching Springboard Diving*; *Camp Management*; *Recreational Programs for Summer Camps*; *Dirt and Disease*; *Polio's Legacy*; *A Paralyzing Fear*; *Polio Voices*; *A Manufactured Wilderness*; *Manual of the Woodcraft Indians*; and, "particularly useful," notes Roth, *The Book of Woodcraft*. Taken together with the novel's at times even parodic Jewish characterizations, this list reveals that *Nemesis*, a book about the body, its physical capabilities, its corporeal limitations, is more emphatically, more eloquently, more starkly, a book about survival. Given the novel's World War II setting, it is a book about the survival of Jews, but at its most grand a novel about the survival of humanity, culture, home, and selfhood.

A corollary to the question regarding the Jewish identity of *Nemesis* is whether it can be considered, in addition to Jewish fiction, a Holocaust novel. Insofar as the novel takes place in 1944 and insofar as it is a text about the Jewish body, both in its singular and collective sense, *Nemesis* has a particularly unique relationship to survival, one that can be read both locally, going no further than the body of Bucky Cantor, and more expansively, as it applies to the body of American Jews born during and after the war and, indeed, even more broadly, to all Americans. Roth challenges precisely the uniqueness of the Jewish body, with its symbolic post-Holocaust lack of wholeness, universalizing it in *Nemesis* by positioning it alongside that of the Native American and the ancient Greek. (It hardly seems coincidental that the setting of the book is described as "Jewish Weequahic," a melding of two ancient traditions that Roth explores in the novel.) In what has become by his own pronouncement his final novel, Roth leaves the reader to determine if the Jewish experience—experienced, as it must be, by the Jewish body—is the human experience, and the Jewish protagonist the heroic figure. In other words, the question Roth presents in the novel is whether survival in some sense universalizes identity or particularizes it—does it make his characters more Jewish or does it make them more like others who have faced extermination, others whose strength in numbers and achievements is largely documented as history?

At the novel's conclusion, Arnie Mesnikoff casts back to the summer of 1944 before the polio epidemic took over and describes Bucky Cantor as, at the age of twenty-three, "the most exemplary and revered authority we [boys] knew, a young man of convictions, easygoing, kind, fair-minded, thoughtful, stable, gentle, vigorous, muscular—a comrade and leader both" (*Nemesis*, 275). Bucky's popularity among his charges and the dedication with which he approached his position as playground, and later waterfront, director are complicated by his own wish to be elsewhere. He "was one of the few young men around who wasn't off fighting in the war" (*Nemesis*, 10)—a wish denied him because of his "poor vision" and "thick eyeglasses" (*Nemesis*, 10). While Arnie and his cohort of local Jewish boys imitate Bucky's "athletic, pigeon-toed trot," copying "his purposeful way of lightly lifting himself as he moved on the balls of his feet," walking, as Bucky did, with a "slight sway . . . of his substantial shoulders" (*Nemesis*, 13), Bucky's strength, agility, and athleticism are insufficient to gain him admission into the U.S. armed forces: "Mr. Cantor had been twenty and a college junior when the US Pacific Fleet was bombed and nearly destroyed in the surprise Japanese attack at Pearl Harbor on Sunday, December 7, 1941. On Monday the eighth he went off to the recruiting station outside City Hall to join the fight. But because of his eyes nobody would have him. . . . He was classified 4-F and sent back to Panzer College to continue preparing to be a phys ed teacher" (*Nemesis*, 26). Indeed, even Bucky Cantor's admittedly limited professional success once he graduates from Panzer College a year later, in 1942, can in part be attributed to the paucity of available and qualified men who are not serving overseas. Marcia Steinberg calls Bucky to recruit him as waterfront director at Indian Hills because a replacement is needed for the current director who "got his draft notice" (*Nemesis*, 84).

Men rejected for military service often suffered a pariah-like status in their community, even as they were in high demand to fill otherwise competitive positions. In *Nemesis*, Bucky occupies a somewhat different role: embraced by his fiancée and her family, admired by his playground charges, tenderly looked after by his grandmother, Bucky's status as an outsider is largely of his own making. Or so it seems. While Bucky is characterized in simple terms—he is unfailingly polite, earnestly believes in the value of exercise and sport, expresses the wonder of a small child at crossing the state line from New Jersey to Pennsylvania—he in fact is situated at the locus of conflict that is not specific only to him, but as if he is the pebble thrown into a pool of water, he stands at the center of graduating rings of conflict. The most intimate of these rings is the conflict presented by Bucky's own body; in the middle distance, Bucky stands as a symbol for the all-American Jew, the object of local, if fairly benign, anti-Semitism; at its most expansive, Bucky stands as a symbol for the havoc wreaked on the Jewish body in all its entirety during the years of World War II. This ruination, the ultimate message borne by the novel, suggests that the consequences of the Holocaust are not limited to the Jewish community or the Jewish body but, rather, affect the heart of civilization.

The irony of Bucky's situation is stark and he feels it keenly: rejected from the U.S. military, he is ordered back to his studies, a program that focuses on physical bodily achievement and one that grants him the authority to lead competitions and games, activities that pit one team against another in contests that test strength, strategy, and nimbleness. In short, few other candidates are as well-groomed for the physical and social challenges that come with active combat and military life. In the privacy of his home, which he shares with the grandmother who raised him, Bucky weeps at the prospect of not being able to join his buddies for basic training. He feels "ashamed to be seen in civilian clothes, ashamed when he watche[s] newsreels of the war at the movies, ashamed when he [takes] the bus home to Newark. . . . He [feels] the shame of someone who might by himself have made a difference" (*Nemesis*, 27).

The 4-F designation was part of the more detailed system of classification for draftees that was developed during World War II to help organize a war effort that ultimately involved close to fifteen million servicemen and several hundred thousand servicewomen. The 4-F classification meant that the individual was found "physically, mentally, or morally unfit for service" and included anything from "flat feet, a hernia, and venereal disease to lack of height (shorter than five feet) or lack of weight (less than 105 pounds)."[52] A range of local articles published during and after World War II confirm the marginalized social status of those not accepted into the military. In March 1944 the *Rotarian Magazine*, a publication of Rotary Clubs, printed an article entitled "A Wartime Casualty on the Homefront: Teen-Age Rejectees": "An apparently healthy young man not in uniform always raises a question. It is one which these teen-age rejectees must constantly answer whether spoken or implied: 'Why aren't you in the service?' "[53]

"Take Ed's case, for instance" the article advises its readers. "His eyes have always been bad. However, when corrected with glasses, he has been able to do school work and to carry on with other activities. Now those eyes are preventing him from joining his pals in military service. . . . Others have been rejected because of childhood injuries or illnesses. These are physical defects that under ordinary circumstances would go unnoticed and offer no serious handicap to normal living. Only the war demand for physical health has made them—and others—conscious of their disability."[54] The article determines that for the roughly 80,000 eighteen-year-old boys inducted into the military annually, "almost that number will fail to pass the physical examination."[55] Elsewhere the number of men designated as 4-F is maintained as "45 per cent."[56] In another local publication, a woman recalls the reaction of her young college classmates toward their male counterparts during the war: "When I started college in the fall of 1944, it was like a girls' school—95 women and only five men students. During the second semester of my sophomore year, more male students were enrolled. By 1948 when I graduated, there were twice as many men as female students. During that first year, several of the girls dated high school seniors because to us the boys on campus were '4-F.' They needed a good reason for not being in the service to be respected by the girls."[57]

Before his death, Bucky's grandfather paid special attention to the boy's "masculine development." He was determined that the weak character of Bucky's father, a gambler who spent time in jail and a figure his grandfather regularly declared "a very shady character," would not exhibit itself in any way in his son—beyond his bad eyesight, which, the narrator tells us more than once, Bucky's father had bequeathed him. "I was the son of a thief," Bucky tells Marcia. "He went to jail for stealing money. He's an ex-convict.... If he had raised me, who's to know if I wouldn't have turned out to be a thief myself?" (*Nemesis*, 167–168). Bucky was an attentive and willing student, and his grandfather's exhortations to "stand up for himself as a man and to stand up for himself as a Jew" stayed close to his heart (*Nemesis*, 25). Yet his poor eyesight complicates matters considerably. Not only do they link him to the disparaged figure of his father, and not only do they prevent him from joining the war effort, but they tie him more generally to a host of Jewish characters whose most memorable, and often despised, trait is located in innate, genetic weakness and malfunction.

Among such of Roth's characters perhaps none is more memorable than Brenda Patimkin in "Goodbye, Columbus," who had her nose "fixed" (it is the only obstacle between her and physical perfection) but still relies on Neil Klugman, the story's poor protagonist, to hold her glasses while she dives into the pool at the country club where she is a member (her family being wealthy enough to buy their way in) and he is a guest. Jewish noses, like Brenda's and Dr. Steinberg's, if he were so inclined, can be "bobbed," as Brenda calls it.[58] Jewish eyes, with their propensity toward weakness, can be corrected in terms of vision; Brenda, Neil, Dr. Steinberg, Bucky, all peer out through thick lenses. What glasses cannot correct is the perception by others. Jews are often portrayed as nearsighted and wearing glasses because they convey a kind of bookishness closely aligned with feebleness or cowardice, which feeds a broader stereotype of Jews as weak. In Thomas Mann's *The Magic Mountain* (1924), the Jewish identity of Leo Naphta is apparent at once from his physical description: "small, skinny," and "corrosively ... ugly," with "the aquiline nose dominating the face; the small, pursed mouth; the pale gray eyes behind thick lenses in the light frames of his glasses."[59] In Arthur Miller's novel *Focus* (1945), the Jewish protagonist, Newman, resists wearing glasses until ordered to do so by his superiors at work. He puts them on and examines himself in his bathroom mirror: "A long time he stood staring at himself, at his forehead, his chin, his nose. It took many moments of detailed inspection of his parts before he could see himself whole.... [H]e was looking at what might very properly be called the face of a Jew.... The glasses did just what he feared they would do to his face.... The frames seemed to draw his flat, shiny-haired skull lower and set off his nose, so that where it had once appeared a trifle sharp it now beaked forth from the nosepiece. He took the glasses off and slowly put them on again to observe the distortion."[60] Eyeglasses not only affect a figure's outwardly physical presentation, affecting the perception and judgment of the viewing public, but the need for glasses suggests a more pervasive, internal weakness or failure. Glasses correct vision through visual distortion and so lend a sense that the innate perception of a glasses-wearer is defective and wanting.

Less intimate but still difficult to bear is the vocal opinion of Bucky's employer, Mr. O'Gara, who had "been running the city playgrounds for years" (*Nemesis*, 137). When Bucky informs him that he is "leaving his job at the end of the week to take over as waterfront director at a summer camp in the Poconos," O'Gara responds by saying, "You're an opportunist, Cancer," mistaking Bucky's last name, Cantor, with its connotation of leadership in prayer and song for a disease, something to be biopsied, excised, and destroyed. "You Jewish boys got all the answers. No, you're not stupid—*but neither is O'Gara, Cancer*" (*Nemesis*, 137–139). The unpleasant encounter with O'Gara, and its suggestion that "Jewish boys" profit from the work and sacrifice of others, casts a pall not only over the professional achievements of "Jewish boys" but also over their role and contributions in larger, more politically inflected tones. "Jewish boys" make good on events like the war and the polio epidemic—this is, in fact, precisely what they do so well. Similar to his weak eyes, which connect him to his estranged father and to a largely foreign world in which Jews are weaklings or wimps, O'Gara positions Bucky at the center of what feels like a morally and professionally significant, even life-defining moment, with Bucky's wish to "face the dangers of running the playground at Chancellor Avenue School in the midst of a polio epidemic" pushing against his desire to forget his betrayal in leaving the playground and to "embrace the security and predictability and contentment of a normal life" with his fiancée, Marcia Steinberg (*Nemesis*, 134, 135).

O'Gara is in fact a spokesperson for the kind of anti-Semitism that was on the rise in America from 1939 through 1945, and these sentiments moved from the civilian population to the military where the notion of "Jewish opportunism" became a source of criticism and dark humor. A parody of the Marine Corps Hymn during this time opens with the following lines:

> From the shores of Coney Island / Looking eastward to the sea / Stands kosher air-raid warden / Wearing a V for victory. / And the gentle breezes fill the air / With the hot dogs from Cohen's stand / Only Christian boys are drafted / From Coney Island's sands. / Oh, we Jews are not afraid to say / We'll stay home and give first aid / Let the Christian saps go fight the Japs / In the uniforms we made.[61]

American anti-Semitism became more formalized during the years in which Europe was at war; before 1933, when anti-Semitic views were articulated, they lacked the intensity, threatening nature, and mass appeal that emerged in the late 1930s. Historian Leonard Dinnerstein notes that beginning in the late 1930s, "for the first time in American history Jews feared that their attackers might acquire the kind of political influence and respectability that anti-Semites had in Europe and achieve similarly devastating results."[62] Indeed, one of the best novels reflecting the distressing atmosphere for American Jews during this period is none other than Roth's *The Plot against America*, which imagines the consequences if aviation hero Charles Lindbergh defeated Franklin Roosevelt and became president in 1940. Roth's novel reflects the all too real systematization of anti-Semitic views that enabled, in an imaginary world inspired by truth, Lindbergh's candidacy to succeed.

Returning to *Nemesis*, in spite of O'Gara's vaguely anti-Semitic insinuations, and in spite of Bucky's vision, "so bad that when he put the glasses away at night to get ready for bed, he could barely make out the shape of the few pieces of furniture in his room," what ultimately defines Bucky before he contracts polio is his strength, agility, and physical power (*Nemesis*, 20). At the end of the novel, Arnie recalls Bucky demonstrating the technique involved in throwing a javelin: "His was the body—the feet, the legs, the buttocks, the trunk, the arms, the shoulders, even the thick stump of the bull neck—that acting in unison had powered the throw. It was as though our playground director had turned into a primordial man, hunting for food on the plains where he foraged, taming the wilds by the might of his hand. Never were we more in awe of anyone" (*Nemesis*, 279). Earlier in the novel the narrator describes Bucky's ears as "shaped much like the ace of spades in a pack of cards, or the wings on the winged feet of mythology" (*Nemesis*, 12). Bucky is mythic, invincible, manly, primordial. At the same time he is nearly blind, an army reject, nicknamed Cancer, regarded as an opportunist, and by the end of the novel, disfigured and crippled by polio.

O'Gara humiliates Bucky by questioning his choice to leave Newark and by more broadly using this moment to fuel his wider claim of existing "Jewish opportunism." O'Gara is described as "a tired old man with a big gut and an antagonistic manner who'd been running the city playgrounds for years and whose prowess as a Central High football player at the time of the First World War still constituted the culmination of his life" (*Nemesis*, 136). In many ways O'Gara is an ironic projection of what Bucky Cantor could turn into if he were less of an opportunist: an embittered civil servant who is identified, to those who remember, with a physical athleticism that has long since ceased to matter in any meaningful way. But Bucky, as he stands in front of Mr. O'Gara a strong, virile young man, opposes the narrow cynical world-view offered up by O'Gara. Bucky sees the world more generously, more openly. "He was raised to be a fearless battler by his grandfather, trained to think he must be a hugely responsible man, ready and fit to defend what was right, and instead, confronted with the struggle of the century, a worldwide conflict between good and evil, he could not take even the smallest part. . . . Yet he *had* been given a war to fight, the war being waged on the battlefield of his playground" (*Nemesis*, 173). Bucky wishes to imbue his charges, whether in the city playground or the Jewish summer camp, not only with a sense of sportsmanship but with the moral valence conveyed by a world easily broken down into binaries, right and wrong, winners and losers, strong and weak.

The characterization of Bucky Cantor as both physically strong and morally upstanding, an image in which the health of the body reflects internal well-being, has long been used, in its inverse, against Jews. Nowhere is this better witnessed than in the caricaturing of the Jewish body as weak, sickly, and inadequate in historical documents, literature, and pamphlets leading up to Nazi Germany. Building on stereotypes that were well-established for many decades—indeed, centuries—that characterized the Jew as physically different, easily identifiable, and repulsive, Nazi propaganda pictured the Jew as abnormal, whether grossly overweight or rail thin, comically short or threateningly large, with distorted and exaggerated features and limbs that combined to suggest that the ugliness and ungainliness found in external features signaled an unseemly, morally corrupt interior. O'Gara's barbed comments to Bucky and, more generally, the rise of anti-Semitism in the United States corresponded to an increase in military engagement with Europe and reflected the characterizations of the Jew that had long been in place in Europe. The Austrian writer and military figure Charles-Joseph Lamoral, the prince de Ligne, describes the Jew at the turn of the nineteenth century as "always sweating from running about selling in public squares and taverns; all hunchbacked, such dirty red or black beards, livid complexions, gaps in their teeth, long, crooked noses, fearful . . . long, pigeon-toed feet, hollow eyes, pointed chins."[63]

The Jew who is pictured as dirty, lame, large-nosed, and flat-footed, was also the Jew believed to be shifty, a sexual misfit, a thief, associated with disease and infestation. Sanders Gilman, in *The Jew's Body*, understands the "construction of the Jewish body in the nineteenth and early twentieth centuries [as] linked to the underlying ideology of antisemitism, to the view that the Jew is inherently different. . . . No aspect of the representation of the Jewish body . . . is free from the taint of the claim of the special nature of the Jewish body as a sign of the inherent difference of the Jew."[64] These differences became especially pertinent and consequential when it came to military service, often a condition of citizenship, and a symbol of true social belonging. In the late eighteenth century the German theologian and Hebraist Johann David Michaelis responded to an initiative that would have included Jews in the military by suggesting that their small stature meant they would be ineffective as soldiers.[65] This was but one of many statements in a sustained debate over citizenship, contributions to the state, and military service that continued well into the nineteenth century with the Jew standing as a symbol of a "bad" citizen because he was deemed physically inadequate for military service and morally too corrosive to be considered a desirable or counted member of the body politic.

In the early twentieth century, a number of Jewish scientists in Europe worked to disprove the claims that Jews were physically unable to contribute actively to the military. In an essay written in 1908 and entitled "The Military Qualifications of the Jew," the German Jewish scientist Dr. Elias Auerbach positioned his research in such a way that he admitted the physical differences of Jews but argued that these should not prevent participation in active military duty. Furthermore, Dr. Auerbach "advocates the only true solution that will make the Jews of equal value as citizens: the introduction of 'sport' and the resultant reshaping of the Jewish body."[66] Other scientists such as the Berlin orthopedist Gustav Muskat similarly worked to suggest that a change in central activity—that is, from merchant to athlete—would work as an enabling force on the Jewish body.[67] That is, taking the Jew away from the conditions that incurred bodily malformation, conditions almost exclusively associated with the grit, disease, and marketplace existence of city life, would positively influence both physical form and malformations associated with Jews. This would enable them eventually to participate physically, civically, and intellectually in public life.

Standing in stark contrast to images such as Jud Süss is the twenty-three-year-old Bucky Cantor, whose frequent showers, strength, and wholesome, even sweet, sexual trysts are repeatedly described.[68] It is this Bucky Cantor who is connected, as he lifts his javelin, to the earliest of societies, to Native Americans, to ancient Greece, and to Hercules, the original javelin thrower and, the narrator reminds readers, "the great warrior and slayer of monsters" (*Nemesis*, 276). It is this Bucky Cantor who, as he hurls the javelin, lets out "a strangulated yowl of effort . . . a noise expressing the essence of him—the naked battle cry of striving excellence" (*Nemesis*, 278). That pre-articulate, preverbal yowl, accompanied by the image of the spear-throwing Bucky Cantor as "primordial man, hunting for food on the plains where he foraged, taming the wilds by the might of his hand," is the image that Roth uses to connect the Jewish experience of self to a universal one. The yowl is what all javelin throwers emit.

Readers are faced with this universalist interpretation of Jewishness elsewhere in the novel, as when Bucky is introduced to Indian Hill camp traditions by the director, Bill Blomback. "This is the bible," Bill tells Bucky as he hands him a "thick volume called *The Book of Woodcraft*" (*Nemesis*, 145–146). These books are "indispensable," Mr. Blomback continues, because they "hold up always a heroic human ideal. They accept the red man as the great prophet of outdoor life and woodcraft and use his methods whenever they are helpful" (*Nemesis*, 146). Bill Blomback, with no sense of irony, willingly and cheerfully, identifies the works of Ernest Thompson Seton as the guidebooks, both moral and practical, for the Jewish boys and girls at Camp Indian Hill. Not only does he read about the Woodcraft Indians as a historical people, but at the weekly Indian Night, campers and staff adorn themselves with Indian regalia, darken their skin with "cocoa powder," gather around a campfire in an event that quite literally identifies the Jewish body with that of another ancient civilization.

The edenic capsule that is Camp Indian Hill is shattered by the insistent intrusion of the war and the polio epidemic. Shortly before his first Indian Night, Bucky Cantor learns that his great college friend, the "indestructible" Jake Garonzik, who Bucky describes as "a brick wall . . . six feet three inches tall and two hundred and fifteen points . . . a powerhouse" (*Nemesis*, 202) has been killed "in action in France" (*Nemesis*, 202). Hours later Bill Blomback begins the campfire ceremony. The opening of the ceremony used to involve an Indian salute, "an upraised right arm with the palm forward" (*Nemesis*, 208). "But this greeting had to be abandoned with the arrival on the world scene of the Nazis, who employed the salute to signify 'Heil Hitler!' " (*Nemesis*, 208–209). Mr. Blomblack begins the ceremony, intoning: "When first the brutal anthropoid stood up and walked erect, . . . there was man! The great event was symbolized and marked by the lighting of the first campfire." Bucky's protégé, Donald Kaplow, whispers to him: "We get this every week. The little kids don't understand a word. No worse, I guess, than what happens in shul." Overhead there is a "roar of an airplane engine" as it passes over the camp. "An army air corps base had opened at the beginning of the war some seventy miles to the north, and Indian Hill was on its flyway" (*Nemesis*, 209). Six days later, Bucky helps a feverish and immobilized Donald to the hospital; polio has reached Camp Indian Hill. Believing himself to be the "healthy infected carrier" (*Nemesis*, 236) who has brought polio to the camp, Bucky undergoes tests that come back positive. Within forty-eight hours he exhibits the unmistakable symptoms of polio: "the monstrous headache, the enfeebling exhaustion, the severe nausea, the raging fever, the unbearable muscle ache . . . paralysis" (*Nemesis*, 238). He spends

> the next fourteen months in rehabilitation at the Kenny Institute, gradually recovering the full use of his right arm and partial use of his legs, though he was left with a twisted lower spine. . . . He was at the Kenny Institute when President Roosevelt unexpectedly died, in April 1945, and the country went into mourning. He was there when defeated Germany surrendered in May. . . . World War II was over, his [other college] buddy Dave would be coming home unscathed from fighting in Europe, America was jubilant, and he was still in the hospital, disfigured and maimed. (*Nemesis*, 240)

When Arnie Mesnikoff spots his former playground director twenty-seven years later on Broad Street, Bucky is wearing "a protective moustache," the "sharp planes of his face were padded by the weight he'd gained. . . . No trace of the compact muscleman remained" (*Nemesis*, 244). He is stout, with a "withered left arm and useless left hand," his left leg is fully encased in a brace and his walking aided with a cane. As he shares with Arnie his belief that he caused the children who were in his care "irrevocable harm," he looks "as if he had lived on this earth seven thousand shameful years" (*Nemesis*, 271). Bucky is no longer the victorious Hercules but, rather, the guilt-laced survivor, a veteran betrayed by his own body, by its very survival. Instead of retaining the identity that linked him not to a specifically Jewish past but to a more universal history and place of origin, as he has aged, experienced, and suffered he has become more identifiably, more tragically, Jewish. Bucky Cantor's postwar self stands as a scarred and fragmented representation of the survivor's body, with all its implications of the Holocaust, and the Jewish body, with its designation as both the individual (Bucky Cantor) and the collective (the larger Jewish community). The two are irretrievably and singularly connected.

# 6 • RECEDING INTO THE DISTANCE

## The Holocaust as Background

> Savta look[ed] at her with a strange expression, saying, "You are a miracle, you and your brother both. You were not supposed to be born." That had made [her] uneasy even though she didn't know what it meant exactly.
>
> —Judith Frank, *All I Love and Know*

Holocaust fiction written by authors who are themselves distanced from the authority of survivor testimony and its inheritance lead readers to question the very value and meaning of the term "Holocaust literature."[1] In his defense of Holocaust fiction more generally, Lawrence Langer notes that its significance can be found in "its ability to evoke the atmosphere of monstrous fantasy that strikes any student of the Holocaust, and simultaneously to suggest the exact details of the experience in a way that forces the reader to fuse and reassess the importance of both. The result is exempted from the claims of literal truth but creates an imaginative reality possessing an autonomous dignity and form that paradoxically immerse us in perceptions about that literal truth which the mind ordinarily ignores or would like to avoid."[2] Leslie Epstein, while recognizing the imbalance between eyewitness testimony of the Holocaust and the majority of fictional accounts on the subject, insists that, "lest those who destroyed European Jewry remain in a crucial sense victorious, [Holocaust fiction] *must* flourish."[3] Aharon Appelfeld notes that to "transmit the dreadful experience we need *all* our memory institutions: history writing as well as testimony, testimony as well as art."[4] Countering these views, Cynthia Ozick insists that depictions of the Holocaust "ought to remain exclusively attached to document and history" (this even as she herself engages in imagining the Holocaust).[5] Or, as Elie Wiesel claims, "A novel about Treblinka is either not a novel or not about Treblinka. A novel about Majdanek is about blasphemy. *Is* blasphemy."[6] It is this wide and contradictory range of responses that fuels Sue Vice's work, *Holocaust Fiction*. Vice plainly states that "Holocaust fictions are scandalous: that is, they invariably provoke controversy by inspiring repulsion and acclaim in equal measure."[7] Indeed, fiction, particularly that which centers on the Holocaust, relies on devices that are familiar to many varieties of fiction and include style, voice, language, and structure, and subjects these particular stories to the critical accusation that rendering fiction out of the Holocaust diminishes its historical reality.

By positioning the Holocaust as peripheral, authors may (ironically) be writing it out of history even as they—justifiably or not, consciously or not—resist tampering with it too much. Unlike earlier fictionalizations of the Holocaust (which often evoked criticism and controversy concerning their representation of evil or concerning the impossibility of representing the unrepresentable precisely because the Holocaust was the direct subject of the eyewitness), third-generation Holocaust fiction reflects on the Holocaust without sparking the accompanying wave of shock that often marked similarly designated fiction of the previous few decades. My notion of a third generation of Holocaust writers provides an explanation for this difference: it is accomplished as the representation of the Holocaust becomes indirect rather than direct and so is not subject to the same sort of analysis. Readers can account for the reason behind this shift: the historical distance between contemporary authors with their audience and the Holocaust transforms these events from a direct experience—the experience of the eyewitness, or even the experience of those closest to them, their children—to an indirect experience.

The most significant consequence of placing the Holocaust in a fictional background is that it reorients the relationship between the readable and the unreadable. Whereas we typically think of the two as oppositional forces, with the former available to decoding and deciphering and the latter resistant to these same efforts, by reducing or restraining the vast trauma and destruction of the Holocaust to the margins of a narrative, the act of reading and the act of unreading draw closer together. Precisely *because* the Holocaust is in the background, there is an understanding that it is not being read, even as it is, to some limited degree, being read. Indeed, its background status, with all of the implied limitation it holds, in some sense means that the Holocaust becomes more readable in these contexts than it does when it is central to the text.

The implication behind this sense of readability can be understood in two deeply conflicting ways as either acutely troubling or bordering on the salvational. Regarding the former, the shift in proximity between the two originally oppositional acts of reading and not reading, of the readable and the unreadable, means that the quality that marks eyewitness accounts, the quality that defines the relationship between the eyewitness and the outside reader, is emptied of meaning. Unreadability in eyewitness narrative is literal, certainly, but also symbolic; it serves to mark the limits of representation but not the limits of meaning or memory. In other words, by identifying unreadable moments, readers still happen on an important—central, even—element of testimony and memoir.

This element clearly exists even as it resists being accessed. In contrast, by moving the Holocaust to the background, third-generation authors render it literally absent—gone—little trace of it is left to be found. Unreadability claims both of these moments, linking them together, and yet the latter dissolves much of the meaning of the former. Even with these troubling implications, however, we can also understand the new proximity of unreadability to readability as bearing a redemptive quality: instead of moving further away from eyewitness testimony, which is the natural and devastating assumption for each successive generation, third-generation literature demands a powerful adjustment to the very terms that define eyewitness literature. It is an imperfect relationship, to be sure, yet a relationship nonetheless.

The indirect experience of the Holocaust that is the marker of third-generation literature can in many ways be best understood through the examination of imaginative Holocaust literature in which the Holocaust is also presented indirectly. Indeed, it is this distance that enables third-generation readers (and, with them, authors) to navigate between the two contradictory and yet inevitable consequences regarding the quality of unreadability, and with it memorialization, as it relates to the Holocaust. As Alvin Rosenfeld notes, part of the problem for any Holocaust writer "is to discover the literary forms most appropriate to representing the extremities of dehumanization and heroism that together begin to define what the Holocaust was."[8] For many third-generation authors, the Holocaust maintains a background role because the stylistic distance reflects the nature of the relationship of the author to the subject. More than any single story that centers on the Holocaust, these texts are built on a tangled triumvirate: the history of a trauma in which there are set limits of representation; the role of abstracted memory; and the presence of an audience longing for an imaginative connection between themselves and the historical event.

## THE HOLOCAUST, QUEER MEMORY, AND THE THIRD GENERATION

Aryeh Lev Stollman's novel *The Far Euphrates* (1997) opens with two oblique references that bring the narrator's voice and identity together with the larger history the novel encompasses.[9] The first occurs before the start of the story and is a citation from the testimony compiled by journalist Lucette Lagnado and the widow of an Auschwitz survivor of Dr. Josef Mengele's devastating experiments on twins: "We heard a terrible cry. The Gypsies knew they were going to be put to death, and they cried all night. They had been at Auschwitz a long time. They had seen the Jews arriving at the ramps, had watched the selections where the old people and the children went to the gas chambers. [And so] they cried. And when the Gypsies cried, all the twins heard them. And even though I was a child, only nine or ten years old, I understood" (*The Far Euphrates*, iii).[10] While this opening citation firmly establishes a vivid connection between the novel and the Holocaust, in fact the role of the Holocaust in *The Far Euphrates* remains sheltered from view, only partially emerging in the second half of the novel. In large part this reflects our growing awareness of the narrator's family's history and his development from childhood to young adulthood. The narrator, Alexander, is raised in the 1950s and 1960s in Windsor, Ontario. His father is the Orthodox rabbi of their community. When Alexander's mother, Sarah, becomes pregnant after having suffered numerous miscarriages, Alexander spends the summer with his mother's best friend, Berenice, and her husband, the cantor of his father's congregation. It is then that Berenice confides in him and tells him the terrible history of her husband and Hannalore, the cantor's sister, twins who have survived Auschwitz and Mengele's inhumane experimentation.

The second oblique reference occurs in the novel's opening line: "At dessert following a holiday lunch, I overheard my mother mention yet again her concern about me" (*The Far Euphrates*, 1). Alexander continues to recall how, as a five-year-old, he became aware of, as he later puts it, his mother resorting to a kind of "code for something she dared not speak" (*The Far Euphrates*, 4). As his mother and Berenice have afternoon tea together, Sarah calls her son "un rêveur," a dreamer. Her concern for him, as she stammeringly reveals to a fortune-teller, is that "He's . . . [a] daydreamer . . . I'm af-fraid for him. Afraid he . . . might turn out wr-wrong. He doesn't always act like a regular child" (*The Far Euphrates*, 21–22). The language describing Alexander's queerness, both in behavior and in identity, is foreign. His mother resorts to French, a language she is not comfortable with or fluent in, as a means of describing her son's differences. Her awkward speech and disruptive ill-timed pauses—illustrated through dashes, commas, spaces, and ellipses—that mark her description reveal her reluctance to articulate his differences. Alexander is a dreamer, his mother is right about that, but he is also oddly aged before his time, picking up on innuendo that ranges from the tragic to the sexually explicit. The child witness in the opening citation comments: "And even though I was a child, only nine or ten years old, I understood." Here the child understands the unspeakable, that which lies outside of language, the cry that precedes the silence. Alexander, also just a child, understands a range of coded messages with a sense of depth and clarity that belie his age. Some of these messages come through as language-oriented, but some come through his ability to read the text of the body, both his own and those around him.

To return to the opening scene in *The Far Euphrates*, joining Sarah and Berenice at tea is Hannalore, the cantor's twin sister, who visits often from Grosse Pointe, Michigan, where she works as a housekeeper in the grand mansion of Henry Ford II and assiduously hides her Jewish identity, even going so far as to wear a small gold cross around her neck. Hannalore's response to Sarah's concerns of her son's "queerness" is to urge the child to "dream on, dream on" (*The Far Euphrates*, 4), which, as the narrative develops, we see that Alexander does.

The scene sets up a complex web of post-Holocaust Jewish gendered identity. Most immediately, Sarah grapples with—and ultimately represses—her understanding that Alexander is different because he is gay. Alexander only reveals his desire to the reader once he is a teenage in, appropriately, a moment of reverie—he is hypnotized by the beauty of a neighborhood boy. The dreaming, the differences, the wrongness, the not being regular, all finally take on an explicit form, namely, a gay Jewish identity in a post-Holocaust world.

While critics have typically understood Alexander's introduction of himself as "different" in *The Far Euphrates* as reflecting his introverted nature and foreshadowing his sustained period of withdrawal from the world around him, this characterization can and should also be understood as symbolic of Alexander's difference as a gay narrator reflecting on a childhood in which he is both celebrated for being special (he is an only child, one who is virtually shared by his parents and by Berenice and the cantor) and at the same time labeled as not normal and taken to a fortune-teller (her authenticity is confirmed by her Gypsy heritage) in an attempt to at least diagnose the reason behind his dreamy strangeness if not to cure it. Indeed, the narrative position is central to the novel: an older Alexander, with a voice of experience and assurance, controls the narration, determining what is said and revealed and what remains withheld. As a narrator, Alexander's control over the body of the text, with all its included histories, imitates his decided control over the text of his body.

Moreover, this interlocking relationship provides the link to the traumatic Holocaust past of Hannalore, which is deeply connected to gender, and to Alexander's own exploration of his sexual identity and its future implications. In a novel that centers, for the reader, on the known and the unknown, the knowable and the unknowable, secrets and public knowledge, Alexander stands as a symbol of the future—Berenice calls him a "real survivor" (*The Far Euphrates*, 70)—as he casts back over his childhood and the past histories of those closest to him. Only from this perspective are readers able to learn of his moments of desire and witness the first stirrings of an emerging sexual identity. The human body in *The Far Euphrates* lies at the intersection of trauma, experience, and knowledge. It is a source of revelation, as Alexander's increasing awareness of masculine beauty illuminates; it is also a vessel that conceals a past marked by loss and trauma. "Self-contraction" is the word that Alexander uses when, on his sixteenth birthday, he retreats into himself and into his room, sews the curtains shut, and becomes himself his own object of study for a year: "Eventually and I suppose inevitably, I myself became an object of study. Every morning at dawn I locked my door and went into my bathroom and took a long shower. Then I stood and examined the container of my soul carefully in the closet mirror. I studied every square inch of my skin with a magnifying glass. . . . I felt and caressed every muscle and palpable bone" (*The Far Euphrates*, 153). It is a withdrawal that each character in the novel enacts in his or her own way, but in particular Alexander's actions resonate with the deaths of the cantor and his twin, Hannalore, the two survivors of Auschwitz and of Dr. Mengele's scientific experimentation.

Born in 1954 in Detroit to a family with ties to the Midwest, Stollman was raised in Windsor, Ontario, where his father, Rabbi Samuel Stollman, served as the rabbi of one of the local Orthodox synagogues and held a position on the English faculty at the University of Windsor. *The Far Euphrates* joins a growing collection of contemporary novels and stories that reference the Holocaust through the lens of a gay Jewish protagonist.[11] As a general marker, the terms "gay" and "Holocaust" have come increasingly to refer to the Nazi persecution of homosexuals, in particular gay men, before and during the Holocaust.[12] Contemporary gay Jewish authors who incorporate both the Holocaust and gender identity into their work, however, almost without exception reflect on the persecution of European Jewry through the voice of a present-day queer protagonist or narrator who operates at a significant distance from the experience of the Holocaust and so, by my terms, can be identified, along with the author, as third-generation.[13] In these texts the quality of unreadability in fact provides one of the few links between the limited role the Holocaust plays in the text and queer identity—that is, the narrative placement and marginalization of the story of the Holocaust mirrors the closeting and closing off of the gay body, which in *The Far Euphrates* is literally enacted when Alexander locks himself in his room for a year of self-study.

The position of the periphery, in spite of its limited view to readers—perhaps because of it—proves central to the protagonist's development. That is, the privacy afforded Alexander in his locked bedroom allows him not only to "survive" but, ultimately, to "come out"—both in the sense that he reemerges from his room and, at the same time, is able to identify himself for who he is. The most powerful assertion of his existence and identity comes through the self-narrated tale that is *The Far Euphrates*, one that relates a history both personal and historical. In his own narration, the events of the Holocaust remain a closed-off space, one Alexander and other readers can rarely access and even then only for the briefest of glimpses. By reading the Holocaust through the lens of his own intimate self-exploration, however, Alexander endows the position of marginality in *The Far Euphrates* with meaning; the presence of the unreadable is accompanied by a sense of profound and personal significance.

Indeed, this quality of unreadability is at least in part confirmed by the lack of recognition in virtually all published reviews or critiques of the novel recognizing it as both a gay and a Holocaust novel—and this in spite of *The Far Euphrates* winning the Lambda Literary Award for Gay Fiction in 1998. In her article entitled "Jewish American Fiction, Act III," in which she considers "the growing heterogeneity of America's Jewry" and, with it, the "latest phase in Jewish American fiction," Susanne Klingenstein establishes six categories that serve "as sources of creative inspiration and Jewish authenticity."[14] While

Klingenstein identifies Stollman as an author who invokes the Holocaust (one of her six categories), he is not included in her discussion of gay Jewish fiction (another category). Reviews of the novel in the *New York Times, Newsday,* the *New York Daily News,* and the *Los Angeles Times* recognize it as a novel that raises the "riddle of God's existence" after the Holocaust; as a "coming-of-age tale [that] is also a coming-home-to-religion story"; as a novel that integrates numerous subplots, "with references to opera, to the Holocaust, to Jewish mystical tradition"; a story that wanders between secrets and revelation. Writing more deeply about the novel, Janet Burstein, in her fine book *Telling the Little Secrets,* identifies the novel as one that "reshape[s] the image of home" as a "place where journeys begin . . . a place so deeply inscribed in the most intimate parts of our brains and feelings that we can neither see it clearly—nor ever look away from it."[15] Burstein never identifies the gendered elements of the novel and only touches glancingly on the role of the Holocaust in the novel. Instead, she understands the novel as one of a number of recently published works of Jewish American fiction that projects an "image of home [that] stirs both personal and collective memory."[16]

As a novel that centers almost obsessively on the body, it is perhaps fitting that readers read the novel as either one that reveals a relationship of the self within a larger landscape of time, both with an awareness of history and in anticipation of the future, or as a novel that is a coming-of-age story, one that gently explores a boy's solitary but growing awareness of homosexuality. Alexander's development occurs in an environment dominated by adults and largely defined by a sense of twinning: his mother and Berenice are jokingly called "the Bobbsey twins"; the cantor and the rabbi are community leaders; the cantor and Hannalore are biological twins. In contrast Alexander stands alone and different in an environment controlled by coupledom and relationships.

Alexander's mother's fears, as she tries—and fails—to articulate what "the problem" is with her son, is met with a quick assessment by the seer, Mademoiselle Dee Dee: "You are such a stupid woman. Just stupid. Now leave the child with Mademoiselle Dee Dee. Now!" (*The Far Euphrates,* 22). At her command, the room clears out and the narrator notes that he liked his mother being screamed at, "it made [him] feel somehow stronger, more grown up. . . . I had never questioned or faulted my mother before, and now I saw her anew, from afar, as other people might have seen her. Perhaps, I like to think, this even saved me, for I did not get caught up in her unexplained worries and fears" (*The Far Euphrates,* 22). The seer's concluding advice to Alexander is to reassure him: "You're a fine little boy. Yes, a little prince. Nothing to be ashamed of. Always take your sweet time when you need to. Time is your loyal servant" (*The Far Euphrates,* 23). Mademoiselle Dee Dee latches on to the concept of shame, even though Alexander has been brought to her out of a sense of fear. Shame, Mademoiselle Dee Dee declares, should not accompany Alexander's sense of difference, however that difference might present itself. And, indeed, this brief scene opens with an intimation that this difference is tied to gender. As Alexander enters the mansion, he notes the presence of a servant, "a handsome young man in a tight uniform . . . [who] winked at me" (*The Far Euphrates*, 18).

References to Alexander's interest in male bodies are spare but undeniably present. The most passionate of these comes shortly after Berenice confides to Alexander about the terrible experiences of her husband and Hannalore in Auschwitz. The doctor who has been tending Alexander's mother during her pregnancy sends his son, Mickey, to inform him and Berenice that Sarah has lost the baby. Mickey is one of few young men whom Alexander comes into contact with and their brief interaction leaves a lasting impression:

> He wore shorts and a thin, rain-soaked tee shirt. . . . At first I hardly listened to what he was saying, because I was staring, hypnotized, at the thick black hair that fell to his broad shoulders, his brown eyes, and at his strong hands as he gestured and spoke quickly. . . . I stood a long while and watched Mickey's back and calves as he walked and settled himself into his car. . . . After Mickey drove down the gravel driveway and swerved onto the main road, I turned around and looked at the ground. My eyes were stinging. And I knew I was crying, not because my mother was losing the baby, but because Mickey had gone and I felt so alone. (*The Far Euphrates*, 94–95)

The idea of companionship for Alexander comes not through the sense of delayed twinning that a sibling might offer but through a longing for unfamilial love, a love that is generated through desire. Adhering to the advice he heard years before from Mademoiselle Dee Dee, Alexander comforts himself, saying: "I am not ashamed. Why should I be? Why should I be?" (*The Far Euphrates*, 95). The connection between Alexander's newfound understanding of himself, the miscarriage of his prospective sibling, and his newly acquired understanding of Hannalore and the cantor's experience in Auschwitz is not at all a haphazard one, but the narrator takes his time to fully reveal the connection. The scene with Mickey and Alexander heightens the novel's already ripened awareness of the body. Together with the potential (and ultimately failed) renewal found in childbirth is the struggle to cope with the physical trauma of the Holocaust. Alexander's awareness of self-love—only achieved when he experiences and reflects upon his desire for another male body, which he does in a more sustained fashion during his year of seclusion as he fantasizes about Mickey's body while touching and examining his own—becomes a source of hope in the novel, carrying with it a sense of futurity and life.

Shortly before seeing Mickey and learning of his mother's miscarriage, Berenice reveals to Alexander the history of her husband and his sister Hannalore. Initiated by Berenice's articulation of her wish to have children, she explains that this is not possible because the cantor has been rendered sterile: "'They did a terrible operation on him, so we can't have children.' . . . Berenice took a photograph out of her purse. It was really half a photograph, cut down a previous center with an unsharp scissors. In the picture was a skeleton in striped rags with a dark, knotlike face. At first I did not realize who it was, but then I knew it was the Cantor. He looked older in the picture than he was now, and this confused me" (*The Far Euphrates*, 86–87). Taken when the camp was liberated, Berenice explains to him that the photograph originally pictured the twin siblings, Hannalore and Bernhard, standing side by side. Before giving it to Berenice, Hannalore carefully cut herself out of the picture and destroyed her half. The silence surrounding the surviving half photo pervades speech, artifact, and narrative. Berenice swears Alexander to secrecy, confessing that she has never told his parents about her husband's or Hannalore's past. The silence of the narrator matches the silence of the half-destroyed photograph itself. Susan Sontag, in *On Photography*, describes the rupture created by viewing photographs of Bergen Belsen and Dachau: "Nothing I have seen—in photographs or in real life—ever cut me as sharply, deeply, instantaneously. Indeed, it seems plausible to me to divide my life into two parts."[17] The torn photograph, the trauma suffered within symbolized by the rough cut done with dull blades, marks not only a before and an after in Alexander's life but also a rupture in the life of the twins who are both pictured through the distorted image of the cantor, Bernhard, and rendered invisible by the absence of Hannalore. The silence of the narrative is only hinted at in this passage: we learn that the cantor "almost starved to death" and was forced to undergo "a terrible operation" resulting in his inability to have children, but nothing is recorded of the torture or trauma suffered by Hannalore (*The Far Euphrates*, 87, 86). Her likeness has disappeared and, correspondingly, her history is made unavailable.

In the final pages of the novel, at the unveiling of Hannalore's gravestone, the reader along with Sarah, Alexander's mother, learns what Berenice revealed to Alexander that day:

> When the cover was withdrawn from the stone, I read the inscription. Hannalore's name was carved on top in English. As I read it I heard her own voice whispering, reading out her name to me. "Hannalore Seidengarn!" . . . I looked underneath the English lettering to the small Hebrew inscription that contained the same honeyed letters that God used to create His universe in seven days: "*Ud mutzal m'aish*." "An ember saved from the fire." Then I read Hannalore's Hebrew name: "Elchanan ben David." Elchanan son of David. . . . I see quickly the full words, a man's name, the son of another man. But at that time it seemed I was reading everything slowly, letter by individual letter, until the ember spared from fire floated before me, burning brightly, phosphorescent like the letters I used to imagine at Creation. (*The Far Euphrates*, 190–192)

Until the final pages of the novel, Hannalore's past is learned although only through inference: born Elchanan, a boy, after the war—because of what she suffered during the war—she adopts an entirely new identity, as a single woman with a husky voice, a housekeeper, adorned by the small golden cross necklace that, contrary to Jewish tradition, she requests to be buried wearing. In reading her history on her gravestone, even a drastically redacted version of it, Alexander describes a process of a gradually diminishing literacy where phrases and names disappear into letters and letters become embers, a spark of presence against a "living darkness" (*The Far Euphrates*, 193). The unreadability of Hannalore's history is accompanied by its unspeakability; the reader, along with the characters in *The Far Euphrates*, never learns anything more than a few sentence fragments regarding the trauma Hannalore suffered. As the gravestone is uncovered, Alexander's mother "began screaming in a high, unnatural voice that resembled no sound I had ever heard from her modest frame, nor any sound I could imagine coming from any human being. . . . 'No one ever told me about Hannalore! No one ever told me!'" (*The Far Euphrates*, 192, 193). The incomprehensibility of Auschwitz is captured as it shifts between inhuman sound and silence, between letters that virtually float away and the embers that remain.

Sarah's reaction to Hannalore's past brings with it a deep sense of uneasiness regarding the connection between queer identity and Holocaust memory in the novel, one that does not end with Hannalore's burial. Determining that Berenice shared Hannalore's past with her son the previous year, Sarah breaks all ties to her dearest friend, blaming her for Alexander's "craz[iness]" (*The Far Euphrates*, 196):

> Finally I said, "[Learning of Hannalore's past] did not affect me."
>
> She thought this over for a moment and then spoke calmly, slowly, as if she was only then figuring something out. As if she were talking to a crazy person.
>
> "No, it did not affect you, Alexander. It did not affect you at all. When you turned sixteen you went into your room and have stayed there for a year. Just like a zombie. . . . Didn't you ever hear of the subconscious? You did what you did at the same age that the Cantor and Hannalore were first taken away. No. It did not affect you." (*The Far Euphrates*, 195–196)

Alexander is rattled by this connection; he has never thought of the cantor or Hannalore as anything other than "middle-aged" and "worn out" (*The Far Euphrates*, 196). What emerges in this exchange are two possible means by which to understand queer identity and Holocaust memory. One, offered by Sarah, connects the two through understanding gay identity as strange, different, crazy, and tragic; the queerness of her son is connected to the violation Hannalore suffered during the war. For Alexander, though, his mother unexpectedly bridges a chasm for him, one he has never been able to cross, connecting his own positive affirmation of queerness with a sudden awareness of the cantor's and Hannalore's prewar identities. By identifying Hannalore as a fellow sixteen-year-old, Alexander reimagines her into the torn photograph he once saw of the young but old-looking cantor. Becoming aware of a past that extends to before the war and putting it together with his knowledge of Hannalore's postwar version of herself, Alexander gains an understanding of the wholeness of Hannalore as an individual that matches his long-sought understanding of himself.

In reflecting on his role as his family's historian in his first autobiographical work, *The Elusive Embrace*, Daniel Mendelsohn brings together his sense of Jewish gendered identity in a way that reflects interestingly on the figure of the narrator in *The Far Euphrates*:

> Because . . . I am the custodian of my family's stories and photographs, I also know exactly which are the faces that haunt my own: the set of my jaw and the shape of my face are the same as that of my mother's uncle, who together with his wife and four teenage daughters was executed by the Germans during the war—a fact, I cannot pretend not to know, that has only enhanced their collective beauty over the past half-century. . . . My homosexuality, when I first acknowledged it, stopped hiding from it, seemed less a surprise than a kind of fulfillment. It seemed appropriate that I now belonged to a world that existed in an eternal present, because it had no generations: the same world I had been inhabiting for years, in my hours among photo albums that were eczematous with age, shedding flakes of black paper every time I picked them up. In a picture, it is always Now. In a picture, if you're lucky, you are always beautiful.[18]

Mendelsohn's sense of connection to the past is to think of it—and him—as arrested in time and place together, a confirmation of being, a compressed moment in time where having existed in the past is yoked to current existence and to the anticipation of existing in the future. Acknowledging his homosexuality, as with Alexander's sense of his identity, serves to connect the present to the past by yoking their presence together.

"Present tense. Eternal tense." The phrase coined by Alexander embodies the kind of "clear statement, the unobstructed, even if tormenting truth" that he has spent his seclusion seeking. "They're dead. Present tense. Eternal tense. Dead," he says, referring to the cantor and Hannalore. Berenice responds: "They both *do* love you and they *do* understand. 'Present tense. Eternal tense' " (*The Far Euphrates*, 188, 189). Alexander's pronouncement, which is meant to capture the current and all future moments, resonates with Mendelsohn's "eternal present." The sense of being, of existing as oneself, permeates *The Far Euphrates*.

For both Mendelsohn and Stollman the question that arises in their work is how history, specifically the traumatic history of the Holocaust, influences or affects our understanding of ourselves. Both authors find recourse in a remarkably simple, irrefutable commonality: the presence of being. It is a dictum that requires some degree of self-awareness and self-acceptance even if these things occur on the margins of the story. Stollman goes a step further, using the language and signs of deviation—words such as "not normal" and a propensity toward silence—to connect the experience of living with a traumatic history with the experience of living with a different gendered identity. The two experiences are far from equitable, and this, too, emerges in *The Far Euphrates*: Alexander's reflections of himself emerge quietly, evenly, and with little sense of revelation. In contrast, the fragmented history of Hannalore is largely withheld until her gravestone is unveiled. In an attempt to comfort Sarah and quiet her screams, Berenice says: "They did terrible things to Hannalore, Sarah. Unspeakable.... She wanted it to be secret while she was alive, and the Cantor promised her. Let her be our Hannalore. Let her be Hannalore" (*The Far Euphrates*, 193). Berenice wants to honor Hannalore by keeping her identity in its most present form its most clearly remembered form. And yet for those who do not know Hannalore's history, for those who wander by her grave and read its Hebrew and English inscription, the identity that is hidden is the one she chose during her postwar life, her identity as a woman, one with a cross around her neck. The process of reading the Holocaust in *The Far Euphrates* is an elusive one, a process that is often and deliberately moved to the side and closed off. And yet in spite of its opaqueness, as Alexander notes on the novel's concluding page, the presence of the cantor and Hannalore, "like so many pillars of cloud and pillars of fire," lead him through his days and nights (*The Far Euphrates*, 206).

## SURVIVING HISTORY: READING NICOLE KRAUSS'S *THE HISTORY OF LOVE*

Nicole Krauss's *The History of Love* (2005) is a novel that both imagines the Holocaust and represents its historical presence in one Jewish family's American identity. The novel represents, without the privilege of direct memory, how the Holocaust can become a historical event in the writer's imagination, even if it is not part of her personal history. Indeed, the representation of the Holocaust in this novel may be read as an early witness to the end of a generation of Holocaust memoirs and to a future of Holocaust literature where imagination and history—both Holocaust and non-Holocaust history—are interpolated. *The History of Love*, one of a number of recently published Jewish American novels to recast the Holocaust, distinguishes itself from older Holocaust fictions in its narrative control, its characterizations, and its style. These differences symbolize a significant point of transition, a point of intersection, where direct memory, that experienced by eyewitnesses, and memory, generated primarily through reading, meet. This, in fact, is the mark or signature of the third generation: within the novel the Holocaust is represented indirectly, positioned as part of one of a number of histories.

The first of two primary narrators introduced in the novel is Holocaust survivor Leopold Gursky who, just as the war is breaking out in his native Poland, entrusts a book manuscript, entitled *The History of Love,* to a friend, Zvi Litvinoff, for safekeeping. After the war, believing Leo has perished, the friend publishes the book under his own name; the only evidence of the work's original author appears in the final chapter, entitled "The Death of Leopold Gursky." Not knowing that his novel has been published, Leopold sets out for New York, determined to find his longtime love, Alma, who in the intervening years has borne his son and married another man.

The second primary narrator is the fourteen-year-old Alma, whose Israeli father died of cancer seven years earlier. Alma is named after the heroine of a book called *The History of Love,* a book her father found while traveling in Spain and the book with which he wooed her mother. Her mother, a translator, has been commissioned to translate *The History of Love* by Isaac, Leo's unacknowledged son, and Alma reads her mother's translation as we read Krauss's *The History of Love.* Thus, the novel is about recent and historical events and, more abstractly, about the writing and reading of all events located in the past. In effect, readers are presented not with an eyewitness account but with an account that reflects on different formative moments in each narrator's history. The young Alma, with help from her brother, Bird, slowly pieces together Leo and the old Alma's past. Leo mourns the loss of his loved ones as Alma mourns the loss of hers. The novel's climax brings the two narrators together in New York City's Central Park Zoo.

Survival links the two primary narrators as do their creative acts: writing and reading. Leo survives the Holocaust; Alma survives the death of her father. Leo writes *The History of Love*; Alma writes *How to Survive in the Wild.* And herein lies the problem of Krauss's novel: the novel works to compress time and history, in some way relating the loss experienced by a survivor with the loss experienced by a child born half a century later. Of all the novels considered here, Krauss's novel most risks what Alvin Rosenfeld calls the "Americanization of the Holocaust," namely, an understanding of the Holocaust that "promote[s] a tendency to individualize, heroize, moralize, idealize, and universalize," for these are the terms "that Americans could readily understand."[19] This quality of Americanization, with all its generic characteristics, is most readily seen in the novel's final page, which records Leo Gursky's obituary, the one that also marks the end of Litvinoff's *History of Love*: "Leopold Gursky started dying on August 18, 1920. He died learning to walk. He died standing at the blackboard. And once, also, carrying a heavy tray. He died practicing a new way to sign his name. Opening a window. Washing his genitals in the bath. He died alone, because he was too embarrassed to phone anyone. Or he died thinking about Alma. Or when he chose not to. Really, there isn't much to say. He was a great writer. He fell in love. It was his life" (*The History of Love,* 255). The obituary neglects any mention of survival and any mention of the Holocaust and is oddly impersonal. Instead it emphasizes death, love, life—universal and even ordinary components that are part of all people's lives.

"And yet"—to use a construction that Krauss employs so effectively in the novel—precisely through its interwoven past and present, its use of various histories and "*History*"s, Krauss's novel pushes back against and complicates Rosenfeld's criticism of Americanizing the Holocaust.[20] In a rare gesture for third-generation fiction, the dedication of the novel features four black-and-white photographs grouped together as two young couples. Written above them are the lines: "For My Grandparents, who taught me the opposite of disappearing." *The History of Love* is in part inspired by the history of Krauss's paternal grandmother—a native of Slonim (Leo's birthplace) who shares her last name, Mereminski, with the "original" Alma, Leo's love. In bringing together multiple histories from different eras, and further yoking biography and fiction, Krauss's novel addresses the complex relationship between historical relevance and contemporary meaning. How is the perception of the Holocaust, the relation of those who experienced it, changed by viewing it from a post-post-Holocaust perspective—a perspective in which knowledge of the Holocaust is removed from both a firsthand account, such as that provided by a survivor, and a secondhand source, one that interacts directly with a primary source? That is, how is the perception of the Holocaust changed when viewed by the third generation? In reading the many layered history of *The History of Love*, one senses that these questions are not only technical, insofar as they relate to constructing a story, but deeply personal in meaning. Krauss struggles with precisely the process that Rosenfeld identifies as "Americanization," identifying with it as a point of accessibility—with all the dangers of trivialization this carries with it—but also recognizing that, two generations later, this inevitable aspect of historical transmission, for all its limitations, can and does prove meaningful. In writing *The History of Love*, Krauss introduces readers to fictional and real histories and through the process of layering one on top of the other both shelters the Holocaust history from over-exposure and uses it to locate the major themes of the novel.[21]

These questions and thus, too, the novel as a whole reflect concerns and tensions associated with the transmission of memory, the cultural and historical inheritance that is inevitably passed on from generation to generation. On the one hand, the transmission of historical memory serves to connect and distinguish distinguish generational memory, reinvigorating each layer. On the other hand, however, the present pushes the past further back into the background. Indeed, perhaps the most "Jewish" aspect of Krauss's novel is not her development of the character of a Holocaust survivor, but the sense that she conveys of the ties linking younger and older generations, those who participated in the events of the Holocaust directly and those who can know it only indirectly. One conversation between Alma and her mother reflects the various ways Alma conceives of herself in response to the question, "What am I?" Alma, impatient with her mother's intellectualized definitions, finally lashes out, shouting: "I'M AMERICAN!" Her brother, witnessing the exchange, corrects her: "No, you're not. You're Jewish" (*The History of Love*, 96–97). Here Alma's sense of identity is challenged by her own family history. Her declaration attempts to detach herself from her past and create herself afresh, from nothingness. That wish, fueled by her father's death and the collapse of her family, is an impossibility, but one that reflects her sense of self and her desire to be, at least momentarily, unaffiliated with *any* culture, simply an individual. Her brother's response—part denial, "No, you're not," and part declaration, "You're Jewish"—encapsulates the thrust of the novel, namely, that history renders impossible an absolute sense of individuality, that those around one will never allow one to be completely alone. Alone as Leo Gursky believes himself to be, and as separate as Alma may strive to be, neither can escape the embrace of the past or the inevitability of the future. Thus a history that reaches far enough back to include the Holocaust, as Leo's does, and the more recent history of Alma Singer, connect and reinforce each other.

This relational concept is expansive and resonates with a much older sense of Jewish history, as seen in an early passage in Ecclesiastes: "One generation passes away and another generation comes, but the earth abides forever" (Eccl. 1:4). Humans are limited by their own mortality, by the shared sense that ultimately no one survives oneself. Although we come from a line of generations and although, like those before us, we will come and go, there is a common foundation on which we depend that not only endures but works to connect us. The Holocaust survivor depends on members of succeeding generations both to remember the past and to live anew, to relate to history that has not been directly experienced by them and also to create their own individual histories.

The experience of history as conveyed in Ecclesiastes, from generation to generation, becomes more fraught when considered in light of Holocaust memory, as illustrated by Krauss's novel. The tension stems from the novel's treatment of all histories, all historical events, with a manner of even-handedness. Alma's history and Leo's history are connected: Alma's very name recalls his world in Poland before it collapsed around him. When Alma introduces herself to Leo in the Central Park Zoo, we see this dramatically acted out: "I stood in front of him. He barely seemed to notice. I said, 'My name is Alma.' And that's when I saw her.... She looked different than I remembered her. And yet. The same. The eyes: that's how I knew her.... Stalled at the age when she loved you most" (*The History of Love*, 241–242). Instead of thinking, "Stalled at the age when she loved *me* most," which would be the most natural construction, Leo pulls the reader into his emotional interior: "Stalled at the age when she loved *you* most." The "you" is all-encapsulating, it refers to Alma and to Leo, certainly, and also to a more collective set of eyes witnessing this meeting, namely, to those who are reading about it. Indeed, the "you" suggests that Leo has joined readers in reading the novel of his own making.

It is this embracing concept of history that makes the novel so compelling: one story doesn't overpower another; one character doesn't reside in the shadow of another. History alone, whether of the Holocaust or of love—an odd conjunction—provides a deep sense of interweaving between individuals otherwise unknown to one another. Out of love, Krauss suggests, history can speak to the insistent inclusion of cultural memory, an inclusion that reaches beyond the pages of *The History of Love*, all four versions (Krauss's, Leo's, Litvinoff's, and Charlotte Singer's, the young Alma's mother), and touches readers as well as authors, translators, and plagiarists.

*The History of Love* repeatedly returns to the view that all histories are not equal. Elie Wiesel writes: "Whoever has not lived through the event can never know it. And whoever has lived through it can never fully reveal it."[22] The challenge faced by first-generation writers of the Holocaust, those with the direct experience of survival, discloses the utter inadequacy of memory and representation for conveying their experience, both for themselves and for their readers.[23] For second-generation writers, situated at a "further temporal and spatial remove from the decimated world of their parents," memory and representation is an imagined re-creation of experience, an "imaginative investment and creation."[24] If the struggle of second-generation writers of the Holocaust involves repopulating a void of memory, the struggle for third-generation Holocaust writers lies in crossing not one but two gaps, that of experience and that of memory. In order to imagine the Holocaust, third-generation writers both rely on text and imagine text. In short, third-generation writers work to represent a text of the text.[25]

This duality, a sense of re-creating the re-created, asserts itself in *The History of Love* insofar as the novel is both the story of one man's life and love, that man being Leo Gursky, and the story of life, of love. The contrast between the two is a contrast between the particular or individual and the universal. Alma's search for the author of *The History of Love* is an attempt to reclaim the particular from the universal, to peel back one layer of text in search of the story, to bridge both the gap of memory and that of experience in order to represent and to remember the Holocaust. Is it even possible to read *The History of Love* as a Holocaust novel?

The answer is twofold: when understanding, and reading the Holocaust in universal terms, that is, with the understanding that it could have happened at another time and another place and involved other victims and perpetrators, then, yes, it is a Holocaust novel. The inheritance of the Holocaust can be read—and understood not only historically (this is what happened to your ancestors) but contemporarily (this is what could and in some sense, *would* have happened to you). The double remove involved in a third-generation text weighs the history of the Holocaust as different from and somewhat more than other independent histories. Leo's feeling of loss colors Alma's life, and while it doesn't prevent her from experiencing her own losses, or her own history, it informs her understanding of them. But *The History of Love* requires readers to view the Holocaust also from a particularist perspective: that is, by understanding the Holocaust as an event that involved individual victims and individual perpetrators. Failing to represent the Holocaust in this way, generalizing it, falsifies it, making it something other, and less, than it was.[26] As a narrative tool, the Holocaust in *The History of Love* becomes an entity marked by a singular kind of agency: one man's story can be—is—accessed and processed and, in effect, runs into the problem of precisely *not* telling the story of the Holocaust it professes to do. In short, the novel's strength—creating a moving and compelling character, Leo Gursky, who survives the Holocaust, is also its weakness—creating a character (whether Leo or Alma) who survives.

The relationship between two generationally distinct characters in *The History of Love* illuminates the position of that book as a third-generation text and, additionally, facilitates the Holocaust's abiding background presence, but the relationship is not the only aspect that establishes this. The playfulness found in *The History of Love,* as evidenced in the novel's often droll tone and its distinctive style involving space and lettering, are two other means by which Krauss works to maintain a carefully worked out balance between Holocaust memory and a contemporary American Jewish world. Humor colors the novel's opening lines and, indeed, is found throughout the novel: "When they write my obituary. Tomorrow. Or the next day. It will say, 'LEO GURSKY IS SURVIVED BY AN APARTMENT FULL OF SHIT.'" Leo's status as a survivor, as alive, is represented in some way by the inert staying power of the inanimate—newspaper clippings, clothes, pots and pans; and this representation seems to diminish the act of living implied by survival, itself an achievement, making it seem dispensable and easy to overlook. There is undeniably a wry sense of laughter in this opening passage, one that is sustained through, for example, references to Leo's nude modeling for an art class or in his attempts to generate attention to himself at drugstores by knocking over the stand holding K-Y Jelly. What is suggested here is that Leo is a survivor in many senses: the survivor of a heart attack, the survivor of numerous mostly unsuccessful visits to the toilet, the survivor of the Nazis. It is not just the scatological humor that marks Leo Gursky's daily life, his observations of his "sagging *knedelach*" (*The History of Love,* 16) or the various descriptions of his bowels that "never cease to appall" him (*The History of Love,* 17). Rather, traces of laughter connect survival and the present.

Who laughs? Not the survivor-writers Leo Gursky, Alma Singer, Zvi Litvinoff, or Charlotte Singer. They write about laughter in a way that recognizes both its elusiveness and its ordinariness. Leo's first attempt for his book title is: "LAUGHING & CRYING" (*The History of Love,* 27). He rejects that for: "LAUGING & CRYING & WRITING" and rejects that one for: "LAUGHING & CRYING & WRITING & WAITING" (*The History of Love,* 29, 31). Alma writes that her father "LIKED TO COOK AND LAUGH AND SING" (*The History of Love,* 41). The two primary narrators not only write of laughter, they create it. Their actions, thoughts, and responses provoke the reader's laughter or, at least, an awareness of irony, humor, wit. The production of laughter serves to draw Alma and Leo together, even as the variations in their lives and histories might separate them. Symbolically, this connection is significant because it serves to make relevant and relative a third-generation perspective in a first-generation context.

Terrence Des Pres, while acknowledging the need to present the Holocaust as solemn, even sacred, also defends representing the Holocaust using humor as "a more flexible mode of response. . . . The paradox of the comic approach is that by setting things at a distance it permits us a tougher, more *active* response."[27] Krauss seems intent on making the reader actively *feel. The History of Love* does not evoke only pathos, although it does that as well. It also evokes laughter, wistfulness, irony, all of which are tied to the tension that is a result of reading about the familiar against the unfamiliar. Unlike fiction that takes place in a Holocaust setting, where the reader's sense of an ending is a foregone conclusion (and can never end well), in *The History of Love* Krauss creates, through emotional range, a sense of capacity, a sense of potential: we do not know how it will end.[28] Leo and Alma confirm this understanding in their concluding dialogue when he asks her about his novel, *The History of Love*: "*Tell me which parts you liked . . . I wanted to make you laugh . . . Also to cry*" (*The History of Love,* 248; italics in the original).

A more ironic example of humor in the novel occurs shortly before Leo's meeting with Alma Singer at the end of the novel, when Leo recounts how he successfully hid from two German soldiers because one was so engrossed in telling the other of his wife's affair:

> Once I was hiding in a potato cellar when the SS came. The entrance was hidden by a thin layer of hay. Their footsteps approached, I could hear them speaking as if they were inside my ears. There were two of them. One said, *My wife is sleeping with another man,* and the other said, *How do you know?* and the first said, *I don't, I only suspect it,* to which the second said, *Why do you suspect it?* while my heart went into cardiac arrest, *It's just a feeling,* the first said and I imagined the bullet that would enter my brain, *I can't think straight,* he said, *I've lost my appetite completely.* (*The History of Love,* 238).

In many ways the passage is emphatically not funny: one man must hide under the threat of death, while two other men talk about the goings on in their daily lives. One man barely lives while the other two live normally. But there is also an interesting irony underlying Leo's description. He lives under fear of discovery; his would-be murderer has just become a discoverer. He imagines the bullet in his brain; his would-be murderer "can't think straight." As a Jew, Leo is a victim; as a cuckold, the soldier is a victim. In short, the passage illuminates commonalities between the people involved and also between the emotions evoked. The idea here is not only that humor and tragedy share positions at the ends of one emotional continuum but that it brings together a Jew and a Nazi effectively (albeit temporarily) mocking the racial superiority of the latter and elevating the position of the former.

Playfulness informs not only tone in *The History of Love* but also its style: Krauss toys with punctuation and typographical convention. In the novel's final meeting between Leo and Alma, the series of exchanges shift between being conventionally and unconventionally recorded. In the exchanges that Leo narrates, dialogue appears as italicized text; in the exchanges that Alma narrates, dialogue appears as it normally would, non-italicized and with indentation and quotation marks:

> [New page] I said, "I was named after every girl in a book called The History of Love."
>
> [New page] I said, *I wrote that book.*
>
> [New page] "Oh," I said. "I'm serious. It's a real book."
>
> [New page] I played along. I said: *I couldn't be more serious.*
>
> [New page] I didn't know what to say. He was so old. Maybe he was joking or maybe he was confused. To make conversation I said, "Are you a writer?"
>
> He said, "In a manner of speaking . . ." (*The History of Love*, 241–247)

Toward the novel's conclusion, for example, very few lines cover each page. Instead, the rhythm of reading achieves a sense of urgency through movement: both the eye and the hand are flexed as the novel rapidly comes to a close. There is an inescapable sense of buildup to the climax, when Alma and Leo finally recognize each other, one that readers participate in actively. The narrative, centered in the middle of the page, is surrounded by blank space. The blankness is a historical record of sorts, one that symbolizes absence and silence, one that recognizes the limitations of language and narrative in a Holocaust context. The absence of conventional punctuation reinforces the sense that, at its most comprehensive, *The History of Love* is the history of the self—"I"—a single story. It is not so much about a Leo, or a soldier, or an Alma, or a Bird. Rather, the narration delivers a sense of meshed identity, a result of the various interactions accumulated over the course of a lifetime. In the passage where Leo hides from the two soldiers, they become part of his history, of his identity. This becomes clear not only through their moments of commonality but also because Leo often identified as the italicized speaker, the position they occupy in that particular exchange.

Krauss cannot resolve the problem that writing about the Holocaust presents, namely, the need to memorialize for the current reader both the particular individual and the idea of the individual. In certain ways Alma takes over Leo's story. This is not the act of appropriation that for some critics is a trademark of

Americanizing the Holocaust. Peter Novick, in his seminal work *The Holocaust in American Life*, argues that increased awareness and attention to the Holocaust took place during the 1970s and 1980s because doing so provided a sense of identity for an increasingly fragmented Jewish community.[29] But Alma's identity, as she herself declares, is a debate between Americanness and Jewishness. What Krauss provides us with here is a means to see the act of taking over memory as one in which a younger generation carries it forward, effectively becoming one of its custodians. This sense of guardianship is imperfect—necessarily so—and its background status is a constant reminder of its limitations. But it also speaks, at times romantically at times realistically, to the future of memory, to its changed form but also to its possibility in future decades, generations, and centuries. Through the character of the two Almas, Krauss creates a sense that generational memory moves not only from the past to the present but from the present to the past, from the old to the young and from the young to the old. This blurring effect between generations bridges the double remove of her position as a third-generation Holocaust writer; and the mirror position of her characters, Alma and Leo, who face the similar problem of making history (and History) relevant to themselves as writers and to each other as readers.

# AFTERWORD

## Reading the Fragments of Memory

When I leaf through these pages I often feel deeply discouraged: . . . these lines, often clumsy, are very far removed, I know, from my memories, and even my memories retrieve only sparse fragments. . . {. Should I go on?}

—Saul Friedlander, *When Memory Comes*

There among the ghosts
between the barracks,
crematorium's ruins,
silence full of murmurs
audible, visible, but
only to me

—Halina Birenbaum, "There Is My Soul"

There is a value in recognizing the limits of reading, or the unreadable, in Holocaust literature.[1] My argument in support of "unreadability" depends on a conventional and presumptive view of contemporary reading: we read in order to experience, to feel, to understand, to learn from, to empathize with, to imitate, to be inspired by text. Reading at its most powerful is a deeply intuitive moment or series of moments of connection and understanding. It is precisely from this background *as* conventional and presumed that my notion of unreadability in connection with traumatic narratives such as those concentrating on the Holocaust gains meaning. As so many survivor-writers note how words fail to convey the breadth of their experience, this book has shown how reading these words carries its own limitations, limitations that, in spite of being unbridgeable, carry deep and symbolic meaning.

There are three modes of unreadability that correlate in both kind and form to the generational structure of Holocaust and post-Holocaust authorship. The notion of unreadability, or textual silence, is most readily identified in the texts of eyewitnesses and survivors for the simple reason that they, the author-eyewitnesses, write not only with an audience in mind but often with a great deal of self-consciousness, admitting to themselves and their readers the inadequacy of language and ability in conveying memory and history and, consequently, acknowledging that just as these limits make a whole representation not possible, these limits make accessibility through reading equally unattainable. Indeed, I go so far as to argue that precisely this awareness on the part of survivor-authors, whose sense of readership is filtered through personal traumatic experience and memory, not only permits us to acknowledge the presence of the unreadable but, even further, elevates its position both literarily and morally.

In his autobiography, *The Story of a Life,* Aharon Appelfeld recognizes the "limit of conscious memory." He continues: "On some occasions I have been able to listen to my body, and then I would write a few chapters, but even they are just fragments of a pulsing darkness that will always be locked inside me."[2] Appelfeld advises his readers not to "expect a sequential and precise account. . . . Much has been lost and corroded by oblivion."[3] I have made a case that enlarges on Appelfeld's and other survivor-authors' gestures regarding reading—namely, identifying what cannot be read, what is "lost and much corroded," is in fact a central part of our reading experience and needs to be more consciously observed as such.

The trope of fragmented memory is often invoked in quite literal terms in literature written by children who have survived the Holocaust. Susan Suleiman, in deciding to write about her wartime memories, notes that they are "fragmentary, incomplete, but possessing a vividness that surprised me."[4] Dori Katz, hidden by a Flemish family in Belgium, never identified as a Holocaust survivor and dismissed her memories of the war as "vague and fragmented"; "inconsequential."[5] In his postwar diary, Michal (Michael) Kraus punctuates his memories of seeing his parents for the last time with reflections around the challenge of writing about the memories, suggesting that the act of narrating itself should be an exercise not in wholeness or entirety but, rather, one that approaches the past and memory in a piecemeal fashion, with gaps, pauses, and interjections registering as part of the narrative:

> At that time—in the summer of 1944, at the beginning of July, I saw my dearest parents for the last time. It is hard for me to describe how I felt at the time. . . . Leaving father was terrible. I see him in front of me, emaciated, sick. How he cried, he who had always been so good to everyone, and now I left him behind, left him to die. I can't think about this because it was the most horrible moment of my life. . . . They led us to the gate, in the direction of the Sauna. . . . It is painful to remember all those who at that time remained . . . those who never returned from the transports.[6]

I turn to the language of children survivors in this final section because traditionally subsequent generational markers of Holocaust literature are defined in relation to one's parents and grandparents. The record left by children survivors is linked to second- and third-generation Holocaust authors, the children and grandchildren of survivors (and those who identify generationally but not in terms of their direct family lineage), by virtue of the designation of all as children. And yet while the sense of fragmentation of memory and narrative is a trope that survivor, second-generation, and post-Holocaust literature all hold in common, it is the written records left by children survivors, and not by their descendants, that exhibit the greatest attentiveness and, if possible, even equanimity with the idea of the impossibility of an incomplete narrative, of a reflection of memory that is punctuated by textual silence.

The presence and role of unreadability or textual silence in second-generation Holocaust literature is complicated by the typically self-identified desire to discover a narrative able to be written—that is, a narrative rendered readable—of their parents' wartime experiences. In effect, second-generation writers attempt to locate a specific kind of trauma they have witnessed but not experienced. Their search for a possible narrative structure reveals them not only as writers telling the narrative of one generation earlier but also as being in the position of readers whose attempts to read have been perpetually and necessarily thwarted. Second-generation writers recognize and even value the boundaries of unreadability, even as they acknowledge a desire to participate more fully in their parents' process of remembering. In her essay "Postmemory, Postmemoir," Leslie Morris examines "the remnants and the echoes and the ruin of the symbiosis in texts that push at the borders between fact and fiction, documentary and memory."[7] In her explanation behind coining the term "postmemory," Marianne Hirsch describes her need to create "a special term to refer to the secondary, belated quality of my relationship with times and places that I had never experienced," but which played a vivid role in her memory. Postmemories, she notes, are "mediated by the stories, images, and behaviors among which [she] grew up, [but they] never added up to a complete picture or linear tale." Rather, their inscrutability was passed down: "unintegrated, conflicting, fragmented, dispersed."[8] Holocaust literature written by children of survivors marks a troubled continuity of the process of writing and reading tied to the survivor generation. Second-generation narrative is predicated on the impossibility of firsthand experience and, instead, evolves as a perpetual mediation between layers of memories and experiences, "a constant interrogation of the nature of the original."[9]

Third-generation or post-Holocaust authors face yet another, different relationship to the historical and traumatic memory of the Holocaust. Because of historical distance, post-Holocaust authors typically have no direct relation to the events, and so recovery occurs through the experience of textuality or artifactuality, that is, through the act of both writing and reading the unreadable. Texts authored by third-generation writers often obscure the fact and nature of unreadability, and this itself is a marker both of the transitional sense of "readability" in relation to Holocaust trauma and an innate human urge to narrate stories that are whole rather than fragmented or piecemeal. It is precisely the ebbing away of *un*readability in third-generation Holocaust literature that marks it as a literature of loss. Such loss of a direct relationship to the events that are unreadable presents this literature as eminently readable—precisely because readability is an essential condition for representation in the absence of the events themselves. Sarah Wildman's *Paper Love* finely documents the author's investigation to uncover the identity and history of Valy, an early love of her grandfather's, a woman who, unable to leave Germany, was murdered in Auschwitz. To Wildman's credit, she opens her concluding findings on Valy by noting what is not and cannot be known: "I can find not further information about what happened to Valy after she boarded the 27th Ost Transport from Putlitzstrasse train station in Berlin Moabit to Auschwitz. She may have died en route. She may have been gassed upon arrival. I know only that she had no number assigned to her, and the vast majority of those who arrived in Auschwitz and received no number were those deemed, immediately, expendable."[10]

Post-Holocaust memoir, in attempting to reinscribe both its own narrative and, in turn, its own sense of readability from the fragmented memories of the past, leads us to fictionalized versions of the past. In terms of the acts of reading that I have grappled with here, I have started as close to the actual event of the Holocaust as one can possibly read and end as far from this point of origin as possible, coming to an examination of Holocaust fiction produced in a different time and place from when and where the events of World War II unfolded. Even further, I examine fiction that relegates the Holocaust to the margins of narrative, so that it both registers its historical presence but at the same time marginalizes or fractures it. Exploring the fiction of American authors who rely on their own memories of the war such as Cynthia Ozick, Philip Roth, and Chaim Potok, as well as of authors born decades later, I make the case that novels that "read" as Holocaust novels and novels that are typically not considered Holocaust novels in fact occupy increasingly overlapping spheres, where imagination and history are interpolated into and read as a hybrid genre. This mode of reading and readability is simultaneously a mode of unreading and unreadability, and this is both a strength and a weakness. The effort to popularize the trauma of the Holocaust in an effort to better understand or draw closer to it in fact accomplishes precisely the opposite, presenting a barrier toward accessing the fragments of memory that are indeed available. And yet symbolically, by holding the Holocaust at a distance, by relegating it to the background, novels such as the ones explored here also recognize the need to treat the Holocaust as a setting that places special burdens—limits—on characters, on words, on sentences, on paragraphs, and so, in turn, on readers.

# ACKNOWLEDGMENTS

In spite of this book's focus on the meaning and presence of the unreadable, I have been supported and nurtured throughout its writing by a community of astute, thoughtful and wonderful readers. The kernel of this study was first defined at the conference for Jewish American and Holocaust Literature. I thank Alan Berger, Victoria Aarons, the late wonderful Dan Walden and, more recently, Ezra Cappell and Holli Levitsky for bringing us together. I am indebted to the United States Holocaust Memorial Museum for supporting my work with two short-term fellowships. Thanks to Dieter Kuntz, Leah Wolfson, and Robert Ehrenreich for welcoming me to the Mandel Center and making my time there so productive. I also wish to thank Dr. Annemarie Nicols-Grinenko and the CUNY Office of Academic Affairs for their support of my scholarship.

Much of the work on this book was done during a sabbatical (2013–2014) and I gratefully acknowledge Baruch College and the City University of New York. Many colleagues at Baruch offered their friendship and support throughout the writing of this book and beyond. Thanks to Ruth Adler, Tim Aubry, Paula Berggren, Roslyn Bernstein, Ellen Block, John Brenkman, Frank Cioffi, Eva Chou, Gerard Dalgish, Gilad Harel, Carmel Jordan, Elaine Kauvar, Susan Locke, Meir Lubetski, Bill McClellan, Mary McGlynn, Corey Mead, Don Mengay, Joshua Mills, Sean O'Toole, Grace Schulman, Ely Shipley, and Cheryl Smith. Barbara Gluck, dear mentor and friend, would surely have celebrated this project's coming to fruition. A special thanks to Jeffrey Peck and Jessica Leitner for their interest, help and support. Jacques Berlinerblau invited me to speak about this project at Georgetown University. Our subsequent conversations helped me develop certain ideas about American Jewish literature. I owe so much to Alyssa Quint and Shelly Eversley, who read and commented on numerous drafts and willingly gave of their time, wisdom and friendship. Josh Levin, Lisa Silverman, Shaindy Aber, Russ Jacobs, Yoni Slonim, Rifki Zable, Esther Sperber, Bruce Goldberger, Aleeza and Dmitry Nemirof, and Alyssa and Howard Shams paired hospitality with a willingness to hear more about this work; their curiosity and conversation spurred me on and helped me to think and write more clearly. Yehuda Levy-Aldema listened to my ideas about silence—and responded in a way that gave me courage to continue. Tal Kastner brightened many solitary days in Butler Library. A special thank you to Barbara Sicherman, Julie Klein, Scott Mankowitz, Shaindy Aber (again!), and Dorota Wojtas for the gift of their many years of friendship, especially over the past year and a half. I recognize with a deep sense of gratitude the many wonderful Baruch students who participated in my Holocaust classes, lectures, and abroad programs. From another circle entirely, thanks to Francine Alfandary, Rachel Berger, Fran Breslauer, George Mannes, and David Wackman, who covered many miles with me while talking me through certain points—both book-related and not.

Portions of chapter 5 were previously published in "Violence, Redemption, and the Shoah," *Studies in American Jewish Literature* 27 (2008): 68–86. © Penn State University Press, 2009. Used by permission of The Pennsylvania State University Press.

Portions of chapter 6 were previously published in "*The History of Love*, the Contemporary Reader, and the Transmission of Holocaust Memory," *Journal of Modern Literature* 33.1 (Fall 2009): 43–56. © Indiana University Press, 2009.

The production of this book was done with wonderful care and attention at Rutgers University Press. Micah Kleit and especially Elisabeth Maselli were responsive, thoughtful and kind, providing just the right kind and amount of guidance throughout the publication process. Jennifer Blanc-Tal helped me through the final stages. I was so pleased to be able to profit from Marilyn Campbell's knowledge and experience before she retired. My thanks go out to them and the entire production team at the press.

My best readers are also those closest to me. My parents, Berel Lang and Helen Lang, my first teachers, inspired within me a lifelong connection to and reverence for language, literacy, and text. Indeed, it was arguing with my father on behalf of writers who write *not* to be read that ultimately led me to this project. Their love has supported me always. I feel so very lucky to have profited from the kindness and generosity of Barbara Estrin, and Almut and Reiner Riegel. Ariella Lang's encouragement and help, her willingness to read and comment on drafts with an amazing combination of generosity and rigor, were so very important to me throughout my work on this book and beyond. I am grateful for my many conversations with Alex Kornfeld, whose own history has informed my thinking. Joerg Riegel's keen analysis, his unwavering enthusiasm, his careful attention to language and form strengthened this project both in style and substance. His companionship and love enrich my life beyond what I can describe here. Our children, Hannah, Leah and David, whose passion for stories is a joy to witness, are an inspiration to my own understanding of the meaning behind reading.

# NOTES

## INTRODUCTION

1. The epigraph is from George Steiner, *On Difficulty and Other Essays* (New York: Oxford University Press, 1980), 45.
2. Ruth Kluger, *Still Alive: A Holocaust Girlhood Remembered* (New York: Feminist Press at the City University of New York, 2003), 18.
3. Wolfgang Iser, *The Act of Reading: A Theory of Aesthetic Response* (Baltimore: Johns Hopkins University Press, 1978), 108.
4. Elie Wiesel, *From the Kingdom of Memory: Reminiscences* (New York: Summit Books, 1990), 14, 15.
5. Robert D. Newman, *Transgressions of Reading: Narrative Engagement as Exile and Return* (Durham, NC: Duke University Press 1993), 1.

## CHAPTER 1—READABILITY AND UNREADABILITY: A FRACTURED DIALOGUE

1. This is Primo Levi's sequel to his memoir *If This Is a Man* (the American title is *Survival in Auschwitz*). The chapter epigraph is from Aharon Appelfeld, *Beyond Despair: Three Lectures and a Conversation with Philip Roth*, trans. Jeffrey M. Green (New York: Fromm International Publishing Corporation, 1994), 79.
2. Primo Levi, *The Reawakening*, trans. Stuart Woolf (New York: Simon and Schuster, 1995), 21.
3. Primo Levi, *Survival in Auschwitz: The Nazi Assault on Humanity*, trans. Stuart Woolf (New York: Simon and Schuster, 1996), 22.
4. Oren Baruch Stier, *Holocaust Icons: Symbolizing the Shoah in History and Memory* (New Brunswick, NJ: Rutgers University Press, 2015), 72.
5. Werner Hamacher, "Working through Working," trans. Matthew T. Hartman, *Modernism/Modernity* 3 (1996): 27.
6. Levi, *The Reawakening*, 25–26.
7. Giorgio Agamben, *Remnants of Auschwitz: The Witness and the Archive*, trans. Daniel Heller-Roazen (New York: Zone Books, 2002), 38.
8. Kalí Tal, *Worlds of Hurt: Reading the Literatures of Trauma* (New York: Cambridge University Press, 1996), 6.
9. M. M. Bakhtin, *The Dialogic Imagination: Four Essays* (Austin: University of Texas Press, 2010), 276–277.
10. Appelfeld, *Beyond Despair*, ix, xii–xiii.
11. Jean-Paul Sartre, "Was ist Literature? Ein Essay," in Jean-Paul Sartre, *Situations Volume II*, trans. Hans Georg Brenner (Hamburg: Rowohlt, 1950), 35.
12. Iser, *The Act of Reading*, 107.
13. Roland Barthes, *Image-Music-Text*, trans. Stephen Heath (New York: Noonday Press, 1977), 148.

**14.** Ibid., 47.
**15.** Peter Smagorinsky, *Vigotsky and Literacy Research: A Methodological Framework* (Boston: Sense Publishers, 2011); L. S. Vygotsky, *Mind in Society: The Development of Higher Psychological Processes*, ed. Michael Cole, Vera John-Stein, Sylvia Scribner, and Ellen Souberman (Cambridge, MA: Harvard University Press, 1978).
**16.** Martin Nystrand, *The Structure of Written Communication: Studies in Reciprocity between Writers and Readers* (Orlando, FL: Academic Press, 1986).
**17.** Frank Smith, *Understanding Reading: A Psycholinguistic Analysis of Reading and Learning to Read* (New York: Routledge, 2004), 28.
**18.** Paul Ricoeur, *Interpretation Theory: Discourse and the Surplus of Meaning* (Fort Worth: Texas Christian University Press, 1976), 72, 75.
**19.** Hayden White, "The Metaphysics of Narrativity: Time and Symbol in Ricoeur's Philosophy of History," in Hayden White, *The Content of the Form: Narrative Discourse and Historical Representation* (Baltimore: Johns Hopkins University Press, 1987), 173.
**20.** Ibid., 178.
**21.** J. A. Appleyard, *Becoming a Reader: The Experience of Fiction from Childhood to Adulthood* (New York: Cambridge University Press, 1994), 9–10.
**22.** Thelma Z. Lavine, "Postmodernism and American Pragmatism," *Journal of Speculative Philosophy* 7 (1993): 111–112.
**23.** I refer here to John Felstiner's translation of "Todesfuge"/"Deathfugue" found in Paul Celan, *Selected Poems and Prose of Paul Celan*, ed. and trans. John Felstiner (New York: W. W. Norton, 2001), 30–33.
**24.** John Felstiner, *Paul Celan: Poet, Survivor, Jew* (New Haven, CT: Yale University Press, 2001), 35.
**25.** Theodor Adorno, "Cultural Criticism and Society," in Theodor Adorno, *Prisms*, trans. Samuel Webber and Shierry Webber (Cambridge, MA: MIT Press, 1983), 33–34.
**26.** Adorno, in a retraction of his initial statement, states that "Perennial suffering has as much right to expression as a tortured man has to scream; hence it may have been wrong to say that after Auschwitz you could no longer write poems. But it is not wrong to raise the less cultural question whether after Auschwitz you can go on living—especially whether one who escaped by accident, one who by rights should have been killed, may go on living." Theodor Adorno, *Negative Dialectics*, trans. E. B. Ashton (New York: Continuum, 1973), 362–363.
**27.** Shoshana Felman and Dori Laub, *Testimony: Crises of Witnessing in Literature, Psychoanalysis, and History* (New York: Routledge, 1991), 3.
**28.** James Young, "Interpreting Literary Testimony: A Preface to Rereading Holocaust Diaries and Memoirs," *New Literary History* 18 (1987): 404.
**29.** Ibid., 412.
**30.** Cynthia Ozick, "Who Owns Anne Frank?" in Cynthia Ozick, *Quarrel and Quandary* (New York: Alfred A. Knopf, 2000), 80.
**31.** Ibid., 102.
**32.** Michael G. Levine, *The Belated Witness: Literature, Testimony, and the Question of the Holocaust* (Stanford, CA: Stanford University Press, 2006), 4.
**33.** George Steiner, *Language and Silence: Essays on Language, Literature, and the Inhuman* (New Haven, CT: Yale University Press, 1998), 11–12.
**34.** Jean Améry, *At the Mind's Limits*, trans. Sidney Rosenfeld and Stella D. Rosenfeld (Bloomington: Indiana University Press, 1980), 20.
**35.** Winifried Georg Sebald, *On the Natural History of Destruction* (New York: Random House, 2003), 162.

**36.** Elie Wiesel, "The Holocaust as Literary Inspiration," in *Dimensions of the Holocaust*, ann. Elliot Lefkovitz (Evanston, IL: Northwestern University Press, 1977); Berel Lang, *Holocaust Representation: Art within the Limits of History and Ethics* (Baltimore: Johns Hopkins University Press, 2000).
**37.** Cynthia Ozick, "The Rights of History and the Rights of Imagination," in Steven T. Katz and Alan Rosen, eds., *Obliged by Memory: Literature, Religion, Ethics* (Syracuse, NY: Syracuse University Press, 2006), 5.
**38.** Ibid., 5, 17.
**39.** J. Hillis Miller, *The Ethics of Reading: Kant, de Man, Eliot, Trollope, James, and Benjamin* (New York: Columbia University Press, 1987), 4.
**40.** Ibid., 2.
**41.** Daniel Schwarz, "The Ethics of Reading: The Case for Pluralistic and Transactional Reading," *NOVEL: A Forum on Fiction* 21 (1988): 198.
**42.** Ibid.
**43.** Adam Zachary Newton, *Narrative Ethics* (Cambridge, MA: Harvard University Press, 1995), 11.
**44.** Ibid., 285.
**45.** Diary entry from Monday, 25 May 1942, in Abraham Lewin, *A Cup of Tears: A Diary of the Warsaw Ghetto*, ed. Antony Polonsky, trans. Christopher Hutton (Oxford: Basil Blackwell, 1988), 97.
**46.** Schwarz, "The Ethics of Reading"; Newton, *Narrative Ethics*.
**47.** Wayne Booth, *The Company We Keep: An Ethics of Fiction* (Berkeley: University of California Press, 1988), 9.
**48.** Ibid., 14.
**49.** Ibid., 16–17.
**50.** Shoshana Felman, "Turning the Screw of Interpretation," *Yale French Studies* 55/56 (1977): 142.
**51.** Ibid., 143.
**52.** Imre Kertész, *Dossier K.*, trans. Tim Wilkinson (Brooklyn, NY: Melville House Publishing, 2013), 1.
**53.** Ibid., 8–9. Italics in the original.
**54.** Cynthia Ozick, *Bloodshed and Three Novellas* (Syracuse, NY: Syracuse University Press, 1976), 38.
**55.** Booth, *The Company We Keep*, 10.
**56.** Berel Lang, "Introduction," *Writing and the Holocaust*, ed. Berel Lang (New York: Holmes and Meier, 1988), 1–2.
**57.** Berel Lang, *Act and Idea in the Nazi Genocide* (Chicago: University of Chicago Press, 1990), 117–118.
**58.** Jakob Lothe, Susan Rubin Suleiman, and James Phelan, "Introduction," in *After Testimony: The Ethics and Aesthetics of Holocaust Narrative for the Future*, ed. Jakob Lothe, Susan Rubin Suleiman, and James Phelan (Columbus: Ohio State University Press, 2012), 10.
**59.** Louise Rosenblatt, *The Reader, the Text, the Poem* (Carbondale: Southern Illinois University Press, 1994), 27.
**60.** James Phelan, "The Ethics and Aesthetics of Backward Narration in Martin Amis's *Time's Arrow*," in Lothe, Suleiman, and Phelan, *After Testimony*, 121–122.
**61.** Ibid., 122.
**62.** Rosenblatt, *The Reader, the Text, the Poem*, 22, 25. Italics in the original.
**63.** Phelan, "Ethics and Aesthetics," 122.

## CHAPTER 2—BEFORE, DURING, AND AFTER: READING AND THE EYEWITNESS

**1.** Alexandra Garbarini, *Numbered Days: Diaries and the Holocaust* (New Haven, CT: Yale University Press, 2006), 1. The epigraph is from Ann Kirschner, *Sala's Gift: My Mother's Holocaust Story* (New York: Free Press, 2006), 7.

**2.** Paul de Man, *Allegories of Reading: Figural Language in Rousseau, Nietzsche, Rilke, and Proust* (New Haven, CT: Yale University Press, 1979), 245.

**3.** Shoshana Felman in "After the Apocalypse: Paul de Man and the Fall to Silence," chapter 5 of *Testimony*, explicitly links de Man's theories of reading to the Holocaust claiming that they "bear implicit witness to the . . . Holocaust's historical disintegration of the witness." Felman and Laub, *Testimony*, 139. Felman develops her argument in part as a way of understanding de Man's silence in light of the revelation that he wrote morally compromising columns for a Belgian pro-Nazi newspaper, *Le Soir*, in 1941 and 1942. That said, Felman's rationalization of de Man's wartime writing, along with those by Jacques Derrida and others, has been seriously criticized. My wish here is not to investigate the controversy but, rather, to trace the use of the word "unreadability." Resources that confront de Man's pro-Nazi writings include the following: Jacques Derrida, "Like the Sound of the Sea Deep within a Shell: Paul de Man's War," *Critical Inquiry* 14 (1988): 590–652; Geoffrey Hartman, "History and Judgment: The Case of Paul de Man," *History and Memory* 1 (1989): 55–84; John Brenkman and Jules David Law, "Resetting the Agenda," *Critical Inquiry* 15 (1989): 804–811; W. Wolfgang Holdheim, "Jacques Derrida's Apologia," *Critical Inquiry* 15 (1989): 784–796; Paul Morrison, "Paul de Man: Resistance and Collaboration," *Representations* 32 (1990): 50–74; Daniel R. Schwarz, "The Narrative of Paul de Man: Texts, Issues, Significance," *Journal of Narrative Technique* 20 (1990): 179–194; Heather Macdonald, "The Holocaust as Text: Deconstruction's Final Solution to the de Man Problem," *Salmagundi* 92 (1991): 160–173; Dominick LaCapra, "The Personal, the Political, and the Textual: Paul de Man as Object of Transference," *History and Memory* 4 (1992): 5–38.

**4.** This sense of haunting filters through a comment Derrida made in an interview conducted toward the end of his life: "Still today there remains in me an obsessive desire to save in uninterrupted inscription, in the form of a memory, what happens—or *fails to happen* . . . of keeping a trace of all the voices which were traversing me—or were *almost doing so*—and which as to be so precious, unique, both specular and speculative. I've just said 'fails to happen' and 'almost doing so' so as to mark the fact that what *happens*—in other words, the unique event whose trace one would like to keep alive—is also the very desire that what does not happen should happen." Jacques Derrida, "An Interview with Jacques Derrida," in Jacques Derrida, *Acts of Literature*, ed. Derek Attridge (New York: Routledge, 1991), 34–35.

**5.** De Man, *Allegories of Reading*, 77; Miller, *The Ethics of Reading*, 47.

**6.** Indeed, one could argue that de Man's anti-Semitic writing makes it impossible for him to have a reader relationship to Holocaust writing.

**7.** Charlotte Delbo, *Days and Memory*, trans. Rosette Lamont (Marlboro, VT: Marlboro Press, 1990), 3–4.

**8.** Charlotte Delbo, *Auschwitz and After*, trans. Rosette C. Lamont (New Haven, CT: Yale University Press, 1995), 70.

**9.** Levi, *Survival in Auschwitz*, 21, 22, 34. The English translation preserves the use of single quotation marks found in the original text.

**10.** Ibid., 34.

**11.** Levi, *The Reawakening*, 37.

**12.** Ibid., 43.

**13.** Ibid., 52.

**14.** David Krell, *Of Memory, Reminiscing, and Writing: On the Verge* (Bloomington: Indiana University Press, 1990), 1.
**15.** Maurice Blanchot, *The Writing of Disaster*, trans. Ann Smock (Lincoln: University of Nebraska Press, 1996), 121.
**16.** U.S. Holocaust Memorial Museum, Steven Spielberg Film and Video Archive, "Eichmann Trial—Sessions 25 and 26—Testimony of Z. Lubetkin, Y. Zuckeran, A. Berman, R. Kuper," available at http://www.ushmm.org/online/film/display/detail.php?file_num=2130&clip_id=CDAEA092-37E3-4F29-8B79-9A9B915990C2/. Minutes: 42:45:20–43:46:22.
**17.** Tim Cole, *Selling the Holocaust: From Auschwitz to Schindler, How History Is Bought, Packaged, and Sold* (New York: Routledge, 2000), 62.
**18.** Jeffrey Feldman, "The Holocaust Shoe: Untying Memory: Shoes as Holocaust Memorial Experience," in Edna Nahshon, ed., *Jews and Shoes* (New York: Berg, 2008), 119.
**19.** Ibid., 119.
**20.** James Young, *The Texture of Memory: Holocaust Memorials and Meaning* (New Haven, CT: Yale University Press, 1993), 132.
**21.** Cole, *Selling the Holocaust*, 111.
**22.** Ibid., 112.
**23.** Links to several such memorial projects are included here: http://mustangnews.net/cal-polys-hillel-hosts-holocaust-memorial/; http://news.mit.edu/1998/hillel; http://sunderlandcollege.ac.uk/2013/01/shoes-help-to-build-bridges-in-sunderland/.
**24.** Michael Bernard-Donals, *Forgetful Memory: Representation and Remembrance in the Wake of the Holocaust* (Albany: State University of New York Press, 2009), 6.
**25.** Levi, *Survival in Auschwitz*, 107.
**26.** The different spellings of Gattermann's name reflect a decision on the part of the translator and publisher of *Survival in Auschwitz*. For more on Gattermann's life and professional contributions please see Ralph E. Oesper, "Ludwig Gattermann," *Journal of Chemical Education* 19 (1942): 444–445.
**27.** Primo Levi, *The Drowned and the Saved*, trans. Raymond Rosenthal (New York: Vintage Books, 1989), 97.
**28.** Ian Mackenzie, *Paradigms of Reading: Relevance Theory and Deconstruction* (New York: Palgrave Macmillan, 2002), 52.
**29.** Iser, *The Act of Reading*, 111.
**30.** I am indebted to the work of Susan Suleiman and Inge Crosman and their collection of essays, *The Reader in the Text: Essays on Audience and Interpretation* (Princeton, NJ: Princeton University Press, 1980).
**31.** Delbo, *Days and Memory*, 1–2.
**32.** Indeed, in the collective biography that Delbo assembled after the war, *Convoy to Auschwitz*, in which she provides sketches for all 230 French women who, because of their activities in the French Resistance, were sent to Auschwitz, one of the 49 survivors, Simone "Poupette" Alizon, responds, when asked how she adapted to life postwar: "'We haven't been spared the thousand difficulties of daily life; they were just added to past sufferings. . . . Yet I have no regrets. You see, in my world, limited to the hotel [her family's business], I would never have met women like you.' She added: 'When I was there, I used to think: "If I get back, I'll read all the books Charlotte talked to me about." And I have.'" Charlotte Delbo, *Convoy to Auschwitz: Women of the French Resistance*, trans. Carol Cosman (Boston: Northeastern University Press, 1997), 19.
**33.** Levi, *Survival in Auschwitz*, 39–40.
**34.** Ibid., 41.
**35.** Ibid., 40.

**36.** Ibid., 41.

**37.** Giuliana Tedeschi, *There Is a Place on Earth: A Woman in Birkenau* (New York: Pantheon, 1992).

**38.** Most of the Jews held in Drancy were deported to Auschwitz-Birkenau. Raymond Berr was arrested and taken to Drancy twice. The second time his wife, Antoinette Berr, and one of his five children, Hélène, were arrested with him. All three of them were deported to Auschwitz-Birkenau. None of them survived.

**39.** Hélène Berr, *The Journal of Hélène Berr*, trans. David Bellos (New York: Weinstein Books, 2008), 78.

**40.** Mariette Job, "Afterword: A Stolen Life," ibid., 275.

**41.** Berr, *The Journal of Hélène Berr*, 78, 79.

**42.** The idea of the "feedback loop" as a means of describing the experience of reading is from Appleyard, *Becoming a Reader*, 9–10.

**43.** All references refer to Imre Kertész, *Kaddish for an Unborn Child*, trans. Tim Wilkinson (New York: Random House, 2004), and will be given parenthetically in the text.

**44.** Traditionally, close male relatives recite the "Kaddish" daily, and only in the presence of a minyan, or quorum, for the eleven months following the death of a parent and then on every anniversary of the date of his or her death.

**45.** The opening lines, *yitgadal v'yitkadash*, are drawn from the book of Ezekiel and celebrate the grandeur of God in the eyes of all the nations (Ezekiel 28:23).

**46.** Cathy Caruth, *Unclaimed Experience: Trauma, Narrative, and History* (Baltimore: Johns Hopkins University Press, 1996), 61.

**47.** Ibid., 62.

**48.** Ibid., 59.

**49.** Elie Wiesel, "The Death Train," in Jacob Glatstein, Israel Knox, and Samuel Margoshes, eds., *Anthology of Holocaust Literature* (New York: Atheneum, 1985), 6–7.

**50.** Garbarini, *Numbered Days*, 155, 155, 155, 154.

**51.** Ibid., 154.

**52.** Feigl Bisberg-Youkelson and Rubin Youkelson eds., *The Life and Death of a Polish Shtetl*, trans. Gene Bluestein (Lincoln: University of Nebraska Press, 2000), 105.

**53.** Garbarini, *Numbered Days*, 154.

**54.** Delbo, *Auschwitz and After*, 238, 239.

**55.** Bisberg-Youkelson and Youkelson, *Life and Death*, 98.

**56.** Garbarini, *Numbered Days*, 154.

**57.** Mackenzie, *Paradigms of Reading*, 52.

## CHAPTER 3—READING TO BELONG: SECOND-GENERATION AND THE AUDIENCE OF SELF

1. The epigraph is from Helen Epstein, *Children of the Holocaust: Conversations with Sons and Daughters of Survivors* (New York: Penguin Books, 2010), 11.

2. Lisa Appignanesi, *Losing the Dead* (Toronto: McArthur, 1999), 78.

3. Phyllis Lassner, *Anglo-Jewish Women Writing the Holocaust: Displaced Witnesses* (New York: Palgrave Macmillan, 2008), 118.

4. Paula Fass, *Inheriting the Holocaust: A Second-Generation Memoir* (New Brunswick, NJ: Rutgers University Press, 2011), 110.

5. Bracha Lichtenberg-Ettinger, *Halala-Autiswork* (Aix-en-Provence: Louis-Jean Depot, 1995), 137.

6. Eva Hoffman, *After Such Knowledge: Memory, History, and the Legacy of the Holocaust* (New York: Public Affairs, 2004), 11–12.
7. Eva Hoffman, *Lost in Translation: A Life in a New Language* (New York: Penguin Books, 1989), 23.
8. Hoffman, *After Such Knowledge*, 16.
9. Marianne Hirsch, "The Generation of Postmemory," *Poetics Today* 29 (2008): 107.
10. Ibid., 103, 106.
11. Ibid., 107.
12. Gary Weissman, *Fantasies of Witnessing: Postwar Efforts to Experience the Holocaust* (Ithaca, NY: Cornell University Press, 2004), 17.
13. Marianne Hirsch, *Family Frames: Photography, Narrative, and Postmemory* (Cambridge, MA: Harvard University Press, 1997), 22–23; Henri Raczymow, "Memory Shot through with Holes," *Yale French Studies* 85 (1994): 98–106.
14. "Afterimages" is the title of Carol Ascher's memoir, which I refer to later in this chapter. The term also is reflected in Nicholas Chare's study, *Auschwitz and Afterimages: Abjection, Witnessing, and Representation* (New York: I. B. Tauris, 2011). "Children of Job" is used by Alan Berger and Naomi Berger in their work on the second generation. Many different sources use some version of the term "secondary witnesses."
15. Hoffman, *After Such Knowledge*, 103, xv.
16. Alan L. Berger, *Children of Job: American Second-Generation Witnesses to the Holocaust* (Albany: State University of New York Press, 1997); Alan L. Berger and Naomi Berger, eds., *Second Generation Voices: Reflections by Children of Holocaust Survivors and Perpetrators* (Syracuse, NY: Syracuse University Press, 2001), 1.
17. Ernst van Alphen, "Second-Generation Testimony, Transmission of Trauma, and Postmemory," *Poetics Today* 27 (2006): 473–488; Janet Handler Burstein, *Telling the Little Secrets: American Jewish Writing since the 1980s* (Madison: University of Wisconsin Press, 2006); Erin Heather McGlothlin, *Second-Generation Holocaust Literature: Legacies of Survival and Perpetration* (Rochester, NY: Camden House, 2006); Marita Grimwood, *Holocaust Literature of the Second Generation* (London: Palgrave Macmillan, 2007).
18. The earliest work on children of Holocaust survivors was done by Canadian psychiatrist Dr. Vivian Rakoff in 1966. Vivian Rakoff, "Long Term Effects of the Concentration Camp," *Viewpoint* (1966): 17–21. The term "second-generation," however, was not regularly used until nearly a decade later.
19. J. J. Sigal, D. Siver, V. Rakoff, and B. Ellin, "Some Second-Generation Effects of Survival of the Nazi Persecution," *American Journal of Orthopsychiatry* 43 (1973): 320–327.
20. "Second-generation" is also a term applied to immigrant families, a term that evolved earlier than its application to children of Holocaust survivors. Alejandro Portes and Rubén G. Rumbaut, *Immigrant America: A Portrait* (Berkeley: University of California Press, 2006); Min Zhou, "Growing Up American: The Challenge Confronting Immigrant Children and Children of Immigrants," *Annual Review of Sociology* 23 (1997): 63–95; Deborah Dash Moore, "At Home in America? Revisiting the Second Generation," *Journal of American Ethnic History* 25 (2006): 156–168.
21. Helen Epstein reviews the early reception to the research of Drs. Sigal and Rakoff in *Children of the Holocaust.*
22. All references are from Art Spiegelman, *Maus I: My Father Bleeds History* (New York: Pantheon, 1986), and Art Spiegelman, *Maus II: A Survivor's Tale: And Here My Troubles Began* (New York: Pantheon, 1992) and will be given parenthetically in the text.
23. For more on the Jewish post-Holocaust body in *Maus,* see Michael Rothberg and Art Spiegelman, "'We Were Talking Jewish': Art Spiegelman's 'Maus' as 'Holocaust' Production," *Contemporary Literature* 35 (1994): 661–687.

**24.** A number of articles have responded to the image of the absent mother in *Maus*: Marianne Hirsch, "Family Pictures: *Maus,* Mourning, and Postmemory," *Discourse* 15 (1992–1993): 3–30; Dominick LaCapra, " 'Twas the Night before Christmas': Art Spiegelman's *Maus,*" in Dominick LaCapra, *History and Memory after Auschwitz* (Ithaca, NY: Cornell University Press, 1998), 139–179; Nancy Miller, "The Art of Survival: Mom, Murder, Memory," in Nancy Miller, *Bequest and Betrayal: Memoirs of a Parent's Death* (New York: Oxford University Press, 1996), 97–125.

**25.** All quotations from *Maus* preserve the author's emphases (either through bold font or capital letters).

**26.** Nancy K. Miller, "Cartoons of the Self-Portrait of the Artist as a Young Murderer: Art Spiegelman's *Maus,*" in *M/E/A/N/I/N/G: An Anthology of Artists' Writings, Theory, and Criticism*, ed. Susan Bee and Mira Schor (Durham, NC: Duke University Press, 2000), 393.

**27.** Alan Rosen, *Sounds of Defiance: The Holocaust, Multilingualism, and the Problem of English* (Lincoln: University of Nebraska Press, 2005), 170.

**28.** All references are to Martin Lemelman, *Mendel's Daughter* (New York: Free Press, 2006), and will be given parenthetically in the text. All quotations preserve the emphases (either through bold font or capital letters) of the author.

**29.** Jill Bennett, *Empathic Vision: Affect, Trauma, and Contemporary Art* (Palo Alto, CA: Stanford University Press, 2005), 36.

**30.** Marianne Hirsch, *The Generation of Postmemory: Writing and Visual Culture after the Holocaust* (New York: Columbia University Press, 2012), 36–37.

**31.** Hirsch, *Family Frames*, 22.

**32.** W. J. T. Mitchell, *Picture Theory: Essays on Verbal and Visual Representation* (Chicago: University of Chicago Press, 1994), 192.

**33.** Here I rely on Hirsch's important definitions for familial and affiliative postmemory, two structures of transmission with familial postmemory limited to the relationship that the second generation bears to their parents' memories and affiliative postmemory encompassing the postgeneration as a whole. Hirsch, *The Generation of Postmemory*, chapter 1.

**34.** Michel Kichka, *Deuxième génération: Ce que je n'ai pas dit à mon père* [*Second generation: What I didn't tell my father*] (Paris: Dargaud, 2012). All translations from the original are mine. I thank Joerg Riegel for his help with the translating.

**35.** Ibid., 29, 74.

**36.** Ibid., 5.

**37.** Several documents are copied in their original form into the text. The most significant of these is an artwork by Kichka's teacher featuring a boy with a masklike face holding a toy train with Birkenau in the background. This powerful image is accompanied by an explanation that his teacher's parents helped Jews during the war. Kichka speculates that the boy in some way represents his teacher. Ibid., 40–41.

**38.** Ibid., 6.

**39.** Ibid., 7.

**40.** Ibid., 8.

**41.** Ibid., 7.

**42.** Rosen, *Sounds of Defiance*, 174.

**43.** Spiegelman, *Maus I*, 158–159.

**44.** Hirsch, *The Generation of Postmemory*, 35.

**45.** Ibid.

**46.** Hillary Chute, " 'The Shadow of a Past Time': History and Graphic Representation in 'Maus,' " *Twentieth Century Literature* 52 (2006): 203.

**47.** Spiegelman, *Maus I*, 104.

48. Bernice Eisenstein, *I Was a Child of Holocaust Survivors* (New York: Riverhead Books, 2006).
49. Most of the originals—drawn while Kantor was in Terezin, Auschwitz, and Schwarzheide, a satellite camp for Sachsenhausen—were lost or destroyed during the war.
50. Ibid., 96–97.
51. Kichka, *Deuxième génération*, 81.
52. Ibid.
53. Kichka also marks foreignness through accents and the incorporation of Yiddish, although to a much lesser extent than Spiegelman or Eisenstein. Kichka's grandfather, a native of Poland, congratulates Michel on his school report card saying "Je svis très contont, Michel!" instead of "Je suis très content, Michel!" ("I am very pleased, Michel!" or, with the accent, something to the effect "I em very heppy, Michel!") (*Deuxième génération*, 18). Another example is found in the rabbi's congratulations at Michel's bar mitzvah: "Ti as très bien récitei!" instead of "Tu as très bien recité!" ("You recited [your Torah portion] very well!") (*Deuxième génération*, 43) In addition to foreignness being marked by an accent in the French text, the character Henri Kichka, who speaks unaccented French, occasionally speaks in Yiddish, which the author Kichka incorporates accurately—that is, not through transliteration, but with the appropriate Hebrew lettering.
54. Iser, *The Act of Reading*, 111.
55. Spiegelman, *Maus I*, 103.
56. Chute, "The Shadow of a Past Time," 199–230.
57. Melvin Jules Bukiet, "The Library of Moloch," in Melvin Jules Bukiet, *While the Messiah Tarries* (Syracuse, NY: Syracuse University Press, 1995), 188.
58. Ibid., 194. For additional information on second-generation literature, see Alan L. Berger, "Bearing Witness: Second Generation Literature of the 'Shoah,'" *Modern Judaism* 10 (1990): 43–63.
59. Carolyn Steedman, *Dust: The Archive and Cultural History* (New Brunswick, NJ: Rutgers University Press, 2002), 21. Here Steedman makes the case that those who spent time in the archive were exposed to dangerous components found in bookmaking that often led to physical illness such as migraine headaches or meningitis and even death.
60. Jacques Derrida, *Archive Fever: A Freudian Impression*, trans. Eric Prenowitz (Chicago: University of Chicago Press, 1996), 11.
61. Ibid., 2.
62. O'Driscoll and Bishop succinctly call this "private histories about encounters with private histories." Michael O'Driscoll and Edward Bishop, "Archiving 'Archiving,'" *English Studies in Canada* 30 (2004): 2.
63. Ibid.
64. Agamben, *Remnants of Auschwitz*, 158.
65. Ibid.
66. O'Driscoll and Bishop, "Archiving 'Archiving,'" 2.
67. Arlene Stein, *Reluctant Witnesses: Survivors, Their Children, and the Rise of Holocaust Consciousness* (New York: Oxford University Press, 2014), 144.
68. Ibid.
69. Ibid., 148–151.
70. Ibid., 151. See also Elisabeth Young-Bruehl, "The Biographer's Empathy with Her Subject," in Elisabeth Young-Bruehl,*Subject to Biography: Psychoanalysis, Feminism, and Writing Women's Lives* (Cambridge, MA: Harvard University Press, 1998).
71. Fass, *Inheriting the Holocaust*, 92.
72. Michel Foucault, *The Archeology of Knowledge*, trans. A. M. Sheridan Smith (New York: Vintage Press, 1982), 129.

**73.** Irving Velody, "The Archive and the Human Sciences: Notes towards a Theory of the Archive," *History of the Human Sciences* 11 (1998): 1–16.
**74.** Hoffman, *After Such Knowledge*, 206–207.
**75.** Ibid., 207.
**76.** Foucault, *The Archeology of Knowledge*, 129.
**77.** Hoffman, *After Such Knowledge*, 214–215.
**78.** Wei-Jue Huang and William J. Haller, "The Journey 'Home': An Exploratory Analysis of Second-Generation Immigrants' Homeland Travel," available at http://scholarworks.umass.edu/cgi/viewcontent.cgi?article=1281&context=gradconf_hospitality/. See also Lynette Russell, "Remembering Places Never Visited: Connections and Context in Imagined and Imaginary," *International Journal of Historical Archaeology* 16 (2012): 401–417; Niamh Moore and Yvonne Whelan, *Heritage, Memory, and the Politics of Identity: New Perspectives on the Cultural Landscape* (Abingdon, UK: Ashgate, 2007); Vicki Bell, ed., *Performativity and Belonging* (Oxford: Sage Publications, 1999).
**79.** Carol Ascher, *Afterimages: A Family Memoir* (Teaneck, NJ: Holmes and Meier, 2008), 105.
**80.** Ibid., 141–142.
**81.** Fass, *Inheriting the Holocaust*, 92.
**82.** Helen Epstein, *Where She Came From: A Daughter's Search for Her Mother's History* (Teaneck, NJ: Holmes and Meier, 2005), 17.
**83.** Ascher, *Afterimages*, 115.
**84.** Appignanesi, *Losing the Dead*, 95.
**85.** Derrida, *Archive Fever*, 2.
**86.** For more on the archive as a system of discursive power, see Foucault, *The Archeology of Knowledge*, 126–131.
**87.** Appignanesi, *Losing the Dead*, 230.
**88.** Epstein, *Where She Came From*, 17.
**89.** Hoffman, *After Such Knowledge*, 3.

## CHAPTER 4—THE THIRD GENERATION'S HOLOCAUST: THE STORY OF TIME AND PLACE

**1.** The epigraph is from Kate Cohen, *The Neppi Modona Diaries: Reading Jewish Survival through My Italian Family* (Hanover, NH: University Press of New England, 1997), 262.
**2.** Demographer and statistician Sergio DellaPergola estimates that the number of Shoah survivors amounted to 1,092,000. See Sergio DellaPergola, *Review of Relevant Demographic Information on World Jewry*, a report for the International Commission on Holocaust Era Insurance Claims (Jerusalem, 2003), 1–65 (hereafter cited as DellaPergola, *Review*). This number was significantly higher than the number prepared a month earlier by Ukeles Associates, whose report concludes that a total of 687,900 Jewish victims were still alive. See Ukeles Associates, *An Estimate of the Current Distribution of Jewish Victims of Nazi Persecution*, a report for the International Commission on Holocaust Era Insurance Claims (New York, 2003), 1–12 (hereafter cited as Ukeles, *Estimate*). The main discrepancy between the two numbers stems from the fact that the former report includes within it "the incorporation of North African and Middle Eastern communities that were mistakenly omitted in previous assessments." DellaPergola, *Review*, 7.
**3.** U.S. Holocaust Memorial Museum, "Survivors and Victims," available at http://www.ushmm.org/remember/the-holocaust-survivors-and-victims-resource-center/survivors-and-victims/.

4. Ukeles, *Estimate,* 4. An earlier report conducted by Ukeles Associates was commissioned in 2000. See the Ukeles Associates, *A Plan for Allocating Successor Organization Resources,* a report for the Conference on Jewish Material Claims against Germany (New York, 2000). Other earlier demographic studies of Holocaust survivors were certainly conducted, with differing results, most of which are addressed in the reports referenced here.

5. DellaPergola, *Review,* 3. Italics in the original.

6. Amiram Barkat, "Who Counts as a Holocaust Survivor?" *Ha'Aretz,* 18 April 2004, available at http://www.haaretz.com/who-counts-as-a-holocaust-survivor-1.119868/.

7. Dori Katz, *Looking for Strangers: The True Story of My Hidden Wartime Childhood* (Chicago: University of Chicago Press, 2013); Dori Katz, "Looking for Strangers" (Paper presented at Baruch College, CUNY, 4 November 2014).

8. Ukeles, *Estimate,* 4; DellaPergola, *Review,* 11–13.

9. Melvin Jules Bukiet, ed., *Nothing Makes You Free: Writings by Descendants of Jewish Holocaust Survivors* (New York: W. W. Norton, 2003), 16.

10. Eric Ehrenreich, *The Nazi Ancestral Proof: Genealogy, Racial Science, and the Final Solution* (Bloomington: Indiana University Press, 2007), 108.

11. Dreifus explores her grandparents' history and her relationship to it in her collection of short stories: Erika Dreifus, *Quiet Americans: Stories* (Boston: Last Light Studio, 2011). The essay I cite from here is Erika Dreifus, "Ever After? History, Healing, and 'Holocaust Fiction' in the Third Generation," in in *Beyond Camps and Forced Labour: Current International Research on Survivors of Nazi Persecution,* edited by Johannes-Dieter Steiner and Inge Weber-Newth (Osnabrück: Secolo Verlag, 2005), 524–30.

12. Gary Weissman prefers to use the term "nonwitness" in an effort to locate the history of a reader or speaker more precisely. While the term is useful because it flattens out the hierarchy of more distant connections to Holocaust victims, it is limiting for this same reason. Many second- and third-generation authors express a need to be identified as such and the word "nonwitness" fails to do this. Weissman, *Fantasies of Witnessing,* 18–24.

13. Iser, *The Act of Reading,* 107.

14. Daniel Mendelsohn, *The Lost: A Search for Six of Six Million* (New York: HarperCollins, 2006), 147.

15. Ibid., 210.

16. Ibid., 210–212.

17. Ioanna Kohler, "The Discovery of Oneself: An Interview with Daniel Mendelsohn," trans. Anna Heyward, *Paris Review,* 1 July 2014, available at http://www.theparisreview.org/blog/2014/07/01/the-discovery-of-oneself-an-interview-with-daniel-mendelsohn/.

18. Ibid.

19. Sidra DeKoven Ezrahi, "Representing Auschwitz," *History and Memory* 7 (1995): 122.

20. Ibid., 121.

21. Mendelsohn, *The Lost,* 112.

22. I am indebted to Bjorn Krondorfer's article "Is Forgetting Reprehensible? Holocaust Remembrance and the Task of Oblivion," *Journal of Religious Ethics* 36 (2008): 233–267. While Krondorfer never turns to versions of remembering and forgetting for the third generation, his argument on the role of oblivion informs my understanding of third-generation narrativity.

23. Mendelsohn, *The Lost,* 503.

24. Vikram Seth, *Two Lives: A Memoir* (New York: HarperCollins, 2005), 234.

25. Ibid., 224–225.

26. Ibid., 225–226.

27. David Laskin, *The Family: Three Journeys into the Heart of the Twentieth Century* (New York: Viking Penguin Group, 2013), 246–247.

**28.** Ibid., 363.
**29.** Edmund de Waal, *The Hare with Amber Eyes: A Hidden Inheritance* (New York: Picador, 2010).
**30.** Ibid., 241.
**31.** Carol Vogel, "Poetry Written in Porcelain," *New York Times*, 29 August 2013, available at http://www.nytimes.com/2013/09/01/arts/design/edmund-de-waal-prepares-for-an-exhibition.html/.
**32.** Felman, "Turning the Screw." Felman's thinking on the relationship of the unreadable to the readable in James's text was helpful to my own understanding of those concepts in a different setting.
**33.** Appignanesi, *Losing the Dead*, 95–96.
**34.** Ascher, *Afterimages*, 123.
**35.** De Waal, *The Hare with Amber Eyes*, 248.
**36.** Mendelsohn, *The Lost*, 19. Italics are in the original. Mendelsohn spells "*kessle*" a few different ways in *The Lost*, but always with the same definition.
**37.** Ibid.
**38.** Ibid., 128.
**39.** Ibid., 482.
**40.** Daniel Asa Rose, *Hiding Places: A Father and His Sons Retrace Their Family's Escape from the Holocaust* (New York: Simon and Schuster, 2002), 33.
**41.** Ibid., 350.
**42.** Ibid., 372.
**43.** My understanding of postmemory (see chapter 2), relies on Marianne Hirsch's most limited definition, one that does not extend past the second generation.
**44.** Mendelsohn, *The Lost*, 112.
**45.** Ibid., 501.
**46.** Ibid., 37.
**47.** Erin Einhorn, *The Pages In Between: Holocaust Legacy of Two Families, One Home* (New York: Simon and Schuster, 2008).
**48.** Ibid., 98.
**49.** Susan Rubin Suleiman, "The 1.5 Generation: Thinking about Child Survivors and the Holocaust," *American Imago* 59 (2002): 277. Emphasis in the original.
**50.** Einhorn, *The Pages In Between*, 24.
**51.** Ibid., 21.
**52.** Ibid., 6.
**53.** Cohen, *The Neppi Modona Diaries*, 262.
**54.** Einhorn, *The Pages In Between*, 6.
**55.** Rutu Modan, *The Property* (Montreal: Drawn and Quarterly, 2013).
**56.** Ibid., 158.
**57.** Marc Sobel, "The Rutu Modan Interview," *Comic Journal*, 29 May 2013, available at http://www.tcj.com/rutu-modan/2/.
**58.** Einhorn, *The Pages In Between*, 250.
**59.** Ibid., 251.
**60.** Ibid., 95.
**61.** Mendelsohn, *The Lost*, 183.
**62.** Elaine Scarry, *The Body in Pain: The Making and Unmaking of the World* (New York: Oxford University Press, 1987), 38.
**63.** Einhorn, *The Pages In Between*, 99, 100.
**64.** Mendelsohn, *The Lost*, 168.

65. Ibid., 180.
66. Einhorn, *The Pages In Between*, 101.

## CHAPTER 5—AMERICAN FICTION AND THE ACT OF GENOCIDE

1. The epilogue is from Elaine M. Kauvar, "An Interview with Cynthia Ozick," *Contemporary Literature* 26 (1985): 378.
2. Geoffrey Hartman suggests that as "even the most faithful memories fade, the question of what sustains Jewish identity is raised with a new urgency." Geoffrey Hartman, ed., *Holocaust Remembrance: The Shapes of Memory* (Cambridge: Blackwell, 1994), 7. Likewise, although limited to Jewish Americans, Walter Benn Michaels argues that in order to "[sustain] identity," Jewish Americans lean toward memory rather than history. Walter Benn Michaels, " 'You Who Never Was There': Slavery and the New Historicism, Deconstruction and the Holocaust," *Narrative* 4, no. 1 (1996): 1–16.
3. Lawrence L. Langer, *The Holocaust and the Literary Imagination* (New Haven, CT: Yale University Press, 1975), xii.
4. Alvin H. Rosenfeld, *A Double Dying: Reflections on Holocaust Literature* (Bloomington: Indiana University Press, 1980), 13. Three writers who first, and most famously, explored this tension are Theodor W. Adorno, "Engagement," in *Gesammelte Schriften* (Frankfurt am Main: Suhrkamp Verlag, 1974); George Steiner, *In Bluebeard's Castle: Some Notes Towards the Redefinition of Culture* (New Haven, CT: Yale University Press, 1971); and Elie Wiesel, "The Holocaust as Literary Inspiration," in *Dimensions of the Holocaust*, ann. Elliot Lefkovitz (Evanston, IL: Northwestern University Press, 1977); Elie Wiesel, "For Some Measure of Humility," *Sh'ma* 5/100 (31 October 1975); Elie Wiesel, *A Jew Today*, trans. Marion Wiesel (New York: Random House, 1978).
5. Sara R. Horowitz, *Voicing the Void: Muteness and Memory in Holocaust Fiction* (Albany: State University of New York Press, 1997), 8, 16.
6. Berel Lang, *Act and Idea in the Nazi Genocide* (Chicago: University of Chicago Press, 1990), xvii–xviii, 146.
7. Critical misgivings are expressed in George Steiner, *Language and Silence: Essays on Language, Literature and the Inhuman* (New Haven, CT: Yale University Press, 1998); Steiner, *In Bluebeard's Castle*; Edward Alexander, *The Resonance of Dust: Essays on Holocaust Literature and Jewish Fate* (Columbus: Ohio State University Press, 1980); Sidra DeKoven Ezrahi, *By Words Alone: The Holocaust in Literature* (Chicago: University of Chicago Press, 1982); Michael Rothberg, *Traumatic Realism: The Demands of Holocaust Representation* (Minneapolis: University of Minnesota Press, 2000); Michael Rothberg, *Multidirectional Memory: Remembering the Holocaust in the Age of Decolonization* (Stanford, CA: Stanford University Press, 2009); Emily Miller Budick, *The Subject of Holocaust Fiction* (Bloomington: Indiana University Press, 2015); Hana Wirth-Nesher and Michael P. Kramer, eds., *The Cambridge Companion to Jewish American Literature* (New York: Cambridge University Press, 2003); Robert Eaglestone, *The Holocaust and the Postmodern* (New York: Oxford University Press, 2005); J. Hillis Miller, *The Conflagration of Community: Fiction before and after Auschwitz* (Chicago: University of Chicago Press, 2011); Ruth Franklin, *A Thousand Darknesses: Lies and Truth in Holocaust Fiction* (New York: Oxford University Press, 2010); Susan Suleiman, *Crises of Memory and the Second World War* (Cambridge, MA: Harvard University Press, 2006).
8. Langer, *The Holocaust and the Literary Imagination*, 8; Alexander, *The Resonance of Dust*; Steiner, *In Bluebeard's Castle*; Sidra Ezrahi, "Holocaust Literature in European Languages," in *Encyclopedia Judaica Yearbook 1973* (Jerusalem: Keter Publishing House, 1973), 104–119; Marie

Syrkin, "The Literature of the Holocaust," *Midstream* 12 (1966): 3–20; Leon Yudkin, *Escape into Siege: A Survey of Israeli Literature Today* (London: Routledge and Kegan Paul, 1974).

**9.** Eaglestone, *The Holocaust and the Postmodern*, 105–106. Italics in the original.

**10.** Rosenfeld, *A Double Dying*, 12, 33. Italics in the original.

**11.** Eaglestone, *The Holocaust and the Postmodern*, 107.

**12.** Rosenfeld, *A Double Dying*, 33–34.

**13.** Ibid., 28.

**14.** Appelfeld quoted from Robert Alter, "Mother and Son, Lost in a Continent," *New York Times*, 2 November 1986, Sunday, Late City Final Edition Section 7, Page 1, Column 1, Book Review Desk.

**15.** Horowitz, *Voicing the Void*, 8.

**16.** Debarati Sanyal, "A Soccer Match in Auschwitz: Passing Culpability in Holocaust Criticism," *Representations* 79 (2002): 21.

**17.** Hartman, *Holocaust Remembrance*, 18.

**18.** J. Hillis Miller, in contrast to this position, goes so far as to write that he is "not exactly an uninvolved bystander. . . . A more universal sense of complicity and guilt may be a sense that these were human beings, like me, lots of them, who committed the atrocity of genocide. I too am a human being. How can I be sure I would not be capable of similar acts? I am old enough to have been alive when the Shoah was occurring and when six million Jews (along with Gypsies, homosexuals, political prisoners, and others) were being murdered in the camps." Miller, *The Conflagration of Community*, 150.

**19.** Lothar Kahn, "The American Jewish Novel Today," *Congress Bi-Weekly* 36 (5 December 1969): 3–4.

**20.** Ezrahi, *By Words Alone*, 176–177.

**21.** Ibid., 179.

**22.** Ibid., 176–216.

**23.** Ian Hamilton, "Interview with the *London Sunday Times*," *London Sunday Times*, 19 February 1984, 41, reprinted in Philip Roth, *Reading Myself and Others*, rev. ed. (New York: Penguin, 1985), 136. See also Peter Novick, *The Holocaust and Collective Memory: The American Experience* (London: Bloomsbury, 1999).

**24.** Emily Miller Budick, "The Holocaust in the Jewish American Literary Imagination," in *The Cambridge Companion to Jewish American Literature*, ed. Hana Wirth-Nesher and Michael P. Kramer (Cambridge: Cambridge University Press, 2003), 215–217. Two earlier comprehensive studies that examine American Holocaust fiction during this time are Dorothy Seidman Bilik, *Immigrant-Survivors: Post-Holocaust Consciousness in Recent Jewish American Fiction* (Middletown, CT: Wesleyan University Press, 1981), and S. Lillian Kremer, *Witness through the Imagination: Jewish American Holocaust Literature* (Detroit: Wayne State University Press, 1989).

**25.** Kremer, *Witness through the Imagination*, 15.

**26.** Elaine Kauvar, "An Interview with Chaim Potok," *Contemporary Literature* 27 (1986): 309. This and other interviews with Chaim Potok can also be found in Daniel Walden, ed., *Conversations with Chaim Potok* (Jackson: University Press of Mississippi, 2001).

**27.** S. Lillian Kremer, "An Interview with Chaim Potok," in Walden, *Conversations*, 39.

**28.** Ibid., 38.

**29.** Sheldon Grebstein, "The Phenomenon of the Really Jewish Best-Seller: Potok's 'The Chosen,'" *Studies in American Jewish Literature* 1 (Spring 1975): 23–31.

**30.** Kauvar, "Interview with Chaim Potok," 309.

**31.** All quotations are from Chaim Potok, *The Chosen* (New York: Ballantine Books, 1967), and page references will be given parenthetically in the text.

**32.** Edward Abramson, *Chaim Potok* (Boston: Twayne, 1986), 10.

**33.** Potok himself comments that he uses the openings of his novels "to make the statement concerning the central metaphor of the novels. The central metaphor of *The Chosen* is combat of various kinds, combat on the baseball field, combat in Europe, and then what happens when the combat in Europe is actually brought home to Brooklyn because of the Holocaust and the subsequent hunger to create the State of Israel." Kauvar, "Interview with Chaim Potok," 296.

**34.** Abramson, *Chaim Potok*, 14. References to this subject can also be found in S. Lillian Kremer's chapter "Eternal Light: The Holocaust and the Revival of Judaism and Jewish Civilization in the Fiction of Chaim Potok," in Kremer, *Witness through the Imagination*, 300–323.

**35.** Chaim Potok, *Wanderings: Chaim Potok's History of the Jews* (New York: Alfred A. Knopf, 1978), 398.

**36.** Kremer, *Witness through the Imagination*, 300. Furthermore, while Jewish American fiction tended to focus more on religious values at the time *The Chosen* was published, Potok distinguishes himself from other contemporary novelists by keeping the Holocaust in the background. As Dorothy Seidman Bilik writes: "In the 1970s . . . Singer, Cohen, and Schaeffer began writing a new kind of immigrant fiction, in which Jewish survivors of the Holocaust were the central figures. In this fiction attention focuses upon Orthodox and traditional Jews and their Eastern European backgrounds, not upon the assimilated characters and American suburban settings that dominated the Jewish-American literature of the fifties." Bilik, *Immigrant-Survivors*, 5.

**37.** Kremer, *Witness through the Imagination*, 308.

**38.** Bilik, *Immigrant-Survivors*, 187.

**39.** Kauvar, "Interview with Chaim Potok," 305.

**40.** Ibid., 298.

**41.** Kauvar, "Interview with Cynthia Ozick," 390.

**42.** Katie Bolick, *Atlantic Unbound: Interviews*, "The Many Faces of Cynthia Ozick," *The Atlantic Online*, 15 May 1997, available at http://www.theatlantic.com/past/docs/unbound/factfict/ozick.htm/.

**43.** In reflecting back on the war years, Ozick notes: "I think back on the four years I was in high school—I was extraordinarily happy, just coming into the exaltations of literature—and then I think about what was going on across the water, with very confused feelings." Ibid.

**44.** John Sutherland, "The Girls Who Would Be James," *New York Times on the Web: Books*, 8 October 2000, available at https://www.nytimes.com/books/00/10/08/reviews/001008.08suthert.html/.

**45.** Maurice Blanchot, *The Space of Literature* (Lincoln: University of Nebraska Press, 1982), 198.

**46.** Cynthia Ozick, "Levitation," in *Levitation: Five Fictions* (Syracuse, NY: Syracuse University Press, 1982), 19. Quotations are from this edition and page references will be given parenthetically in the text.

**47.** Michael Bernard-Donals and Richard Glejzer, *Between Witness and Testimony: The Holocaust and the Limits of Representation* (Albany: State University of New York Press, 2012), 90. See also Michael Andre Bernstein, *Foregone Conclusions: Against Apocalyptic History* (Berkeley: University of California Press, 1994), 42–52.

**48.** All quotations are from Cynthia Ozick, *Foreign Bodies* (New York: Mariner Books, Houghton Mifflin, 2011), and page references will be given parenthetically in the text.

**49.** Shlomo Katz, "What Should We Write?" *Jewish Frontier* 7 (1940): 16.

**50.** All quotations are from Philip Roth, *Nemesis* (New York: Houghton Mifflin Harcourt, 2010), 1, and page references will be given parenthetically in the text.

**51.** Found in Celestine Bohlen, "Rare Unfurling of the Reluctant Philip Roth," *New York Times*, 15 September 2011, available at http://www.nytimes.com/2011/09/16/arts/16iht-Roth16.html?pagewanted=all/.

**52.** Michael E. Haskew, ed., *The World War II Desk Reference* (New York: Grand Central Press, 2004), 383.
**53.** Carrol C. Hall, "A Wartime Casualty on the Homefront: Teenage Rejectees," *Rotarian Magazine* (March 1944): 23.
**54.** Ibid.
**55.** Ibid.
**56.** G. St. J. Perrott, "Findings of Selective Service Examinations," *Milbank Memorial Fund Quarterly* 22 (1944): 358.
**57.** "Recruits: The 4-F Classification," available at http://www.nebraskastudies.org/0800/frameset_reset.html/ and http://www.nebraskastudies.org/0800/stories/0801_0106.html/.
**58.** Sander Gilman writes that Brenda's nose surgery illustrates "Roth's image of a supposedly malleable Jewish identity in 1959." I would argue that Brenda's willingness to talk about her nose suggests her willingness to identify herself not only as a Jew but as a Jew of a defined social standing. Sander Gilman, *Multiculturalism and the Jews* (New York: Routledge, 2006), 127.
**59.** Thomas Mann, *The Magic Mountain* (New York: Alfred A. Knopf, 2005), 442.
**60.** Arthur Miller, *Focus* (Syracuse, NY: First Syracuse University Press, 1997), 24–25.
**61.** Found in Leonard Dinnerstein, *Antisemitism in America* (New York: Oxford University Press, 1994), 140.
**62.** Ibid., 126–127.
**63.** Charles-Joseph Lamoral, prince de Ligne, "Mémoire sur les Juifs du Prince Ch. de Ligne," in Léon Poliakov, *The History of Anti-Semitism*, vol. 3: *From Voltaire to Wagner*, trans. Miriam Kochan (Philadelphia: University of Pennsylvania Press, 2003), 48.
**64.** Sander Gilman, *The Jew's Body* (New York: Routledge 1991), 38.
**65.** Poliakov, *History of Anti-Semitism*, 3:177.
**66.** Gilman, *The Jew's Body*, 47–48.
**67.** Ibid., 48–49.
**68.** *Jud Süss*, a 1940 Nazi propaganda film, centers on the grossly anti-Semitic portrayal of a Jewish moneylender Joseph Süss Oppenheimer.

## CHAPTER 6—RECEDING INTO THE DISTANCE: THE HOLOCAUST AS BACKGROUND

**1.** The epigraph is from Judith Frank, *All I Love and Know* (New York: William Morrow, 2014), 278.
**2.** Langer, *The Holocaust and the Literary Imagination*, 30.
**3.** Leslie Epstein, "Writing about the Holocaust," in Lang, *Writing and the Holocaust*and, 261.
**4.** Appelfeld, *Beyond Despair*, 22.
**5.** Kauvar, "An Interview with Cynthia Ozick," 390.
**6.** Wiesel, "The Holocaust as Literary Inspiration," 7.
**7.** Sue Vice, *Holocaust Fiction* (New York: Routledge, 2000), 1. A list of Holocaust fiction that spans multiple generations and has evoked controversies includes stories that center on memorializing the Holocaust through the eyes of non-Jews, stories such as William Styron, *Sophie's Choice* (New York: Random House, 1979), Emily Prager, *Eve's Tattoo* (New York: Random House, 1991), and Jonathan Littell, *The Kindly Ones* (New York: Harper Perennial, 2010); novels that fetishize the Holocaust such as Philip Roth, *The Ghost Writer* (New York: Farrar Straus and Giroux, 1979), and D. M. Thomas, *The White Hotel* (New York: Viking, 1981); and novels that laugh at the Holocaust such as Melvin Jules Bukiet, *After* (New York: St. Martin's Press, 1996), and Shalom Auslander, *Hope: A Tragedy* (New York: Riverhead Books, 2012).

8. Rosenfeld, *A Double Dying*, 27.
9. All citations are from Aryeh Lev Stollman, *The Far Euphrates* (New York: Riverhead Trade, 1997), and page references will be given parenthetically in the text.
10. This citation is from Lucette Matalon Lagnado and Sheila Cohn Dekel, *Children of the Flames: Dr. Josef Mengele and the Untold Story of the Twins of Auschwitz* (New York: Penguin Books, 1992).
11. Second-generation author Lev Raphael consistently uses his fiction and nonfiction to investigate the implications behind being gay, Jewish, and second-generation. In his first memoir, *The Elusive Embrace*, Daniel Mendelsohn partly addresses the intersection of the Holocaust through a queer Jewish lens, although this perspective is notably absent from his second memoir, *The Lost*. Daniel Mendelsohn, *The Elusive Embrace: Desire and the Riddle of Identity* (New York: Vintage, 2000). Lesléa Newman's fiction often confronts the intersection of lesbian Jewish identity, with the Holocaust occupying a background role in a number of them. In her recent novel *All I Love and Know*, Judith Frank positions the Holocaust in the background of a story about queer partnership and parenting.
12. Kai Hammermeister compellingly documents the origins of gay Holocaust literature in his article "Inventing History: Toward a Gay Holocaust Literature," *German Quarterly* 70 (1997): 18–26.
13. One exception to this rule is the work by second-generation author Raphael Lev.
14. Susanne Klingenstein, "Jewish American Fiction, Act III: Eccentric Sources of Inspiration," *Studies in American Jewish Literature* 18 (1999): 84.
15. Burstein, *Telling the Little Secrets*, 93, 108.
16. Ibid., 76.
17. Susan Sontag, *On Photography* (New York: Anchor Doubleday Books, 1989), 19.
18. Mendelsohn, *The Elusive Embrace*, 132–133.
19. Alvin H. Rosenfeld, "The Americanization of the Holocaust," in *Thinking about the Holocaust: After Half a Century*, ed. Alvin H. Rosenfeld (Bloomington: Indiana University Press, 1997), 123.
20. Krauss's novel is more in keeping with the argument that Hilene Flanzbaum makes about Americanization, namely, that while the Holocaust "as image and symbol, seems to have sprung loose from its origins," this "does not mean we should decry Americanization; rather, the pervasive presence of representations of the Holocaust in our culture demands responsible evaluation and interpretation." Hilene Flanzbaum, "Introduction: The Americanization of the Holocaust," in *The Americanization of the Holocaust*, ed. Hilene Flanzbaum (Baltimore: Johns Hopkins University Press, 1999), 8.
21. Michael Berenbaum makes the point that while "popularizers of the Holocaust have tended to look for cheap grace, for easy sources of consolation," those who tell the story as "faithful to the historical event" as possible produce valuable work. Berenbaum, formerly the project director of the U.S. Holocaust Memorial Museum, was surely directing his comments more toward historical writing, but his point resonates with Krauss's novel, too. Michael Berenbaum, *After Tragedy and Triumph: Essays in Modern Jewish Thought and the American Experience* (New York: Cambridge University Press, 1990), 13.
22. Wiesel, *A Jew Today*, 234.
23. This is (at least partly) the implication of Theodor Adorno's oft-repeated line that to "write poetry after Auschwitz is barbaric." For a helpful discussion of Adorno and post-Holocaust modernism see Rothberg, *Traumatic Realism*, 19–58.
24. Marianne Hirsch, "Past Lives: Postmemories in Exile," *Poetics Today* 17 (1996): 659. Hirsch calls this second-generation formation of memory "postmemory," a topic I discuss at greater length in chapter 2.

**25.** This formulation intentionally resonates with the lines from ee cummings: "here is the deepest secret nobody knows / (here is the root of the root and the bud of the bud and the sky of the sky or a tree called life . . ." ee cummings, "i carry your heart with me," available at https://www.poetryfoundation.org/poetrymagazine/poems/detail/49493/.
**26.** Berel Lang, *Post-Holocaust: Interpretation, Misinterpretation, and the Claims of History* (Bloomington: Indiana University Press, 2005), 102.
**27.** Terrence Des Pres, "Holocaust Laughter," in Terrence Des Pres, *Writing into the World: Essays, 1973–1987* (New York: Viking, 1991), 280, 286. Also see Adam Rovner, "Instituting the Holocaust: Comic Fiction and the Moral Career of the Survivor," *Jewish Culture and History* 5 (2002): 1–24.
**28.** Transforming victimization into laughter is one of the defining features of Jewish humor. Martin Grotjahn writes: "The Jewish joke constitutes victory by defeat . . . one can almost see how a witty Jewish man carefully and cautiously takes a sharp dagger out of his enemy's hands, sharpens it so that it can split a hair in mid-air, polishes it so that it shines brightly, stabs himself with it, then returns it gallantly to the anti-Semite with the silent reproach: Now see whether you can do half so well." Martin Grotjahn, *Beyond Laughter: Humor and the Subconscious* (New York: Blakiston Division, 1966), 22–23.
**29.** Peter Novick, *The Holocaust in American Life* (Boston: Houghton Mifflin, 1999).

## AFTERWORD: READING THE FRAGMENTS OF MEMORY

**1.** The epigraphs are from Saul Friedlander, *When Memory Comes*, trans. Helen R. Lane (New York: Farrar Straus Giroux, 1979; reprinted 1991), 134; Halina Birenbaum, "There Is My Soul," in Halina Birenbaum, *Sounds of Guilty Silence: Selected Poems*, trans. June Friedman (Krakow: Centrum Dialogu, 1997), 35.
**2.** Aharon Appelfeld, *The Story of a Life*, trans. Aloma Halter (New York: Schocken Books, 2004), vii.
**3.** Ibid., ix.
**4.** Susan Suleiman, *Budapest Diary: In Search of the Motherbook* (Lincoln: University of Nebraska Press, 1997), 32.
**5.** Katz, *Looking for Strangers*, 8.
**6.** Diary of Michal (Michael) Kraus, handwritten with illustrations (1945–1947), 54–60, U.S. Holocaust Memorial Museum Archive, Acc. 2006.51, Michael Kraus Collection (translated from the Czech), found in Patricia Heberer, *Children during the Holocaust*, intro. Nechama Tec (New York: AltaMira Press in association with the U.S. Holocaust Memorial Museum, 2011), 165–166.
**7.** Leslie Morris, "Postmemory, Postmemoir," in *Unlikely History: The Changing German-Jewish Symbiosis, 1945–2000*, ed. Leslie Morris and Jack Zipes (New York: Palgrave Macmillan, 2002), 292.
**8.** Marianne Hirsch, *Ghosts of Home: The Afterlife of Czernowitz in Jewish Memory* (Berkeley: University of California Press, 2010), 9.
**9.** Morris, "Postmemory, Postmemoir," 293.
**10.** Sarah Wildman, *Paper Love: Searching for the Girl My Grandfather Left Behind* (New York: Riverhead Books, 2014), 362–363.

# BIBLIOGRAPHY


Abramson, Edward. *Chaim Potok*. Boston: Twayne, 1986.

Adorno, Theodor. *Gesammelte Schriften*. Frankfurt am Main: Suhrkamp Verlag, 1974.

———. *Negative Dialectics*. Translated by E. B. Ashton. New York: Continuum, 1973.

———. *Prisms*. Translated by Samuel Webber and Shierry Webber. Cambridge, MA: MIT Press, 1983.

Agamben, Giorgio. *Remnants of Auschwitz: The Witness and the Archive*. Translated by Daniel Heller-Roazen. New York: Zone Books, 2002.

Alexander, Edward. *The Resonance of Dust: Essays on Holocaust Literature and Jewish Fate*. Columbus: Ohio State University Press, 1980.

Alter, Robert. "Mother and Son, Lost in a Continent." *New York Times*, 2 November 1986. Sunday, Late City Final Edition Section 7, Page 1, Column 1, Book Review Desk.

Amery, Jean. *At the Mind's Limits*. Translated by Sidney Rosenfeld and Stella D. Rosenfeld. Bloomington: Indiana University Press, 1980.

Appelfeld, Aharon. *Beyond Despair: Three Lectures and a Conversation with Philip Roth*. Translated by Jeffrey M. Green. New York: Fromm International Publishing, 1993.

———. *The Story of a Life*. Translated by Aloma Halter. New York: Schocken Books, 2004.

Appignanesi, Lisa. *Losing the Dead*. Toronto: McArthur, 1999.

Appleyard, J. A. *Becoming a Reader: The Experience of Fiction from Childhood to Adulthood*. New York: Cambridge University Press, 1994.

Ascher, Carol. *Afterimages: A Family Memoir*. Teaneck, NJ: Holmes and Meier, 2008.

Auslander, Shalom. *Hope: A Tragedy*. New York: Riverhead Books, 2012.

Bakhtin, M. M. *The Dialogic Imagination: Four Essays*. Austin: University of Texas Press, 2010.

Barkat, Amiram. "Who Counts as a Holocaust Survivor?" *Ha'Aretz*, 18 April 2004. Available at http://www.haaretz.com/who-counts-as-a-holocaust-survivor-1.119868/.

Barthes, Roland. "The Death of the Author." In *Image-Music-Text*, translated by Stephen Heath, 142–148. New York: Noonday Press, 1977.

Bell, Vicki, ed. *Performativity and Belonging*. Oxford: Sage Publications, 1999.

Bennett, Jill. *Empathic Vision: Affect, Trauma, and Contemporary Art*. Palo Alto, CA: Stanford University Press, 2005.

Berenbaum, Michael. *After Tragedy and Triumph: Essays in Modern Jewish Thought and the American Experience*. New York: Cambridge University Press, 1990.

Berger, Alan L. "Bearing Witness: Second Generation Literature of the 'Shoah.'" *Modern Judaism* 10 (1990): 43–63.

———. *Children of Job: American Second-Generation Witnesses to the Holocaust*. Albany: State University of New York Press, 1997.

Berger, Alan L., and Naomi Berger, eds. *Second Generation Voices: Reflections by Children of Holocaust Survivors and Perpetrators*. Syracuse, NY: Syracuse University Press, 2001.

Bernard-Donals, Michael. *Forgetful Memory: Representation and Remembrance in the Wake of the Holocaust*. Albany: State University of New York Press, 2009.

Bernard-Donals, Michael, and Richard Glejze. *Between Witness and Testimony: The Holocaust and the Limits of Representation*. Albany: State University of New York Press, 2012.

Bernstein, Michael Andre. *Foregone Conclusions: Against Apocalyptic History*. Berkeley: University of California Press, 1994.

Berr, Hélène. *The Journal of Hélène Berr*. Translated by David Bellos. New York: Weinstein Books, 2008.

Bilik, Dorothy Seidman. *Immigrant-Survivors: Post-Holocaust Consciousness in Recent Jewish American Fiction*. Middletown, CT: Wesleyan University Press, 1981.

Birenbaum, Halina. *Sounds of Guilty Silence: Selected Poems*. Translated by June Friedman. Krakow: Centrum Dialogu, 1997.

Bisberg-Youkelson, Feigl, and Rubin Youkelson, eds. *The Life and Death of a Polish Shtetl*. Translated by Gene Bluestein. Lincoln: University of Nebraska Press, 2000.

Blanchot, Maurice. *The Space of Literature*. Lincoln: University of Nebraska Press, 1982.

———. *The Writing of Disaster*. Translated by Ann Smock. Lincoln: University of Nebraska Press, 1996.

Bohlen, Celestine. "Rare Unfurling of the Reluctant Philip Roth." *New York Times*, 15 September 2011. Available at http://www.nytimes.com/2011/09/16/arts/16iht-Roth16.html?pagewanted=all/.

Bolick, Katie. *Atlantic Unbound: Interviews*. "The Many Faces of Cynthia Ozick." *The Atlantic Online*. 15 May 1997. Available at http://www.theatlantic.com/past/docs/unbound/factfict/ozick.htm/.

Booth, Wayne. *The Company We Keep: An Ethics of Fiction*. Berkeley: University of California Press, 1988.

Brenkman, John, and Jules David Law. "Resetting the Agenda." *Critical Inquiry* 15 (1989): 804–811.

Budick, Emily Miller. "The Holocaust in the Jewish American Literary Imagination." In *The Cambridge Companion to Jewish American Literature*, edited by Hana Wirth-Nesher and Michael P. Kramer, 212–230. Cambridge: Cambridge University Press, 2003.

———. *The Subject of Holocaust Fiction*. Bloomington: Indiana University Press, 2015.

Bukiet, Melvin Jules. *After*. New York: St. Martin's Press, 1996.

———. "The Library of Moloch." In Melvin Jules Bukiet, *While the Messiah Tarries*, 184–197. Syracuse, NY: Syracuse University Press, 1995.

———, ed. *Nothing Makes You Free: Writings by Descendants of Jewish Holocaust Survivors*. New York: W. W. Norton, 2003.

Burstein, Janet Handler. *Telling the Little Secrets: American Jewish Writing since the 1980s*. Madison: University of Wisconsin Press, 2006.

Caruth, Cathy. *Unclaimed Experience: Trauma, Narrative, and History*. Baltimore: Johns Hopkins University Press, 1996.

Celan, Paul. *Selected Poems and Prose of Paul Celan*. Edited and translated by John Felstiner. New York: W. W. Norton, 2001.

Chare, Nicholas. *Auschwitz and Afterimages: Abjection, Witnessing, and Representation*. New York: I. B. Tauris, 2011.

Chute, Hillary. " 'The Shadow of a Past Time': History and Graphic Representation in 'Maus.' " *Twentieth Century Literature* 52 (2006): 199–230.

Cohen, Kate. *The Neppi Modona Diaries: Reading Jewish Survival through My Italian Family*. Hanover, NH: University Press of New England, 1997.

Cole, Tim. *Selling the Holocaust: From Auschwitz to Schindler, How History Is Bought, Packaged, and Sold*. New York: Routledge, 2000.

Delbo, Charlotte. *Auschwitz and After*. Translated by Rosette C. Lamont. New Haven, CT: Yale University Press, 1995.

———. *Convoy to Auschwitz: Women of the French Resistance*. Translated by Carol Cosman. Boston: Northeastern University Press, 1997.

———. *Days and Memory*. Translated by Rosette Lamont. Marlboro, VT: Marlboro Press, 1990.

DellaPergola, Sergio. *Review of Relevant Demographic Information on World Jewry*. Report for the International Commission on Holocaust Era Insurance Claims, 1–65. Jewish People Policy Institute (JPPI). Jerusalem, November 2003. Available at http://www.bjpa.org/Publications/details.cfm?PublicationID=907/.

de Man, Paul. *Allegories of Reading: Figural Language in Rousseau, Nietzsche, Rilke, and Proust*. New Haven, CT: Yale University Press, 1979.

Derrida, Jacques. *Archive Fever: A Freudian Impression*. Translated by Eric Prenowitz. Chicago: University of Chicago Press, 1996.

———. "An Interview with Jacques Derrida." In *Acts of Literature*, edited by Derek Attridge, 33–75. New York: Routledge, 1991.

———. "Like the Sound of the Sea Deep within a Shell: Paul de Man's War." *Critical Inquiry* 14 (1988): 590–652.

Des Pres, Terrence. "Holocaust Laughter." In Terrence Des Pres, *Writing into the World: Essays, 1973–1987*, 77–86. New York: Viking, 1991.

de Waal, Edmund. *The Hare with Amber Eyes: A Hidden Inheritance*. New York: Picador, 2011.

Dinnerstein, Leonard. *Antisemitism in America*. New York: Oxford University Press, 1994.

Dreifus, Erika. "Ever After? History, Healing, and 'Holocaust Fiction' in the Third Generation." In *Beyond Camps and Forced Labour: Current International Research on Survivors of Nazi Persecution*, edited by Johannes-Dieter Steiner and Inge Weber-Newth, 524–30. Osnabrück: Secolo Verlag, 2005.

———. *Quiet Americans: Stories*. Boston: Last Light Studio, 2011.

Eaglestone, Robert. *The Holocaust and the Postmodern*. New York: Oxford University Press, 2005.

Ehrenreich, Eric. *The Nazi Ancestral Proof: Genealogy, Racial Science, and the Final Solution*. Bloomington: Indiana University Press, 2007.

Einhorn, Erin. *The Pages In Between: Holocaust Legacy of Two Families, One Home*. New York: Simon and Schuster, 2008.

Eisenstein, Bernice. *I Was a Child of Holocaust Survivors*. New York: Riverhead Books, 2006.

Epstein, Helen. *Children of the Holocaust: Conversations with Sons and Daughters of Survivors*. New York: Penguin Books 2010.

———. *Where She Came From: A Daughter's Search for Her Mother's History*. Teaneck, NJ: Holmes and Meier, 2005.

Epstein, Leslie. "Writing about the Holocaust." In *Writing and the Holocaust*, edited by Berel Lang, 261–270. New York: Holmes and Meier, 1988.

Ezrahi, Sidra DeKoven. *By Words Alone: The Holocaust in Literature*. Chicago: University of Chicago Press, 1982.

———. "Holocaust Literature in European Languages." In *Encyclopedia Judaica Yearbook 1973*, edited by Cecil Roth, Geoffrey Wigoder, and Raphael Posner, 104–119. Jerusalem: Keter Publishing House, 1973.

———. "Representing Auschwitz." *History and Memory* 7 (1995): 121–154.

Fass, Paula. *Inheriting the Holocaust: A Second-Generation Memoir*. New Brunswick, NJ: Rutgers University Press, 2011.

Feldman, Jeffrey. "The Holocaust Shoe: Untying Memory: Shoes as Holocaust Memorial Experience." In *Jews and Shoes*, edited by Edna Nahshon. New York: Berg, 2008.

Felman, Shoshana. "Turning the Screw of Interpretation." *Yale French Studies* 55/56 (1977): 94–207.

Felman, Shoshana, and Dori Laub. *Testimony: Crises of Witnessing in Literature, Psychoanalysis, and History*. New York: Routledge, 1991.

Felstiner, John. *Paul Celan: Poet, Survivor, Jew*. New Haven, CT: Yale University Press, 2001.

Flanzbaum, Hilene. "Introduction: The Americanization of the Holocaust." In *The Americanization of the Holocaust*, edited by Hilene Flanzbaum, 1–17. Baltimore: Johns Hopkins University Press, 1999.

Foucault, Michel. *The Archeology of Knowledge*. Translated by A. M. Sheridan Smith. New York: Vintage Press, 1982.

Frank, Judith. *All I Love and Know*. New York: William Morrow, 2014.

Franklin, Ruth. *A Thousand Darknesses: Lies and Truth in Holocaust Fiction*. New York: Oxford University Press, 2010.

Friedlander, Saul. *When Memory Comes*. Translated by Helen R. Lane. New York: Farrar Straus Giroux, 1979.

Garbarini, Alexandra. *Numbered Days: Diaries and the Holocaust*. New Haven, CT: Yale University Press, 2006.

Gilman, Sander. *The Jew's Body*. New York: Routledge 1991.

———. *Multiculturalism and the Jews*. New York: Routledge, 2006.

Glatstein, Jacob, Israel Knox, and Samuel Margoshes, eds. *Anthology of Holocaust Literature*. New York: Atheneum, 1985.

Grebstein, Sheldon. "The Phenomenon of the Really Jewish Best-Seller: Potok's 'The Chosen.'" *Studies in American Jewish Literature* 1 (Spring 1975): 23–31.

Grimwood, Marita. *Holocaust Literature of the Second Generation*. London: Palgrave Macmillan, 2007.

Grotjahn, Martin. *Beyond Laughter: Humor and the Subconscious*. New York: Blakiston Division, 1966.

Hall, Carrol C. "A Wartime Casualty on the Homefront: Teenage Rejectees." *Rotarian Magazine* (March 1944): 23–24.

Hamacher, Werner. "Working through Working." Translated by Matthew T. Hartman. *Modernism/Modernity* 3 (1996): 23–56.

Hamilton, Ian. "Interview with the *London Sunday Times*." *London Sunday Times*, 19 February 1984, 41.

Hammermeister, Kai. "Inventing History: Toward a Gay Holocaust Literature." *German Quarterly* 70 (1997): 18–26.

Hartman, Geoffrey. "History and Judgment: The Case of Paul de Man." *History and Memory* 1 (1989): 55–84.

———, ed. *Holocaust Remembrance: The Shapes of Memory*. Cambridge: Blackwell, 1994.

Haskew, Michael E., ed. *The World War II Desk Reference*. New York: Grand Central Press, 2004.

Hirsch, Marianne. *Family Frames: Photography, Narrative, and Postmemory*. Cambridge, MA: Harvard University Press, 1997.

———. "Family Pictures: *Maus*, Mourning, and Postmemory." *Discourse* 15 (1992–1993): 3–30.

———. "The Generation of Postmemory." *Poetics Today* 29 (2008): 103–128.

———. *The Generation of Postmemory: Writing and Visual Culture after the Holocaust*. New York: Columbia University Press, 2012.

———. *Ghosts of Home: The Afterlife of Czernowitz in Jewish Memory*. Berkeley: University of California Press, 2010.

———. "Past Lives: Postmemories in Exile." *Poetics Today* 17 (1996): 659–686.

Hoffman, Eva. *After Such Knowledge: Memory, History, and the Legacy of the Holocaust*. New York: Public Affairs, 2004.

———. *Lost in Translation: A Life in a New Language*. New York: Penguin Books, 1989.

Holdheim, W. Wolfgang. "Jacques Derrida's Apologia." *Critical Inquiry* 15 (1989): 784–796.

Horowitz, Sara R. *Voicing the Void: Muteness and Memory in Holocaust Fiction*. Albany: State University of New York Press, 1997.

Huang, Wei-Jue, and William J. Haller. "The Journey 'Home': An Exploratory Analysis of Second-Generation Immigrants' Homeland Travel." Available at http://scholarworks.umass.edu/gradconf_hospitality/2011/Presentation/21/.

Iser, Wolfgang. *The Act of Reading: A Theory of Aesthetic Response*. Baltimore: Johns Hopkins University Press, 1978.

Kahn, Lothar. "The American Jewish Novel Today." *Congress Bi-Weekly* 36 (5 December 1969).

Katz, Dori. "Looking for Strangers." Paper presented at Baruch College, CUNY, 4 November 2014.

———. *Looking for Strangers: The True Story of My Hidden Wartime Childhood*. Chicago: University of Chicago Press, 2013.

Katz, Shlomo. "What Should We Write?" *Jewish Frontier* 7 (1940): 15–17.

Kauvar, Elaine M. "An Interview with Chaim Potok." *Contemporary Literature* 27 (1986): 296–317.

———. "An Interview with Cynthia Ozick." *Contemporary Literature* 26 (1985): 375–401.

———. "An Interview with Cynthia Ozick." *Contemporary Literature* 34 (1993): 376–401.

Kertész, Imre. *Dossier K*. Translated by Tim Wilkinson. Brooklyn, NY: Melville House, 2013.

———. *Kaddish for an Unborn Child*. Translated by Tim Wilkinson. New York: Random House, 2004.

Kichka, Michel. *Deuxième génération: Ce que je n'ai pas dit à mon père* [*Second generation: What I didn't tell my father*]. Paris: Dargaud, 2012.

Kirschner, Ann. *Sala's Gift: My Mother's Holocaust Story*. New York: Free Press, 2006.

Klingenstein, Susanne. "Jewish American Fiction, Act III: Eccentric Sources of Inspiration." *Studies in American Jewish Literature* 18 (1999): 83–92.

Kluger, Ruth. *Still Alive: A Holocaust Girlhood Remembered*. New York: Feminist Press at the City University of New York, 2003.

Kohler, Ioanna. "The Discovery of Oneself: An Interview with Daniel Mendelsohn." Translated by Anna Heyward. *Paris Review*, 1 July 2014. Available at http://www.theparisreview.org/blog/2014/07/01/the-discovery-of-oneself-an-interview-with-daniel-mendelsohn/.

Kraus, Michal. "Diary of Michal (Michael) Kraus." Handwritten with illustrations, 1945–1947. U.S. Holocaust Memorial Museum Archive, Acc. 2006.51, Michael Kraus Collection (translated from the Czech). Found in Patricia Heberer, *Children during the Holocaust*, introduction by Nechama Tec. AltaMira Press in association with the U.S. Holocaust Memorial Museum, 2011.

Krell, David. *Of Memory, Reminiscing, and Writing: On the Verge*. Bloomington: Indiana University Press, 1990.

Kremer, S. Lillian. "An Interview with Chaim Potok." In *Conversations with Chaim Potok*, edited by Daniel Walden, 31–45. Jackson: University Press of Mississippi, 2001.

———. *Witness through the Imagination: Jewish American Holocaust Literature*. Detroit: Wayne State University Press, 1989.

Krondorfer, Bjorn. "Is Forgetting Reprehensible? Holocaust Remembrance and the Task of Oblivion." *Journal of Religious Ethics* 36 (2008): 233–267.

LaCapra, Dominick. "The Personal, the Political, and the Textual: Paul de Man as Object of Transference." *History and Memory* 4 (1992): 5–38.

———. "'Twas the Night before Christmas: Art Spiegelman's *Maus*." In Dominick LaCapra, *History and Memory after Auschwitz*, 139–179. Ithaca, NY: Cornell University Press, 1998.

Lagnado, Lucette Matalon, and Sheila Cohn Dekel. *Children of the Flames: Dr. Josef Mengele and the Untold Story of the Twins of Auschwitz*. New York: Penguin Books, 1992.

Lang, Berel. *Act and Idea in the Nazi Genocide*. Chicago: University of Chicago Press, 1990.

———. *Holocaust Representation: Art within the Limits of History and Ethics*. Baltimore: Johns Hopkins University Press, 2000.

———. "Introduction." In *Writing and the Holocaust*, edited by Berel Lang, 1–6. New York: Holmes and Meier, 1988.

———. *Post-Holocaust: Interpretation, Misinterpretation, and the Claims of History*. Bloomington: Indiana University Press, 2005.

———, ed. *Writing and the Holocaust*. New York: Holmes and Meier, 1988.

Langer, Lawrence L. *The Holocaust and the Literary Imagination*. New Haven, CT: Yale University Press, 1975.

Laskin, David. *The Family: Three Journeys into the Heart of the Twentieth Century*. New York: Viking Penguin, 2013.

Lassner, Phyllis. *Anglo-Jewish Women Writing the Holocaust: Displaced Witnesses*. New York: Palgrave Macmillan, 2008.

Lavine, Thelma Z. "Postmodernism and American Pragmatism." *Journal of Speculative Philosophy* 7 (1993): 110–113.

Lemelman, Martin. *Mendel's Daughter*. New York: Free Press, 2006.

Levi, Primo. *The Drowned and the Saved*. Translated by Raymond Rosenthal. New York: Vintage Books, 1989.

———. *The Reawakening*. Translated by Stuart Woolf. New York: Simon and Schuster, 1995.

———. *Survival in Auschwitz: The Nazi Assault on Humanity*. Translated by Stuart Woolf. New York: Simon and Schuster, 1996.

Levine, Michael G. *The Belated Witness: Literature, Testimony, and the Question of the Holocaust*. Stanford, CA: Stanford University Press, 2006.

Lewin, Abraham. *A Cup of Tears: A Diary of the Warsaw Ghetto*. Edited by Antony Polonsky, translated by Christopher Hutton. Oxford: Basil Blackwell, 1988.

Lichtenberg-Ettinger, Bracha. *Halala-Autiswork*. Aix-en-Provence, France: Louis-Jean Depot, 1995.

Littell, Jonathan. *The Kindly Ones*. New York: Harper Perennial, 2010.

Lothe, Jakob, Susan Rubin Suleiman, and James Phelan. "Introduction." In *After Testimony: The Ethics and Aesthetics of Holocaust Narrative for the Future*, edited by Jakob Lothe, Susan Rubin Suleiman, and James Phelan, 1–19. Columbus: Ohio State University Press, 2012.

Macdonald, Heather. "The Holocaust as Text: Deconstruction's Final Solution to the de Man Problem." *Salmagundi* 92 (1991): 160–173.

Mackenzie, Ian. *Paradigms of Reading: Relevance Theory and Deconstruction*. New York: Palgrave Macmillan, 2002.

Mann, Thomas. *The Magic Mountain*. New York: Alfred A. Knopf, 2005.

McGlothlin, Erin Heather. *Second-Generation Holocaust Literature: Legacies of Survival and Perpetration*. Rochester, NY: Camden House, 2006.

Mendelsohn, Daniel. *The Elusive Embrace: Desire and the Riddle of Identity*. New York: Vintage, 2000.

———. *The Lost: A Search for Six of Six Million*. New York: HarperCollins, 2006.

Michaels, Walter Benn. "'You Who Never Was There': Slavery and the New Historicism, Deconstruction and the Holocaust." *Narrative* 4, no. 1 (1996): 1–16.

Miller, Arthur. "Focus." Syracuse, NY: Syracuse University Press, 1997.

Miller, J. Hillis. *The Conflagration of Community: Fiction before and after Auschwitz*. Chicago: University of Chicago Press, 2011.

———. *The Ethics of Reading: Kant, de Man, Eliot, Trollope, James, and Benjamin*. New York: Columbia University Press, 1987.

Miller, Nancy K. "The Art of Survival: Mom, Murder, Memory." In Nancy K. Miller, *Bequest and Betrayal: Memoirs of a Parent's Death*, 97–125. New York: Oxford University Press, 1996.

———. "Cartoons of the Self-Portrait of the Artist as a Young Murderer: Art Spiegelman's *Maus*." In *M/E/A/N/I/N/G: An Anthology of Artists' Writings, Theory, and Criticism*, edited by Susan Bee and Mira Schor, 388–404. Durham, NC: Duke University Press, 2000.

Mitchell, W. J. T. *Picture Theory: Essays on Verbal and Visual Representation*. Chicago: University of Chicago Press, 1994.

Modan, Rutu. *The Property*. Montreal: Drawn and Quarterly, 2013.

Moore, Deborah Dash. "At Home in America? Revisiting the Second Generation." *Journal of American Ethnic History* 25 (2006): 156–168.

Moore, Niamh, and Yvonne Whelan. *Heritage, Memory, and the Politics of Identity: New Perspectives on the Cultural Landscape*. Abingdon, UK: Ashgate, 2007.

Morris, Leslie. "Postmemory, Postmemoir." In *Unlikely History: The Changing German-Jewish Symbiosis, 1945–2000*, edited by Leslie Morris and Jack Zipes, 291–306. New York: Palgrave Macmillan, 2002.

Morrison, Paul. "Paul de Man: Resistance and Collaboration." *Representations* 32 (1990): 50–74.

Newman, Robert D. *Transgressions of Reading: Narrative Engagement as Exile and Return*. Durham, NC: Duke University Press 1993.

Newton, Adam Zachary. *Narrative Ethics*. Cambridge, MA: Harvard University Press, 1995.

Novick, Peter. *The Holocaust and Collective Memory: The American Experience*. London: Bloomsbury, 1999.

———. *The Holocaust in American Life*. Boston: Houghton Mifflin, 1999.

Nystrand, Martin. *The Structure of Written Communication: Studies in Reciprocity between Writers and Readers*. Orlando, FL: Academic Press, 1986.

O'Driscoll, Michael, and Edward Bishop. "Archiving 'Archiving.'" *English Studies in Canada* 30 (2004): 1–16.

Oesper, Ralph E. "Ludwig Gattermann." *Journal of Chemical Education* 19 (1942): 444–445.

Ozick, Cynthia. *Bloodshed and Three Novellas*. Syracuse, NY: Syracuse University Press, 1976.

———. *Foreign Bodies*. New York: Mariner Books, Houghton Mifflin, 2011.

———. "Levitation." In Cynthia Ozick, *Levitation: Five Fictions*, 3–38. Syracuse, NY: Syracuse University Press, 1982.

———. "The Rights of History and the Rights of Imagination." In *Obliged by Memory: Literature, Religion, Ethics*, edited by Steven T. Katz and Alan Rosen, 3–18. Syracuse, NY: Syracuse University Press, 2006.

———. "Who Owns Anne Frank?" In Cynthia Ozick, *Quarrel and Quandary*, 74–102. New York: Alfred A. Knopf, 2000.

Perrott, G. St. J. "Findings of Selective Service Examinations." *Milbank Memorial Fund Quarterly* 22 (1944): 358–366.

Phelan, James. "The Ethics and Aesthetics of Backward Narration in Martin Amis's *Time's Arrow*." In *After Testimony: The Ethics and Aesthetics of Holocaust Narrative for the Future*, edited by Jakob Lothe, Susan Rubin Suleiman, and James Phelan, 120–139. Columbus: Ohio State University Press, 2012.

Poliakov, Leon. *The History of Anti-Semitism*, vol. 3: *From Voltaire to Wagner*. Translated by Miriam Kochan. Philadelphia: University of Pennsylvania Press, 2003.

Portes, Alejandro, and Rubén G. Rumbaut. *Immigrant America: A Portrait*. Berkeley: University of California Press, 2006.

Potok, Chaim. *The Chosen*. New York: Ballantine Books, 1967.

———. *Wanderings: Chaim Potok's History of the Jews*. New York: Alfred A. Knopf, 1978.

Prager, Emily. *Eve's Tattoo*. New York: Random House, 1991.

Raczymow, Henri. "Memory Shot through with Holes." *Yale French Studies* 85 (1994): 98–106.

Rakoff, Vivian. "Long-Term Effects of the Concentration Camp." *Viewpoint* (1966): 17–21.

Ricoeur, Paul. *Interpretation Theory: Discourse and the Surplus of Meaning*. Fort Worth: Texas Christian University Press, 1976.

Rose, Daniel Asa. *Hiding Places: A Father and His Sons Retrace Their Family's Escape from the Holocaust*. New York: Simon and Schuster, 2000.

Rosen, Alan. *Sounds of Defiance: The Holocaust, Multilingualism, and the Problem of English*. Lincoln: University of Nebraska Press, 2005.

Rosenblatt, Louise. *The Reader, the Text, the Poem*. Carbondale: Southern Illinois University Press, 1994.

Rosenfeld, Alvin H. "The Americanization of the Holocaust." In *Thinking about the Holocaust: After Half a Century*, edited by Alvin H. Rosenfeld, 119–150. Bloomington: Indiana University Press, 1997.

———. *A Double Dying: Reflections on Holocaust Literature*. Bloomington: Indiana University Press, 1980.

Roth, Philip. *The Ghost Writer*. New York: Farrar Straus and Giroux, 1979.

———. *Nemesis*. New York: Houghton Mifflin Harcourt, 2010.

———. *Reading Myself and Others*. Rev. ed. New York: Penguin, 1985.

Rothberg, Michael. *Multidirectional Memory: Remembering the Holocaust in the Age of Decolonization*. Stanford, CA: Stanford University Press, 2009.

———. *Traumatic Realism: The Demands of Holocaust Representation*. Minneapolis: University of Minnesota Press, 2000.

Rothberg, Michael, and Art Spiegelman. "'We Were Talking Jewish': Art Spiegelman's 'Maus' as 'Holocaust' Production." *Contemporary Literature* 35 (1994): 661–687.

Rovner, Adam. "Instituting the Holocaust: Comic Fiction and the Moral Career of the Survivor." *Jewish Culture and History* 5 (2002): 1–24.

Russell, Lynette. "Remembering Places Never Visited: Connections and Context in Imagined and Imaginary." *International Journal of Historical Archaeology* 16 (2012): 401–417.

Sanyal, Debarati. "A Soccer Match in Auschwitz: Passing Culpability in Holocaust Criticism." *Representations* 79 (2002): 1–27.

Sartre, Jean-Paul. *Situations Volume II*. Translated by Hans Georg Brenner. Hamburg: Rowohlt, 1950.

Scarry, Elaine. *The Body in Pain: The Making and Unmaking of the World*. New York: Oxford University Press, 1987.

Schwarz, Daniel R. "The Ethics of Reading: The Case for Pluralistic and Transactional Reading." *NOVEL: A Forum on Fiction* 21 (1988): 197–218.

———. "The Narrative of Paul de Man: Texts, Issues, Significance." *Journal of Narrative Technique* 20 (1990): 179–194.

Sebald, Winifried Georg. *On the Natural History of Destruction*. New York: Random House, 2003.

Seth, Vikram. *Two Lives: A Memoir*. New York: HarperCollins, 2005.

Sigal, J. J., D. Siver, V. Rakoff, and B. Ellin. "Some Second-Generation Effects of Survival of the Nazi Persecution." *American Journal of Orthopsychiatry* 43 (1973): 320–327.

Smagorinsky, Peter. *Vigotsky and Literacy Research: A Methodological Framework.* Boston: Sense Publishers, 2011.

Smith, Frank. *Understanding Reading: A Psycholinguistic Analysis of Reading and Learning to Read.* New York: Routledge, 2004.

Sobel, Marc. "The Rutu Modan Interview." *Comic Journal,* 29 May 2013. Available at http://www.tcj.com/rutu-modan/2/.

Sontag, Susan. *On Photography.* New York: Anchor Doubleday Books, 1989.

Spiegelman, Art. *Maus I: My Father Bleeds History.* New York: Pantheon, 1986.

———. *Maus II: A Survivor's Tale: And Here My Troubles Began.* New York: Pantheon, 1992.

Steedman, Carolyn. *Dust: The Archive and Cultural History.* New Brunswick, NJ: Rutgers University Press, 2002.

Stein, Arlene. *Reluctant Witnesses: Survivors, Their Children, and the Rise of Holocaust Consciousness.* New York: Oxford University Press, 2014.

Steiner, George. *In Bluebeard's Castle: Some Notes towards the Redefinition of Culture.* New Haven, CT: Yale University Press, 1971.

———. *Language and Silence: Essays on Language, Literature, and the Inhuman.* New Haven, CT: Yale University Press, 1998.

———. *On Difficulty and Other Essays.* New York: Oxford University Press, 1980.

Stier, Oren Baruch. *Holocaust Icons: Symbolizing the Shoah in History and Memory.* New Brunswick, NJ: Rutgers University Press, 2015.

Stollman, Aryeh Lev. *The Far Euphrates.* New York: Riverhead Trade, 1998.

Styron, William. *Sophie's Choice.* New York: Random House, 1979.

Suleiman, Susan Rubin. *Budapest Diary: In Search of the Motherbook.* Lincoln: University of Nebraska Press, 1997.

———. *Crises of Memory and the Second World War.* Cambridge, MA: Harvard University Press, 2006.

———. "The 1.5 Generation: Thinking about Child Survivors and the Holocaust." *American Imago* 59 (2002): 277–295.

Suleiman, Susan, and Inge Crosman. *The Reader in the Text: Essays on Audience and Interpretation.* Princeton, NJ: Princeton University Press, 1980.

Sutherland, John. "The Girls Who Would Be James." *New York Times on the Web: Books,* 8 October 2000. Available at https://www.nytimes.com/books/00/10/08/reviews/001008.08suthert.html/.

Syrkin, Marie. "The Literature of the Holocaust." *Midstream* 12 (1966): 3–20.

Tal, Kalí. *Worlds of Hurt: Reading the Literatures of Trauma.* New York: Cambridge University Press, 1996.

Tedeschi, Giuliana. *There Is a Place on Earth: A Woman in Birkenau.* New York: Pantheon, 1992.

Thomas, D. M. *The White Hotel.* New York: Viking, 1981.

Ukeles Associates, Inc. *An Estimate of the Current Distribution of Jewish Victims of Nazi Persecution.* New York: International Commission on Holocaust Era Insurance Claims, 2003.

———. *A Plan for Allocating Successor Organization Resources.* Report for the Conference on Jewish Material Claims against Germany. New York, 2000.

U.S. Holocaust Memorial Museum. "Eichmann Trial—Sessions 25 and 26—Testimony of Z. Lubetkin, Y. Zuckeran, A. Berman, R. Kuper." Steven Spielberg Film and Video Archive. Available at http://www.ushmm.org/online/film/display/detail.php?file_num=2130andclip_id=CDAEA092-37E3-4F29-8B79-9A9B915990C2/.

———. "Survivors and Victims." Available at http://www.ushmm.org/remember/the-holocaust-survivors-and-victims-resource-center/survivors-and-victims/.

van Alphen, Ernst. "Second-Generation Testimony, Transmission of Trauma, and Postmemory." *Poetics Today* 27 (2006): 473–488.

Velody, Irving. "The Archive and the Human Sciences: Notes towards a Theory of the Archive." *History of the Human Sciences* 11 (1998): 1–16.

Vice, Sue. *Holocaust Fiction*. New York: Routledge, 2000.

Vogel, Carol. "Poetry Written in Porcelain." *New York Times*, 29 August 2013.

Vygotsky, L. S. *Mind in Society: The Development of Higher Psychological Processes*. Edited by Michael Cole, Vera John-Stein, Sylvia Scribner, and Ellen Souberman. Cambridge, MA: Harvard University Press, 1978.

Walden, Daniel, ed. *Conversations with Chaim Potok*. Jackson: University Press of Mississippi, 2001.

Weissman, Gary. *Fantasies of Witnessing: Postwar Efforts to Experience the Holocaust*. Ithaca, NY: Cornell University Press, 2004.

White, Hayden. "The Metaphysics of Narrativity: Time and Symbol in Ricoeur's Philosophy of History." In Hayden White, *The Content of the Form: Narrative Discourse and Historical Representation*, 169–184. Baltimore: Johns Hopkins University Press, 1990.

Wiesel, Elie. "The Death Train." In *Anthology of Holocaust Literature*, edited by Jacob Glatstein, Israel Knox, and Samuel Margoshes, 3–10. New York: Atheneum, 1985.

———. "For Some Measure of Humility." *Sh'ma* 5/100, 31 October 1975.

———. *From the Kingdom of Memory: Reminiscences*. New York: Summit Books, 1990.

———. "The Holocaust as Literary Inspiration." In *Dimensions of the Holocaust*, annotated by Elliot Lefkovitz, 5–19. Evanston, IL: Northwestern University Press, 1977.

———. *A Jew Today*. Translated by Marion Wiesel. New York: Random House, 1978.

Wildman, Sarah. *Paper Love: Searching for the Girl My Grandfather Left Behind*. New York: Riverhead Books, 2014.

Wirth-Nesher, Hana, and Michael P. Kramer, eds. *The Cambridge Companion to Jewish American Literature*. New York: Cambridge University Press, 2003.

Young, James. "Interpreting Literary Testimony: A Preface to Rereading Holocaust Diaries and Memoirs." *New Literary History* 18 (1987): 403–423.

———. *The Texture of Memory: Holocaust Memorials and Meaning*. New Haven, CT: Yale University Press, 1993.

Young-Bruehl, Elisabeth. "The Biographer's Empathy with Her Subject." In Elisabeth Young-Bruehl, *Subject to Biography: Psychoanalysis, Feminism, and Writing Women's Lives*, 17–42. Cambridge, MA: Harvard University Press, 1998.

Yudkin, Leon. *Escape into Siege: A Survey of Israeli Literature Today*. London: Routledge and Kegan Paul, 1974.

Zhou, Min. "Growing Up American: The Challenge Confronting Immigrant Children and Children of Immigrants." *Annual Review of Sociology* 23 (1997): 63–95.

# INDEX

Page numbers in italics refer to images.

# ABOUT THE AUTHOR

JESSICA LANG is an associate professor of English at Baruch College, City University of New York, where she also serves as the founding William Newman Director of the Wasserman Jewish Studies Center. She lives in New York City with her husband and three children.